Green Woodworking
Pattern Book

Ray Tabor

BATSFORD

First published 2005

Copyright © Ray Tabor 2005

The right of Ray Tabor to be identified as Author of this work has been asserted by him in accordance with the Copyright, Designs and Patents Act 1988.

ISBN 0 7134 8914 6

A CIP catalogue record for this book is available from the British Library.

Printed in Singapore by Kyodo Printing Co. Ltd

for the publishers

B T Batsford
Chrysalis Books Group
The Chrysalis Building
Bramley Road
London W10 6SP
www.chrysalisbooks.co.uk

An imprint of Chrysalis Books Group plc

Distributed in the United States and Canada
by Sterling Publishing Co.,
387 Park Avenue South, New York, NY 10016, USA

Acknowledgements

During the 30 years in which I have researched and practised woodmanship, I have received unstinting help from a large number of people. Many have become lifelong friends. Too many have passed on. Much that this book contains is a tribute to their unique skills.

I also owe a particular debt of gratitude to: The late Charles West, Dorset hurdle maker; Noel Cullum, Suffolk rake and hurdle maker; the late Frank Bird, Suffolk hurdle maker; the late Sidney Lukehurst, Kent hurdle maker; the late Cyril Mummery, expert in Kent woodmanship; the late Alex Mummery, Kentish woodman; Richard Edwards, coppice craftsman; Malcolm Lee, pole lathe turner; Hugh Spencer, pole lathe designer; Janet Spencer for introducing me to wooden spoons; Peter Lambert, Kent pole lathe turner and woodman; Jon Warnes, Suffolk stick and living wood furniture maker; Barry Gladwell, Suffolk master thatcher; the late Raphael Salaman, tool historian; the late Phillip Walker, tool historian; Fred Hams, Kentish edge tool historian; the late Alec Morris, Devon tool maker; the late Bryony Driver, tool maker; Andrew Breese, Sussex tool maker; Simon Leatherdale, Essex forester; and Professor Ted Collins, rural historian.

There remain many craftsmen with whom I have spoken, or whose products I have seen either in the flesh or in print, and whose names are lost or were never known. I thank them for their work. I hope through this book that their skills are not lost and I thank them all for their inspiration, direct or indirect. I am only sorry I cannot thank them by name. I hope that I have recorded correctly the patterns of all of these green woodworkers past and present – I apologise for any errors, the fault for which lies with me.

A special thanks is due to the staff at Batsford whose enthusiasm and commitment made this book possible.

Thank you to my team members at Shadwell Wood, Tony Morton and Mark Hinton in particular, who have helped so much in developing markets for our green wood products.

And finally my biggest debt is to my wife, Judith, without who's forbearance this book would not have seen the light of day.

Ray Tabor, August 2004

Contents

Introduction to a Green Woodworking Pattern Book

About Green Woodworking: The title of this book is quite specific. It is a pattern book for green woodworkers. Not cabinet-makers, not carpenters in sawn soft wood, but green woodworkers. So what is green woodworking?

Working with green or unseasoned wood is the oldest form of woodworking – an ancient craft of woodmanship that has survived to the present day. By green I mean wood that is not fully seasoned but that still contains much, if not all, of the moisture present in the living tree at the time it was felled. Normally trees are felled during the winter months once their leaves have dropped and the sap is not flowing. At this time the tree's moisture content is lower (it is highest in the spring when the leaves are fully open and the tree is growing vigorously) and the wood is at its prime for many craft purposes. Some craftsmen, such as hurdle makers, do cut wood in the summer when it is in full leaf in order that they can work all year, but this can cause problems with the regeneration of the stump from which the poles have been cut. For some jobs, such as the removal of oak bark or lime and elm bast, the sap does need to be rising to enable the wood man to remove these items cleanly for tanning and weaving chair seats respectively. For some craft products wood can be used as soon as it is felled. For others, the wood needs to be held and partially seasoned over a period of between four weeks and six months, during which time the loss of moisture toughens the wood, making it more suitable for some uses.

It is easy to understand how and why our Neolithic ancestors started woodworking with green wood. Once tools such as flint axes and chisels became available, wood could be worked in larger sizes than just small rods that could be wrenched from the tree stool. And, of course, with primitive tools it was much easier to work green wood that is softer and more pliable than seasoned or sere wood. The remains of hazel wattle trackways from this period have been discovered in Somerset and are dated at 3100 BC. In

those 5,000 years during which woodmanship has evolved, an enormous range of artefacts – elegant, functional, ingenious, beautiful and all made from green wood, have been developed. Their patterns have been honed and modified by years of use to those that we know today. Who cannot wonder at a product such as the hazel wattle hurdle? A tough, resilient fencing panel used to restrain sheep, made from small rods by a craftsman using only a billhook. No nails, wire or other aids are needed to make this marvel of ingenuity that can be regularly manhandled and still last up to 10 years in the open. This book contains many more examples like this, where it is hard to believe that a better pattern can be designed. Working wood while it is still green has allowed craftsmen to develop a number of techniques that are both fast and produce better products than when using sawn scasoned wood. These advantages include:

- Green wood can be worked faster than seasoned wood since it works more easily with edge tools.
- It rives (splits) well, which is faster than sawing and reveals hidden faults in the wood. Riven wood is also more water repellent since the wood fibres have not been severed.
- Because many green wood products can be made in the wood, the offal is left behind, minimising the weight to be moved when the job is done.
- Small rods of various species can be wound (twisted) whilst still green to make ties.
- Pushing young green rods into the ground so that they take root can produce living artefacts and offers a whole new range of outdoor products.
- Green wood has a fast turn round, being used the year it is felled. This means little cash is tied up in stocks of seasoned wood.
- Green woodworking uses mainly small, round wood, which is quick to grow and is lighter and easier to work.

Of course there are some drawbacks to using green wood. After working green wood will continue to shrink, so that where very accurate turnery is required it may be necessary to turn, season, and then turn a final time. Also some warping of finished products may occur, although this can also result from normal use, such as frequent contact with very hot liquids. Joints in green wood can shrink and come loose unless cutting patterns and pegging are used to mitigate the problem. The existence of so many timber-framed buildings of great age in Britain would indicate that this problem is more an aesthetic than practical one. Finally, care is needed in the manufacture of turned products to avoid radial splitting as a result of products drying too quickly.

Why have a pattern book? Traditionally the patterns and skills associated with wood crafts were handed down from father to son. This was not done in writing but rather by practical training in the wood or workshop, starting with the simplest tasks and graduating to a whole job. Unfortunately the decline in the woodland trades during the second half of the 20th century has broken this essential chain. Full time chair bodgers or bowl turners in the traditional sense, producing essential products for a mass market, no longer exist. Those trades still in use are practised by a new wave of green woodworkers, many of whom are new to the trade, with no familial history to support them, and with a mere handful of craftsmen remaining from whom they can learn the details of their craft. Thus the first important role for this book is to record the patterns of once common products, together with the key features that made them work so well. Where possible the book explains the function of the artefact and what is important in its design. This record will provide a baseline, charting our knowledge of the patterns of green wood products at the start of the 21st century and to which new generations of green woodworkers can refer.

Secondly a pattern book is for practical reference. If a product has not been made for a long period, here are the notes that will allow workers to check the shape, the size, and the subtle nuances of that product so they can make it again. It is like a notebook in which

a craftsman has jotted a sketch and the dimensions of a product they have made; it is noted down so that in the future it is there to refer to.

Lastly a pattern book provides a catalogue of options that a craftsman can offer to the customer. Whether it is the pattern of a garden fence, the shape of a vase, or the decoration on a chair leg, a pattern book attempts to offer a range of choices. Pattern books started in the 18th century with furniture designs, when in 1762 Thomas Sheraton produced his 'Drawing Book' and Thomas Chippendale his 'Director'. By Victorian times it was a *sine qua non* for most companies large and small to have a catalogue illustrating all of the available patterns of their particular product. Although it may still be the case that the customer requires something slightly different, the illustrations in a pattern book or catalogue help to focus their ideas.

What does this pattern book contain? This book is unique in that it is the first to cover patterns for the whole range of green wood products. It ranges from the humblest pea stick for the vegetable garden, via fencing, wooden tools and treen, to furniture turned on the pole lathe. In addition there is a chapter describing the essential tools and devices traditional devised by craftsmen to help them do the job. They were masters of innovation and, either themselves or with the help of the local blacksmith, produced a range of unique tools and devices with names such as 'engines', 'brakes', or 'horses'. Each tool had a key role in the process. Perhaps the best known and most influential of these is the pole lathe, upon which many of the products in this book are dependent. Patterns and key dimensions for these tools are described, since they will not be found in any catalogue.

Under each section a range of products and patterns is described, together with, in most cases, an illustration. The illustrations are simple line drawings so that the key points of the artefact are clear. In some cases the drawings are from two perspectives where this is needed to make the design clear. Not all of the products described are in current use – not many of us use 'crow starvers' today! However, some of these older products are shown, however, firstly to ensure that a historical record maintained, but also to show how more modern versions have evolved. And who can tell when a similar pattern may be needed in the future? On each pattern is added the most important dimensions. The finished shape and size of a piece is, in many instances, down to the preference of the customer or the eye of the craftsman. Thus the height of a chair seat will be adjusted to the height of the user, as will the length of an axe handle. Dimensions are given in both metric and imperial measures, but it will be clear to users that, due to the history of the products, their sizes were originally imperial.

This book also tries to put each of the products in some social and historic context. Where possible there are notes on the history of the artefact and its original use(s). This helps to show the reasons why a particular pattern evolved, for invariably there are good, functional reasons for a particular design. Long feet, for example, on a Kentish gate hurdle are so the hurdle can be driven into the ground; this in turn requires a ferrule to avoid the head splitting. In some instances by looking at patterns of old and new, one can see how the product evolved. Lemon juicers, for example, have changed as the size of lemons has gradually increased over the last 300 years.

Understanding this process of evolution is important, for the process is still carrying on today. It remains a basic truth that customers will beat a path to the door of a craftsman who has a better product. If this book is repeated in 100 years time, there will be many new and interesting patterns to add to those illustrated here.

Where does the information come from? The patterns for the artefacts shown in this book came from a number of sources. While I have seen most products 'in the flesh', there are a number that have come from published sources. The difficulty, as

always, is in deciding what to include and what to leave out. The end result is a personal choice, but I have tried to choose patterns that show the functional properties of good design, the effectiveness of different woods and the opportunities offered to the craftsman by the warmth and beauty of wood itself. The best products have, as Walter Rose described it, 'a little touch of beauty engraved on the article of utility'.

The greatest source of data on green wood products has come from my own records, collected in over 30 years of both working wood and in meeting craftsmen practising a wide range of trades. I always carry a note book and there are many of these on my shelf, full of quick sketches of products, lists of dimensions and notes on how the products were made, all of which I made in the field. In addition I have collected over the years cuttings from newspapers and magazines, photographs and catalogues that show patterns for products that I have not seen before.

Another great source of information has come from visiting museums in many parts of the country. There is not a single rural museum that does not contain one or more unique items that are of interest to the woodworker. Some, however, such as the Mary Rose Trust, the Weald and Downland Museum, the Chiltern Furniture Museum and Museum of English Rural Life are outstanding. Here one can see historical artefacts in the flesh, exactly as used by our forebears as far back as the 16th century. Some museums have been good enough to open their reserve collections, which contain some real gems not usually seen by the public.

Catalogues provide a veritable mine of information. Some of the best are those Victorian editions published by tool and furniture makers. They are full of drawings illustrating almost every pattern made. Readers bitten by the bug are recommended to seek these out, for they will offer more ideas than has been possible to incorporate in this volume. Even rural workshops in some areas, such as the renowned Suffolk rake factory, produced catalogues of their wares, and have proven useful for detailed patterns. Lastly there are a number of books that I have referred to over the years, and which contain descriptions and photographs of many products. The most important of these are listed in the bibliography (see page 236). Most of these books concentrate on one subject area, but are excellent references for different patterns.

Who should use this book and how? This book does not tell the reader how to make a particular product. There are numerous excellent books on the market that already do this, the best of which are included in the bibliography (see page 236). This book is for those who are starting in green woodworking and are looking for products to make, as well as those competent at the basic elements of the craft and looking to broaden the range of what they produce. It will give the reader ideas for a variety of products across the whole range of green woodworking. It will also be of great use to those with experience who are teaching newcomers what they can do and how. It is all here – the complete range of green wood products to choose from.

This book is best used as a reference. It is like my note books and files – full of sketches and key dimensions that remind me what size and shape a stable fork should be, or how to weave the rods at the bottom of a hurdle, or a favourite pattern for a turned chair leg. Using this book acts as a reminder for these key features that make the product both work and look right. Also, browsing through the book will refresh your mind as to the patterns and ideas you can use.

Any artefact should be designed by the craftsman who will make it – it should have the creator's stamp on it. No one has to slavishly follow the patterns that are illustrated here. They can, and should, be modified and improved to reflect the design skills of the worker and the taste of the customer. For this reason only the most important dimensions are shown on the products. I expect that every craftsman will take the time to design in some detail the product they are going to make. It is not possible in a book of this scale to show fully dimensioned drawings and cutting plans, but worked examples for a garden bench and a chair are shown in the appendix (see page 227). If you go to the trouble of working out your plans to this level of detail, you will have to face any difficult issues and solve them before you put saw to wood. It also gives you the chance to alter the design to improve the product and give it your own style. It is worth taking the time to do this, whether for a whistle or a chair, because you will understand the design of green wood products better and this will be reflected in the quality of what you make.

I hope the text and the tips make it clear where you can apply flexibility in your design and where it is best to stick to traditional wisdom. The shapes and sizes of many features, such as the height of the arms on a chair, can be changed, but the height of a cricket stump is fixed!

The interest in green woodworking continues to increase year by year, although it will never return to the pre-eminence it held up to the 1920s. However, these ancient woodland crafts still have much to offer 21st century society – not only fine products in beautiful wood, but also a role in conserving our ancient woodland heritage and an opportunity for many to enjoy satisfying, physical work in an environment of often unparalleled beauty. All of those who work so hard training green wood workers or pursuing these trades deserve our support. I hope this book will contribute to their efforts and introduce more people to what green woodworking can achieve. And when I see copies of this book well thumbed and with pencilled notes in the margin denoting new sizes or patterns, then I shall know it was worth while.

Chapter 1 Tools, Devices, Patterns and Gauges

Introduction

Before looking at the range of products made by green wood craftsmen, we need to look at some of the tools and devices that are used to produce those products. Traditional woodworkers have always been masters at devising the best means of manufacture. The devices they used enable their artefacts to be made, not only very quickly and efficiently, but also to repeatable quality and dimensions. A good hurdle-maker, for instance, can tell the quality of the hurdles made by another simply by the straightness of the stack in which they are stored; a leaning stack means there is a problem! Doing the job repeatedly, speedily and effectively requires exactly the right tool or device.

A majority of these tools were either made by the craftsman himself, or by a blacksmith under his instruction. Because of this there is a wide range of tool patterns varying, not just between regions, but also between individual craftsmen. These tools often cannot be found in catalogues, new or old, so I have described the best here so that their patterns and unique properties are not lost, and so that modern craftsmen can reproduce them.

The devices that are described are more ephemeral, but no less important. Invariably made of wood, and, in many cases, designed to last only one season, their often rustic appearance belies the efficiency of their operation. Indeed it would not be possible to rind, rive or shave wood properly without an appropriate 'horse' or 'brake'. The examples described are all designed and used by woodworkers and are extremely effective.

Tools

Froes are tools for splitting wood (**fig 1.1**). They are based on a moderately long but narrow blade fitted at right angles to a longer handle that enables the blade to be levered from side to side. The thickness of the blade is determined by the fineness of the work – coarser clefts require a thicker blade and a longer handle. Relatively short clefts (shingles) only need a short handle (**fig 1.2**), while lathes that are very narrow only require a short-bladed froe (**fig 1.3**). The end of the blade may be sharpened so it can be inserted into a split, or used as a chopper in the case of a froe for lathes.

Cleaves or bond splitters (**fig 1.4**) are beautiful, egg-shaped, hardwood splitters designed to make fine clefts from small rods of hazel, willow or cane. It is usual for them to have either three or four 'wedge faces' producing a similar number of clefts. Somewhat larger splitters (**fig 1.5**) are used for splitting oak rods in order to make lathes. Bond splitters are also used to split cane for basket-making, and because this material is tougher, it is common for the ends of the 'wedges' to be tipped with metal (**fig 1.6**).

Stail engines were the universal means of making long, smooth handles (called stails) for rakes and hoes (**fig 1.7**). They are rotary wooden planes, using a plane blade, and work like a pencil sharpener, being rotated around the handle and removing a shaving in the process. The size of the finished product is determined by setting the gap between the two parts of the tool body using the screw wing nuts. This is the only tool that allows a long, tapered handle to be made by gradually adjusting the aperture as the shaving progresses. Modern, all-metal versions of this tool can now be purchased (**fig 1.8**).

Rounders are a simpler form of the stail engine (**fig 1.9**). In a rounder, the diameter of the finished product cannot be changed. Also, the hole in a rounder is usually tapered to produce a slight conical end to the piece. The main use for this tool was to shape the ends of ladder rungs, which it does to perfection. Today an important use for the tool is in jointing rustic furniture, the rounder making the round 'tenon' fit in a drilled round 'mortice'. Modern, metal versions can be purchased to a number of standard sizes.

Curved shaves come in various patterns, but all with the same objective of a smooth, curved surface without 'flats', giving a round pole or handle. The simplest shaves are made from old grass-hook blades fitted with two handles (**fig 1.10**) and are designed to remove the bark from large poles when making hurdles. A one-handed tool was much used in Kent for removing the bark from poles for broom handles (**fig 1.11**), thus avoiding the need for a brake. Smaller shaves are used for a variety of handles (besoms and rakes for example) and other smoothing jobs (**fig 1.12**). These tools may be designed to be used with the sharpening bevel either against the work or not.

The Twybil is a tool designed to make mortices in green wood (**fig 1.13**). It comprises a blade that is designed to cut along the grain between two pre-drilled holes. At the opposite end to the blade is usually a hook used to 'huck out' the waste wood. A handle at right angles to the blade allows leverage to be applied. Some twybils have two handles to hold (**fig 1.14**), but in my view are less effective since this is at the expense of the hook to remove the waste wood.

Side axes are still made, albeit not to all of the traditional patterns (**fig 1.15**). The key to the operation of this tool is that there is no sharpening bevel on one side (the one nearest your body as you hold the tool). This makes the tool either right- or left-handed. It is always fitted with a short handle, particularly by chair bodgers, since the tool is more accurate if held close to its head. A small nug axe (**fig 1.16**) is also illustrated; this is used by wattle hurdle makers to trim the finished hurdle, and has two sharpening bevels.

Tips

- Make sure the socket on a froe is tapered to prevent the handle pulling out.
- Bond splitters must be made from the hardest wood – box is best.
- The blade in a stail engine or rounder should be slightly curved so that the ends do not dig into the wood.
- Get the heaviest side axe you can comfortably use and let the weight do the work.
- Make sure when sharpening any blade with one sharpening bevel that the 'flat' side is kept perfectly flat.
- Make sure that any hook on a twybil to remove waste has a curve towards the side with the handle – it cannot work if it curves the other way.

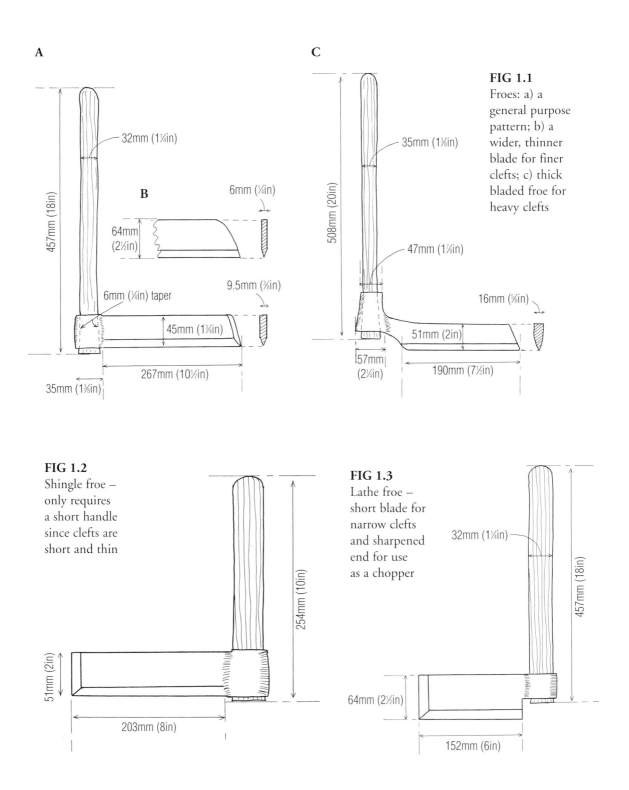

A

32mm (1¼in)

B

6mm (¼in)

457mm (18in)

64mm (2½in)

6mm (¼in) taper

9.5mm (⅜in)

45mm (1¾in)

267mm (10½in)

35mm (1⅜in)

C

508mm (20in)

35mm (1⅜in)

47mm (1⅞in)

16mm (⅝in)

51mm (2in)

57mm (2¼in)

190mm (7½in)

FIG 1.1
Froes: a) a
general purpose
pattern; b) a
wider, thinner
blade for finer
clefts; c) thick
bladed froe for
heavy clefts

FIG 1.2
Shingle froe –
only requires
a short handle
since clefts are
short and thin

254mm (10in)

51mm (2in)

203mm (8in)

FIG 1.3
Lathe froe –
short blade for
narrow clefts
and sharpened
end for use
as a chopper

32mm (1¼in)

457mm (18in)

64mm (2½in)

152mm (6in)

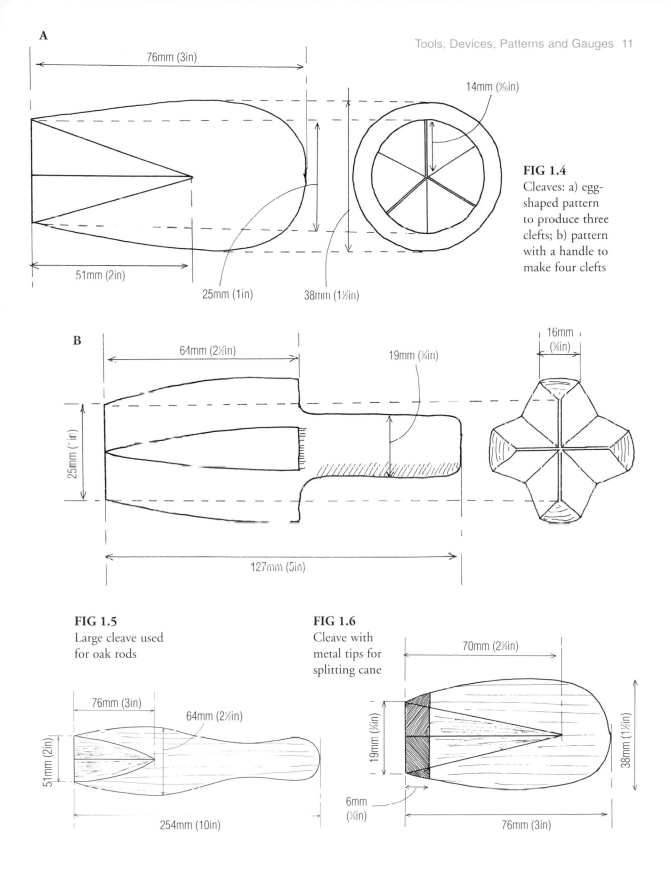

A

76mm (3in)

51mm (2in)

25mm (1in)

38mm (1½in)

14mm (⁹⁄₁₆in)

FIG 1.4
Cleaves: a) egg-shaped pattern to produce three clefts; b) pattern with a handle to make four clefts

B

64mm (2½in)

19mm (¾in)

16mm (⅝in)

25mm (in)

127mm (5in)

FIG 1.5
Large cleave used for oak rods

76mm (3in)

64mm (2½in)

51mm (2in)

254mm (10in)

FIG 1.6
Cleave with metal tips for splitting cane

70mm (2¾in)

19mm (¾in)

38mm (1½in)

6mm (¼in)

76mm (3in)

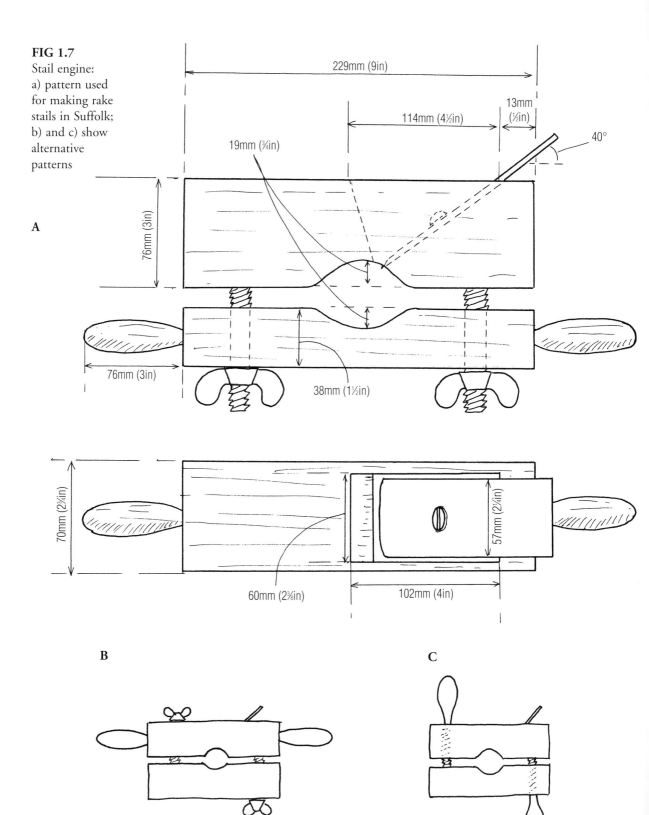

FIG 1.7
Stail engine:
a) pattern used
for making rake
stails in Suffolk;
b) and c) show
alternative
patterns

A

229mm (9in)

114mm (4½in)

13mm (½in)

40°

19mm (¾in)

76mm (3in)

76mm (3in)

38mm (1½in)

70mm (2¾in)

57mm (2¼in)

60mm (2⅜in)

102mm (4in)

B

C

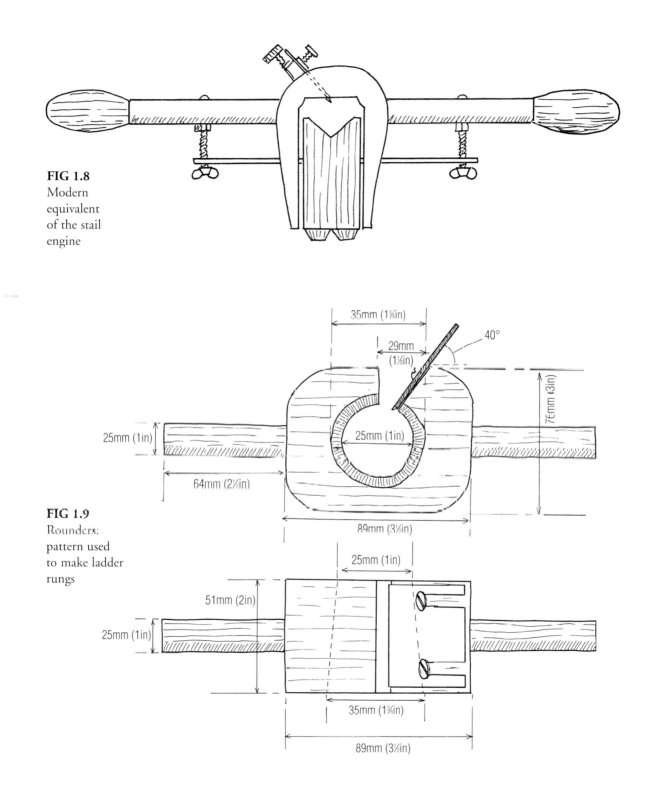

FIG 1.8
Modern
equivalent
of the stail
engine

35mm (1⅜in)

29mm
(1⅛in)

40°

25mm (1in)

76mm (3in)

25mm (1in)

64mm (2½in)

89mm (3½in)

FIG 1.9
Rounders:
pattern used
to make ladder
rungs

25mm (1in)

51mm (2in)

25mm (1in)

35mm (1⅜in)

89mm (3½in)

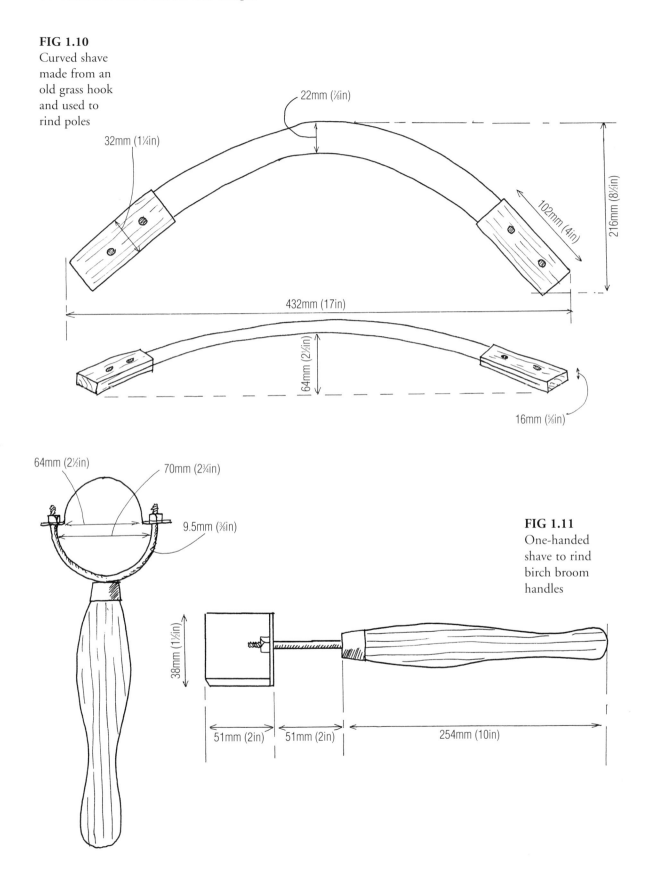

FIG 1.10
Curved shave
made from an
old grass hook
and used to
rind poles

22mm (⅞in)

32mm (1¼in)

102mm (4in)

216mm (8½in)

432mm (17in)

64mm (2½in)

16mm (⅝in)

64mm (2½in)

70mm (2¾in)

9.5mm (⅜in)

FIG 1.11
One-handed
shave to rind
birch broom
handles

38mm (1½in)

51mm (2in)

51mm (2in)

254mm (10in)

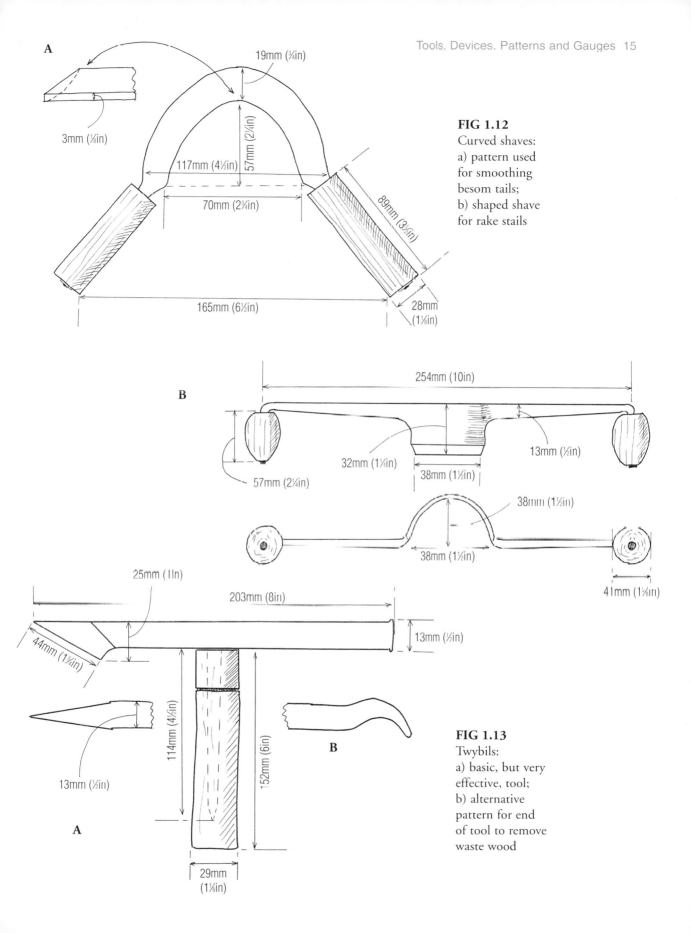

A

19mm (¾in)

3mm (⅛in)

117mm (4½in)

57mm (2¼in)

70mm (2¾in)

89mm (3½in)

165mm (6½in)

28mm (1⅛in)

FIG 1.12
Curved shaves:
a) pattern used
for smoothing
besom tails;
b) shaped shave
for rake stails

B

254mm (10in)

57mm (2¼in)

32mm (1¼in)

38mm (1½in)

13mm (½in)

38mm (1½in)

38mm (1½in)

41mm (1⅝in)

25mm (1in)

203mm (8in)

44mm (1¾in)

13mm (½in)

114mm (4½in)

152mm (6in)

13mm (½in)

B

A

29mm
(1⅛in)

FIG 1.13
Twybils:
a) basic, but very
effective, tool;
b) alternative
pattern for end
of tool to remove
waste wood

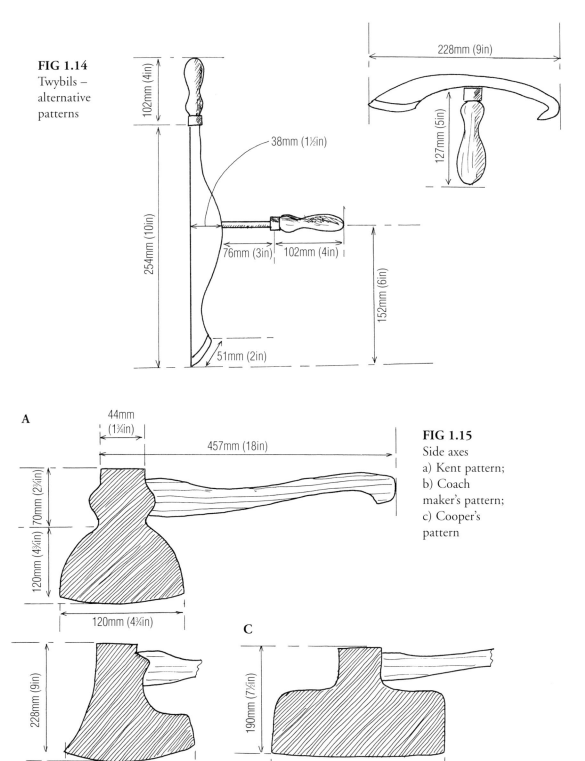

FIG 1.14
Twybils –
alternative
patterns

FIG 1.15
Side axes
a) Kent pattern;
b) Coach
maker's pattern;
c) Cooper's
pattern

A

B

C

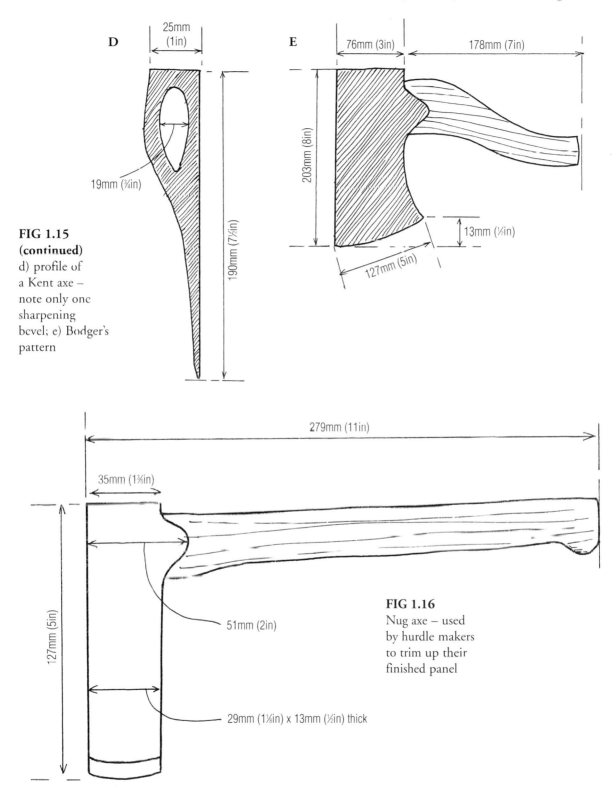

D

25mm (1in)

19mm (¾in)

190mm (7½in)

E

76mm (3in)

178mm (7in)

203mm (8in)

13mm (½in)

127mm (5in)

**FIG 1.15
(continued)**
d) profile of
a Kent axe –
note only one
sharpening
bevel; e) Bodger's
pattern

279mm (11in)

35mm (1⅜in)

127mm (5in)

51mm (2in)

29mm (1⅛in) x 13mm (½in) thick

FIG 1.16
Nug axe – used
by hurdle makers
to trim up their
finished panel

Devices

Tension grips are designed to hold the work piece so it can be shaved, drilled or mortised (**fig 1.17**). It relies on bending the work piece slightly so that it is held under tension, and is stopped from moving sideways, either by a 'V' in the top of the post, or by the use of a sharpened nail. A metal device called a hop dog (**fig 1.17c**) can also be used to hold one end of the work.

Shaving brakes support round poles from which the bark has to be removed (**fig 1.18**). The work piece has to be rotated as required and also turned from end to end to shave the whole piece. This is best used where there are large numbers of long poles to be processed.

Shaving horses are sit-on devices with a foot-operated grip or vice that holds the work piece so it can be shaved or shaped (**fig 1.19**). Different sizes of work piece are accommodated by moving the wedge under the work board backwards and forwards (**fig 1.20a**). For small, round poles a forked support should be used in place of the normal flat board (**fig 1.20b**). Designs popular in Europe and the United States have a slightly tighter grip due to longer leverage, but are less flexible in the size of piece they hold (**fig 1.21**).

Knee vices are designed to hold very long clefts that require shaving, but cannot be handled on a small horse (**fig 1.22**). The work is held by applying pressure with the knee to the flat board, which is also long enough to support long, thin clefts and achieve an even thickness.

Spindle grips are essential for holding items, such as axe handles, so that they can be shaped (**fig 1.23**). The work piece is held between two spindle points (as in a lathe), which allows the work to be rotated, and to be worked along its whole length without being removed from the spindles.

Riving brakes allow the worker to control the riving of wood to produce even clefts (**fig 1.24**). The essence of the device is two horizontal poles that allow leverage to be applied to the work piece. The more distance between the poles, the more leverage can be applied. These poles should also be set to have different horizontal spacing along their length so that they can handle pieces of different diameters (**fig 1.24c**). Alternative patterns are shown in **fig 1.25**.

Spar splitters provide possibly the quickest means of splitting hazel sticks to make thatching spars (**fig 1.26**). They are either mounted on a horse or left as free-standing posts to a height just above the waist. Once a split has been started in the gad it is continued by pushing each of the clefts to either side of the splitter. Steady forward pressure will continue the splitting process.

Tips

- It is best to angle the horizontal bars on the tension grip so that it can cope with different sizes of work.
- Where 'V' cut-outs are used to provide lateral support, make sure they are deep enough to prevent the piece from rolling out.
- Make the wedge under the plate of the shaving horse moveable so the gap under the vice can be adjusted to different sizes of material.
- Adjust the size of a horse to fit the user – it is most important to have enough leg room to apply full pressure when required.
- It will help the vice on a horse to grip if a metal plate is added to it or metal strips are added to the plate.
- Triangulated riving brakes work better than those using two posts – you can achieve more leverage.

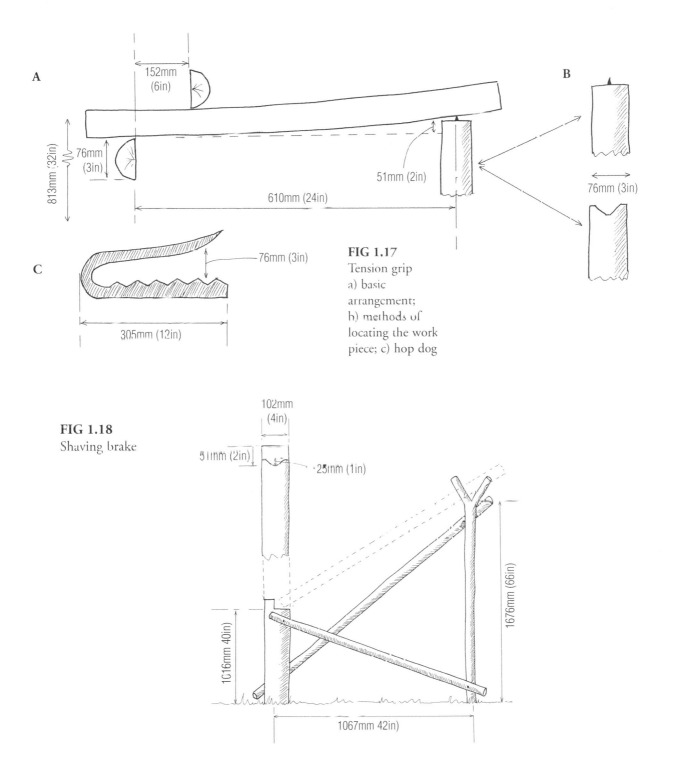

A

152mm (6in)

76mm (3in)

813mm (32in)

610mm (24in)

51mm (2in)

B

76mm (3in)

C

76mm (3in)

305mm (12in)

FIG 1.17
Tension grip
a) basic
arrangement;
b) methods of
locating the work
piece; c) hop dog

FIG 1.18
Shaving brake

102mm
(4in)

51mm (2in)   25mm (1in)

1676mm (66in)

1016mm (40in)

1067mm 42in

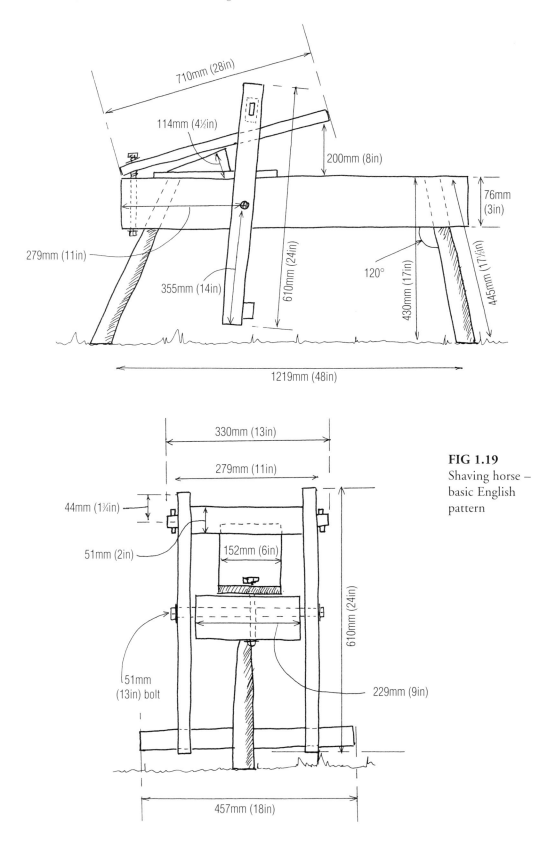

FIG 1.19
Shaving horse –
basic English
pattern

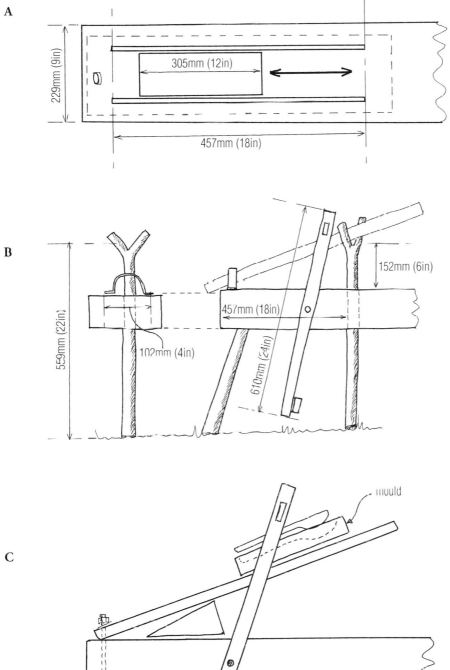

A

229mm (9in)

305mm (12in)

457mm (18in)

B

559mm (22in)

102mm (4in)

152mm (6in)

457mm (18in)

610mm (24in)

C

mould

FIG 1.20
Detail of the
shaving horse:
a) design to move
the wedge in
order to change
the aperture of
the vice;
b) modifications
to hold round
poles; c) how to
hold a spoon
in a mould for
carving

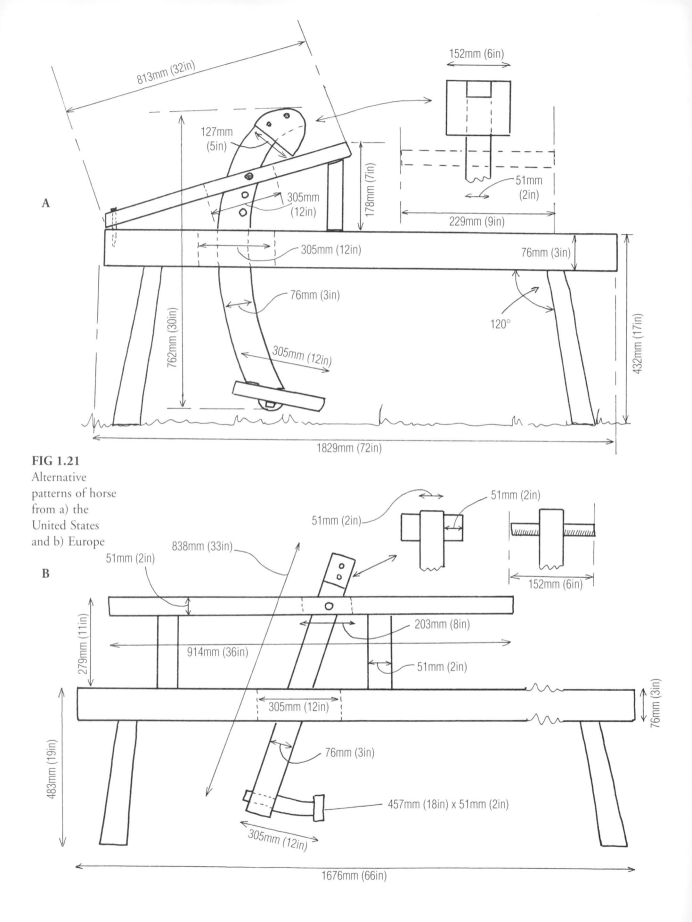

FIG 1.21
Alternative
patterns of horse
from a) the
United States
and b) Europe

813mm (32in)

152mm (6in)

127mm (5in)

305mm (12in)

178mm (7in)

51mm (2in)

229mm (9in)

305mm (12in)

76mm (3in)

120°

762mm (30in)

76mm (3in)

305mm (12in)

432mm (17in)

1829mm (72in)

A

51mm (2in)

51mm (2in)

838mm (33in)

51mm (2in)

152mm (6in)

279mm (11in)

914mm (36in)

203mm (8in)

51mm (2in)

305mm (12in)

76mm (3in)

483mm (19in)

76mm (3in)

457mm (18in) x 51mm (2in)

305mm (12in)

1676mm (66in)

B

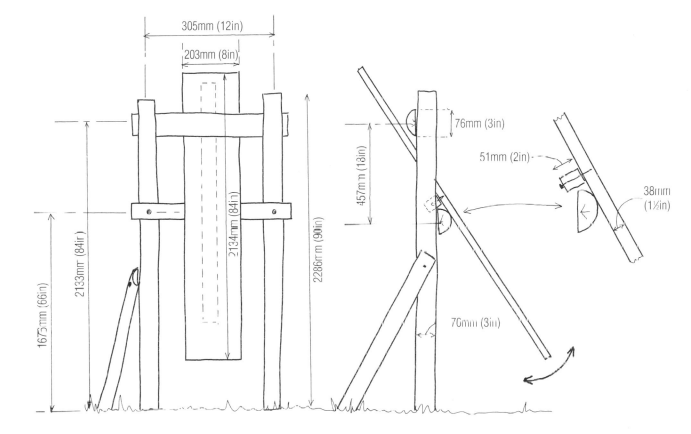

FIG 1.22
Knee vice (work
piece shown by
dotted lines)

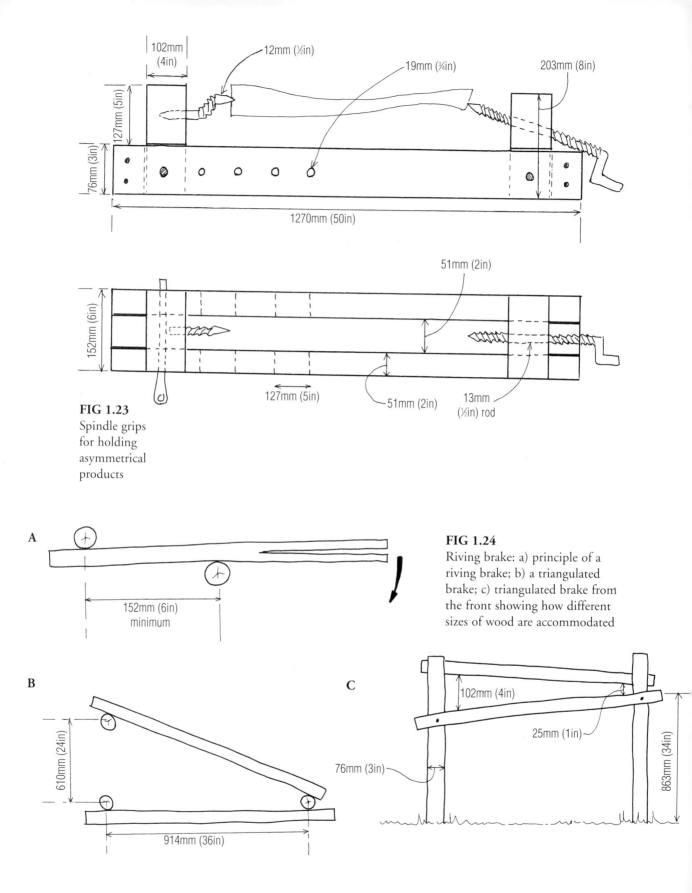

102mm (4in)

12mm (½in)

19mm (¾in)

203mm (8in)

127mm (5in)

76mm (3in)

1270mm (50in)

51mm (2in)

152mm (6in)

127mm (5in)

51mm (2in)

13mm (½in) rod

FIG 1.23
Spindle grips
for holding
asymmetrical
products

A

152mm (6in)
minimum

FIG 1.24
Riving brake: a) principle of a
riving brake; b) a triangulated
brake; c) triangulated brake from
the front showing how different
sizes of wood are accommodated

B

610mm (24in)

914mm (36in)

C

102mm (4in)

25mm (1in)

76mm (3in)

863mm (34in)

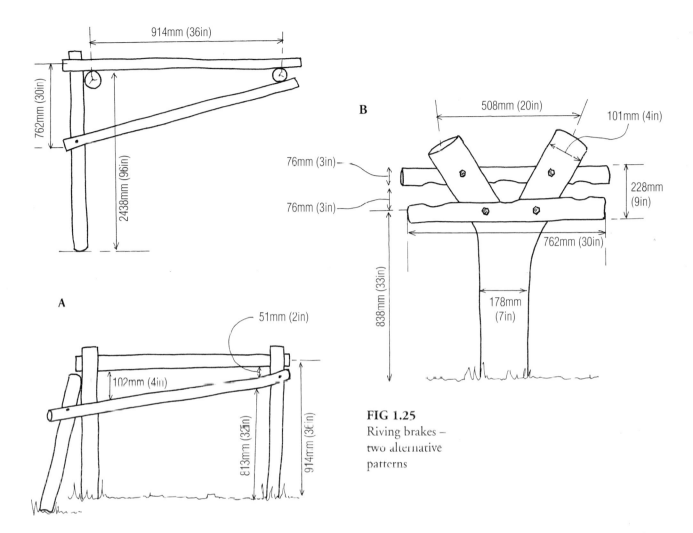

914mm (36in)

762mm (30in)

2438mm (96in)

B

508mm (20in)

101mm (4in)

76mm (3in)

76mm (3in)

228mm (9in)

838mm (33in)

762mm (30in)

178mm (7in)

A

51mm (2in)

102mm (4in)

813mm (32in)

914mm (36in)

FIG 1.25
Riving brakes –
two alternative
patterns

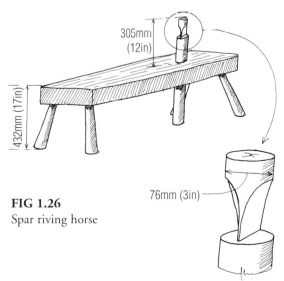

305mm (12in)

432mm (17in)

76mm (3in)

FIG 1.26
Spar riving horse

Pole lathe

The pole lathe is the *sine qua non* of the modern green woodworker, and traditionally was the tool of the chair bodger (**fig 1.27**). The basis of the lathe is a 'bed', comprising two parallel members with a gap between them, supported at either end by an 'A' frame. This must be bolted and jointed to ensure the structure is rigid, and the length of the bed can be fixed to suit the user.

The work piece is held between two threaded 'centres' that are fitted into the 'stocks' or 'poppets' (**fig 1.28**). The centre in the head-stock is fixed, but that in the tail-stock can be rotated to tighten or release the work piece. Both stocks are moveable along the bed, but are held in place during turning by wedges under the bed. A tool rest set at the same height as the centres (**fig 1.29**) is also located on the bed, to which it is held by a wedge or screw bolt. A longer pattern of rest is illustrated in **fig 1.30**. Long, thin work pieces tend to bow under the pressure of the chisel, so that a back support is essential. A pattern for a back support is shown in **fig 1.31** (designed by Hugh Spencer), the key to which is the wedge at the back which, being loose, is able to take up any slack and keep the support in contact with the work piece. Both head and tail stock centres in a pole lathe are 'dead', meaning that neither of them drives the work piece round.

This is accomplished by a cord, which is actually wound around the work piece with one end attached to the pole and the other to the treadle (**fig 1.32a**). The motive force to rotate the work piece is the bodger's leg pushing on the treadle; the function of the pole is to rotate the work back to its start point. This means of course that the bodger's chisel can only cut as he pushes down on the treadle, but not as the pole returns. Because a normal pole is so long it is common to replace it with a 'bungee' cord, particularly for indoor work (**fig 1.32b**).

Tips

- Cover the top face of the wedges with leather to help stop them working loose.
- Use hard wood if possible for the bed, frame and poppets.
- Fix a small metal strip to the top of the tool rest where the chisel will contact – this will reduce wear.
- Use double bolts and tight joints between bed and 'A' frame to avoid movement.
- Hinge the treadle to its board using two pieces of leather and notch the top of the treadle so that the cord cannot pull off.
- The pole must be green – sere wood will snap under tension.

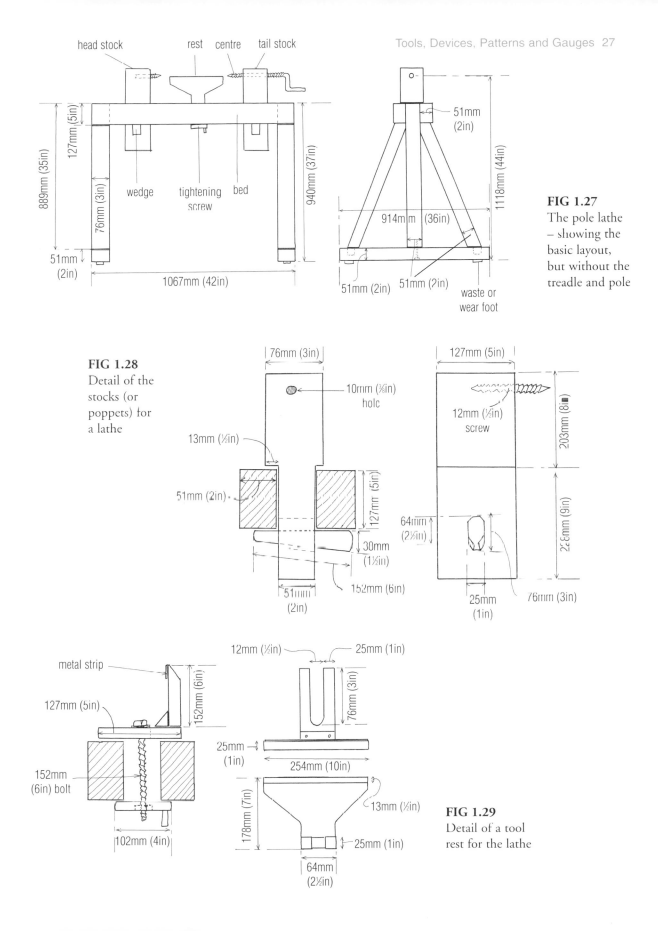

head stock · rest · centre · tail stock

127mm (5in)
889mm (35in)
76mm (3in)
51mm (2in)
1067mm (42in)
940mm (37in)

wedge · tightening screw · bed

51mm (2in)
1118mm (44in)
914mm (36in)
51mm (2in)
51mm (2in)
waste or wear foot

FIG 1.27
The pole lathe – showing the basic layout, but without the treadle and pole

FIG 1.28
Detail of the stocks (or poppets) for a lathe

76mm (3in)
10mm (⅜in) hole
13mm (½in)
51mm (2in)
127mm (5in)
30mm (1½in)
51mm (2in)
152mm (6in)

127mm (5in)
12mm (½in) screw
203mm (8in)
64mm (2½in)
229mm (9in)
25mm (1in)
76mm (3in)

metal strip
127mm (5in)
152mm (6in) bolt
152mm (6in)
102mm (4in)

12mm (½in)
25mm (1in)
76mm (3in)
25mm (1in)
254mm (10in)
178mm (7in)
13mm (½in)
25mm (1in)
64mm (2½in)

FIG 1.29
Detail of a tool rest for the lathe

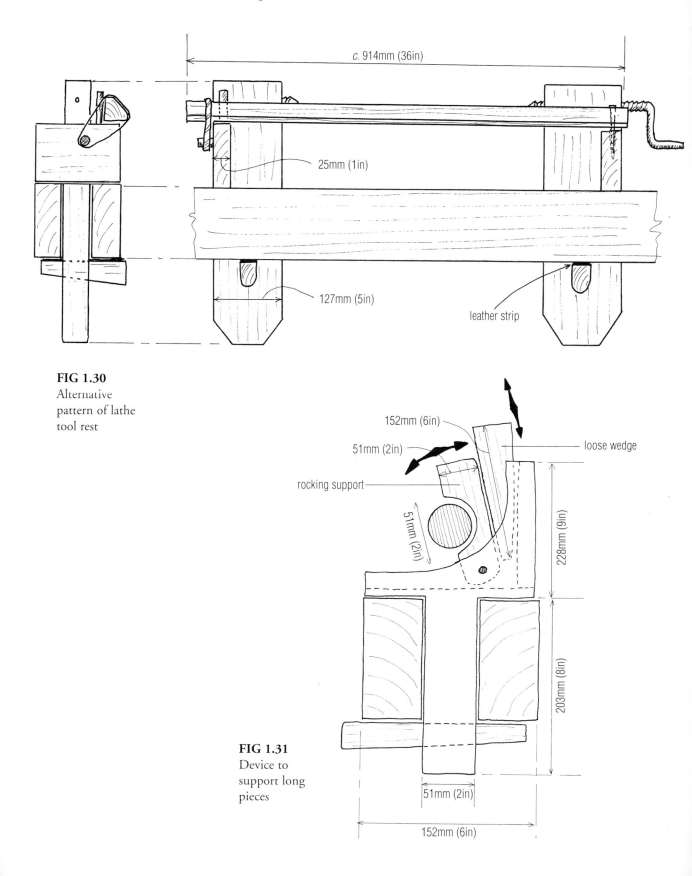

FIG 1.30
Alternative
pattern of lathe
tool rest

FIG 1.31
Device to
support long
pieces

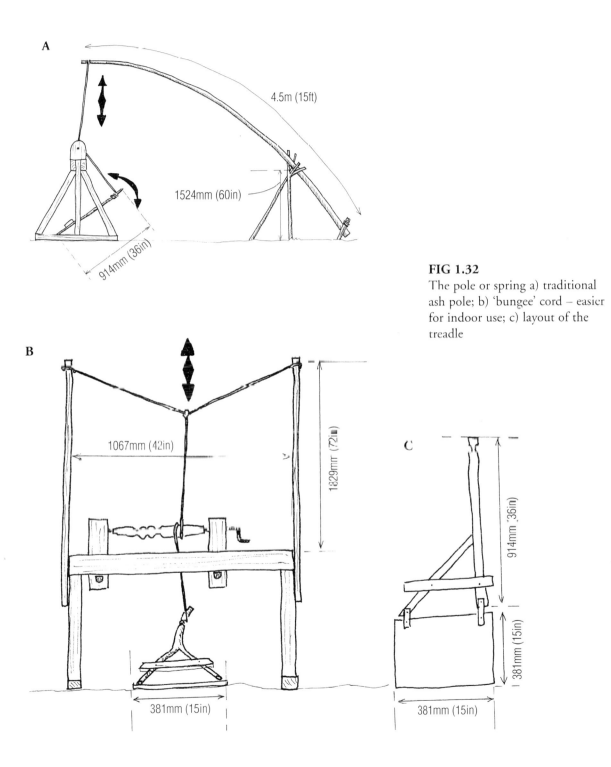

A

4.5m (15ft)

1524mm (60in)

914mm (36in)

B

1067mm (42in)

1829mm (72in)

381mm (15in)

C

914mm (36in)

381mm (15in)

381mm (15in)

FIG 1.32
The pole or spring a) traditional
ash pole; b) 'bungee' cord – easier
for indoor use; c) layout of the
treadle

Gauges and Patterns

Sticks are frequently used where repetitive measuring of material is undertaken (**fig 1.33**) – it is a lot quicker and easier than using a tape, particularly where quite long lengths are involved. These devices can be used on sawing horses to mark a cutting point. Long sticks, with a fork at one end, are used by hurdle makers to check that the length of their wattle is correctly maintained.

Simple gauges are often used where a part of a product has to be shaped to fit in a hole (mortice) in another member. An example (**fig 1.34**) is shown of a gauge used to confirm that the ends of the rails of a gate hurdle will fit the mortices in the heads. Such gauges are all 'home made' by the craftsman. In **fig 1.35** are two simple gauges, made in plywood, and used for repetitive turnery jobs on the lathe, or for gauging, for example, that the diameter of a long handle is consistent.

Patterns can range from a sketch on a sheet of paper to a durable pattern upon which an artefact is actually made. An example of this is in **fig 1.36a**, which shows a wooden pattern for marking out the head of a gate hurdle with the points of the mortices drilled through it so that they can be marked onto the work piece. **Fig 1.36b** shows the wooden form on which the pieces are nailed together, and which helps to ensure that the dimensions of each hurdle are the same. Patterns

for spoons (**fig 1.37**), a chair leg (**fig 1.38**) and a splat for a chair (**fig 1.39**) are all illustrated, and would normally be kept in the craftsman's workshop in cut-out form. They are made in plywood, or in the case of smaller patterns, a very stiff card. This enables them to be used to mark around in order to transfer the pattern to the material being worked. Over time they will wear out and need to be replaced.

The cutting positions for the design on a turned leg may be marked on the leg blank by means of a pattern using sharpened nails (**fig 1.38**), and which is carefully held against the blank on its return rotation.

Tips

- Slightly curved sticks make very good gauges since the end can be formed into a hook to locate over the end of a work piece.
- A nail in one end of a gauge makes a very good means of marking the work piece.
- Gauges for tenons will wear if used a lot and need to be changed to keep tight, fitting joints.
- Don't worry if the products are not absolutely identical – it is one of the beauties of green woodworking that almost every product is unique.
- Keep a file of your patterns and ideas – memory is very fickle!

FIG 1.33
Measuring sticks
– these are cut to
size for the work
required

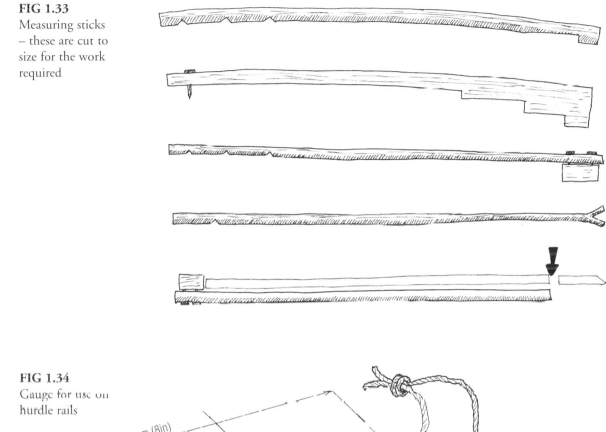

FIG 1.34
Gauge for use on
hurdle rails

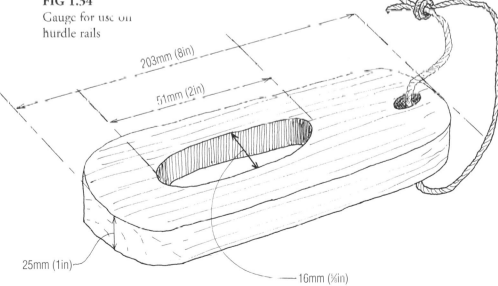

203mm (8in)

51mm (2in)

25mm (1in)

16mm (⅝in)

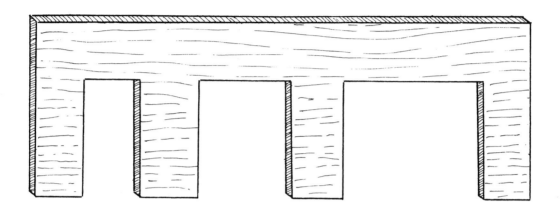

FIG 1.35
Two gauges for
use on the lathe

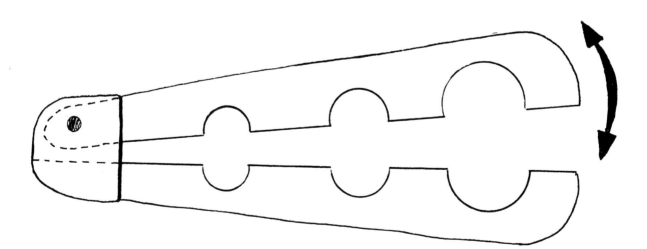

A

B

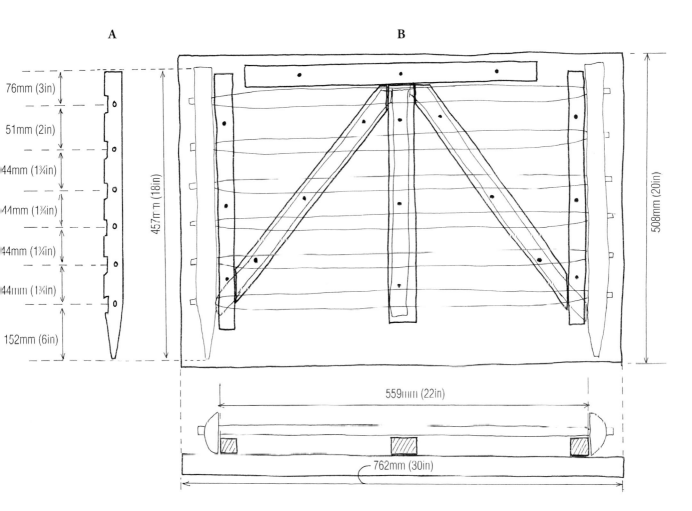

76mm (3in)

51mm (2in)

44mm (1¾in)

44mm (1¾in)

44mm (1¾in)

44mm (1¾in)

152mm (6in)

457mm (18in)

508mm (20in)

559mm (22in)

762mm (30in)

FIG 1.36
Pattern stock for hurdle heads
a) and b) a form in which the
hurdle is assembled, ensuring
consistent shape

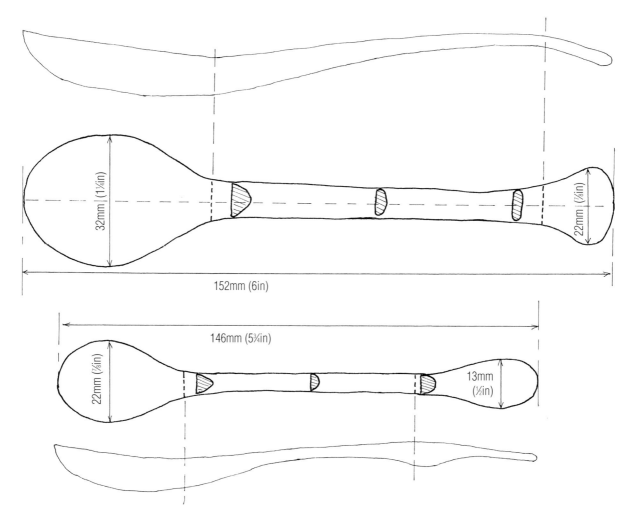

32mm (1¼in)

22mm (⅞in)

152mm (6in)

146mm (5¾in)

22mm (⅞in)

13mm (½in)

FIG 1.37
Patterns for spoons

FIG 1.38
Patterns for chair legs: a) Pattern
for a chair leg; b) finished leg;
c) 'pin' pattern used to mark
the leg blank

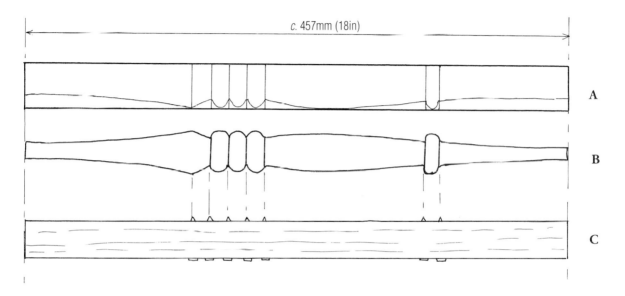

c. 457mm (18in)

A

B

C

FIG 1.39
Pattern for a chair splat

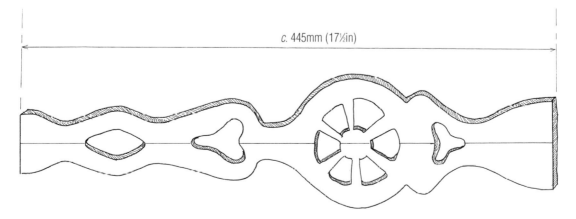

c. 445mm (17½in)

Chapter 2 Fences and Gates

Introduction

Fencing is among the oldest of the green wood products. As soon as our ancestors developed a more settled lifestyle involving crops and animals, the need for fencing to contain yet separate the two became essential. Perhaps the very earliest fencing was made of twiggy boughs laid horizontally on top of one another to make a 'dead hedge'. More sophisticated forms of this hedge, in which the boughs are interwoven between upright stakes, were common in medieval copses and are still used today to keep deer away from young tree shoots. In the medieval coppice, stakes and rods for fencing came second only to firewood in the uses for coppice wood.

Variations of post and rail have always been the most common fencing. The addition of flat cleft palings resulted in the use of pale fencing around estates and deer parks, where its effective height was increased by erecting the fence on top of the boundary bank.

As farming developed, so did the need for moveable fencing that allowed animals, particularly sheep, to be contained while feeding on arable and pasture fields. Gate hurdles and wattle sheep hurdles filled the need, and were made in their thousands across the south and east of England. They soon became synonymous with shepherds and their flocks, and with slightly different patterns in different areas. Although farming methods have changed and fewer hurdles are required, wattle panels remain popular as a form of garden fencing.

Most other fencing around cottage gardens relied on small round wood cut from the coppice and hedge. Here, craftsmen were not tied to a particular pattern and could express their own ideas, constrained only by function. As a result there are many patterns for garden fences, all designed to look attractive in their setting.

In damp climates the durability of wood out of doors has always been a problem. Heartwood of oak and sweet chestnut is without doubt the best type of wood for resisting damp. Chestnut in particular produces very little sapwood, so that even small clefts are very durable. Without this property, making the pale and wire fencing we all know would not be possible.

Post and Rail Fencing

As the name suggests, this fencing is based on vertical posts set in the ground and joined by horizontal rails. The posts can be quite light, around 75mm (3in) diameter, sharpened at the butt and driven into the ground. More robust posts, of around 128mm x 76mm (5in x 3in), require a hole to be dug and the earth tamped back around the post. Spacing between posts can vary from 1.8m (6ft) to 2.7m (9ft), mainly depending on the strength of fence required.

It is most common to use two parallel rails in the fence, although three are used in taller fences. In the simplest (and least attractive) fence the rails are simply nailed to the sides of the posts (**fig 2.1**). It is commoner and more effective to mortise the posts and insert the ends of the rails into these. At their simplest, mortices can be round drilled holes (**fig 2.2** and **2.3**). For more robust fencing, use either one mortice hole into which two rails are inserted and overlap, or two mortices side by side (**fig 2.4** and **2.5**). Since the ends of the rails are tapered to fit the mortices, the rails cannot be removed without lifting the posts once erected.

A paling fence is erected by nailing cleft pales to the rails, spaced according to the level of protection required (**fig 2.6–2.8**).

A whole range of garden fences in round and cleft wood have developed from the basic pale fence, a selection of which are illustrated in **fig 2.9**.

Tips

- Use chestnut or oak, particularly where the wood is in contact with the ground.
- Cleft wood will always last longer than sawn.
- Use wooden wedges to tighten the ends of the rails in their mortices (**fig 2.4**).
- Place rails cleft face uppermost in order to shed water better (**fig 2.4**).
- Keep the bottom rails and ends of the pales clear of the ground.

FIG 2.1
Basic post and rail fencing with rail nailed to posts

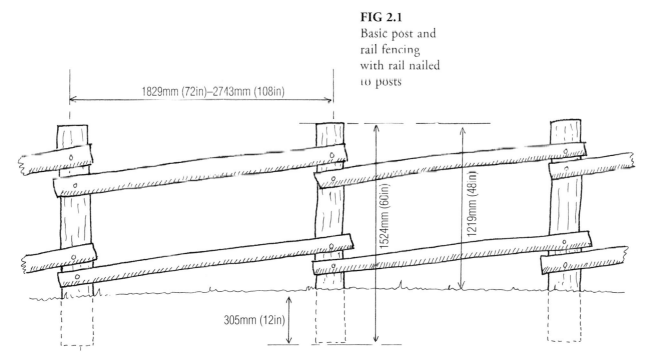

1829mm (72in)–2743mm (108in)

1524mm (60in)

1219mm (48in)

305mm (12in)

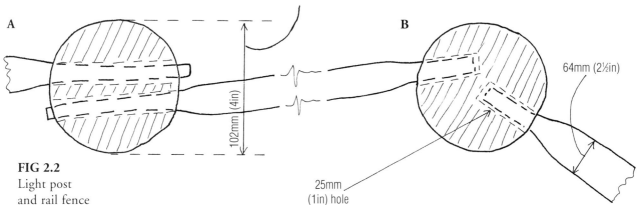

A

102mm (4in)

B

64mm (2½in)

25mm
(1in) hole

FIG 2.2
Light post
and rail fence
a) using round
poles and
b) how to
turn a corner

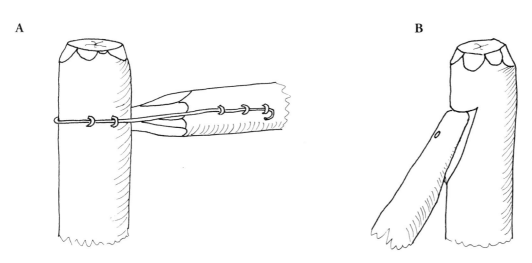

A

B

FIG 2.3
Fencing detail:
a) using fencing
wire to secure
the last post
to the rail;
b) securing an
angled brace to
a post; c) a
sharpened stake
(spile) for light
fencing and a
stout post for
normal post
and rail

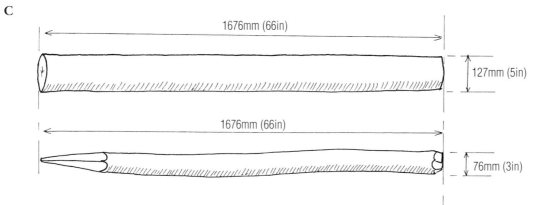

C

1676mm (66in)

127mm (5in)

1676mm (66in)

76mm (3in)

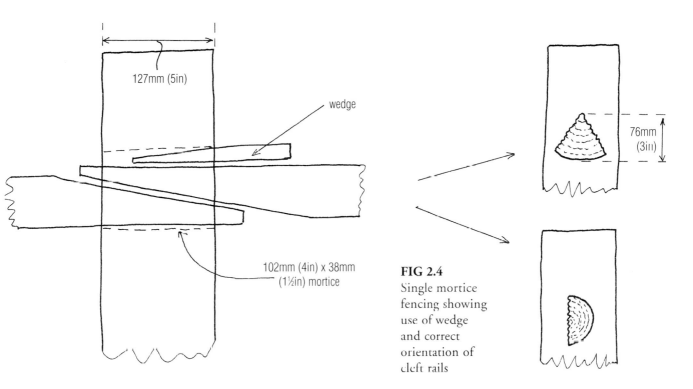

127mm (5in)

wedge

102mm (4in) x 38mm
(1½in) mortice

76mm
(3in)

FIG 2.4
Single mortice
fencing showing
use of wedge
and correct
orientation of
cleft rails

FIG 2.5
Comparison
of a) single
and b) double
mortising

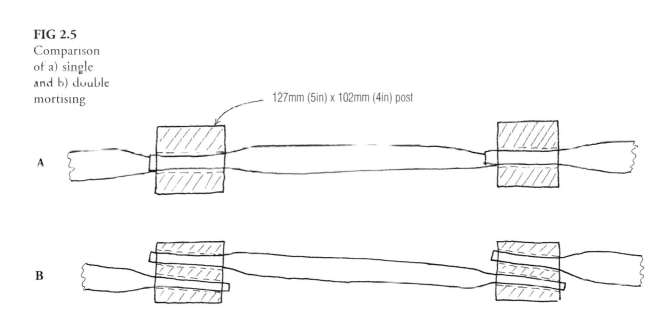

127mm (5in) x 102mm (4in) post

A

B

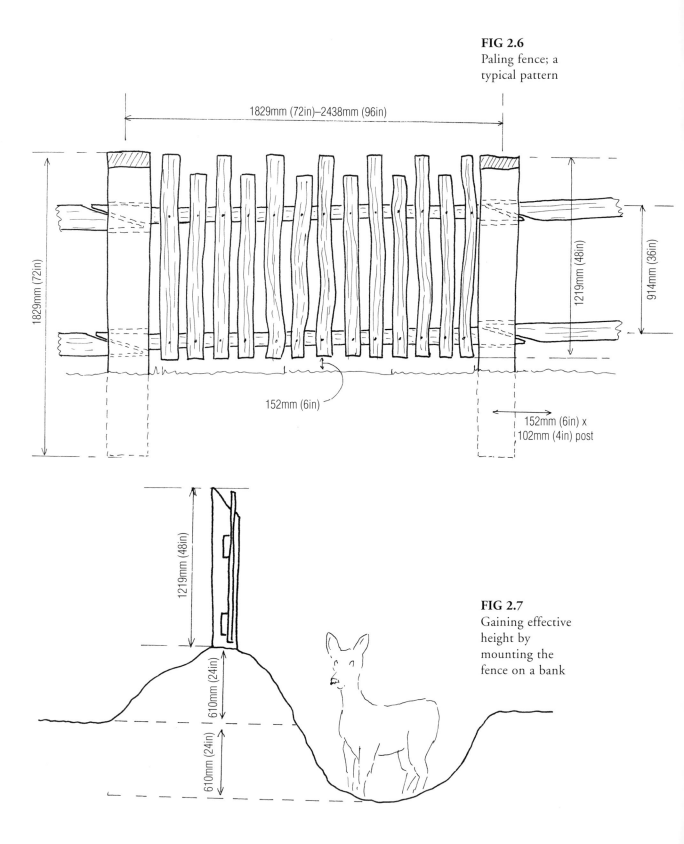

FIG 2.6
Paling fence; a typical pattern

1829mm (72in)–2438mm (96in)

1829mm (72in)

1219mm (48in)

914mm (36in)

152mm (6in)

152mm (6in) x
102mm (4in) post

1219mm (48in)

610mm (24in)

610mm (24in)

FIG 2.7
Gaining effective
height by
mounting the
fence on a bank

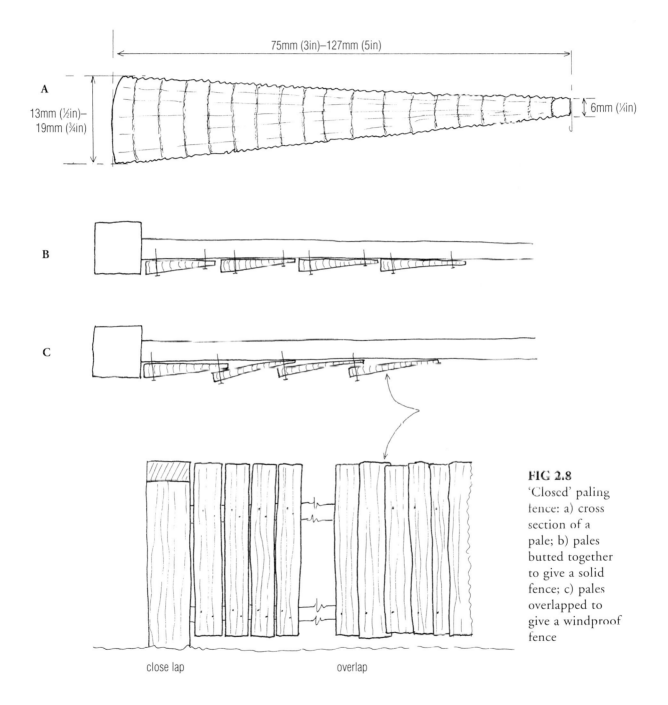

75mm (3in)–127mm (5in)

A

13mm (½in)–
19mm (¾in)

6mm (¼in)

B

C

close lap   overlap

FIG 2.8
'Closed' paling
fence: a) cross
section of a
pale; b) pales
butted together
to give a solid
fence; c) pales
overlapped to
give a windproof
fence

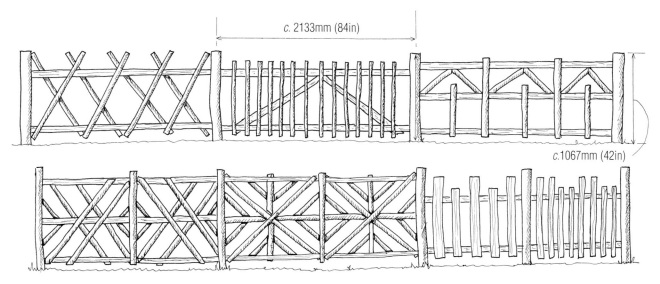

FIG 2.9
Patterns for rustic and pale garden fences

Gate Hurdles

Gate hurdles are light field gates made from small cleft poles (**figs 2.10** and **11**). Usually 1.8m (6ft) long by 1.2m (4ft) high, they have two upright 'heads' that are mortised to take five, six or seven rails (or ledges). The rails are then strengthened by means of one central upright 'strop' and two diagonal 'braces'. The whole is nailed together with the ends of the nails being clenched over to prevent them pulling out. An alternative is for the ends of the rails to be taken right through the heads and secured with wooden pegs (**fig 2.12**). The base of the heads are sharpened so they can be lightly driven into the ground (**fig 2.13**), and often the hurdle is fitted with a metal loop that is placed over a stake to hold the hurdle upright. Kentish hurdles, which are longer, have longer points on their heads that are also fitted with a ferrule at the top (**figs 2.14**), allowing them to be firmly driven into the ground without the use of supporting stakes. It is usual for the lower rails to be more closely spaced. This not only makes the bottom stronger, but also restrains older animals from grazing outside the fold.

Gate hurdles are primarily designed for creating folds in which sheep can be contained, allowing the grazing of grasslands and field crops, such as beet, to be controlled. Pens are also used at shearing and market time to restrain the animals. Hurdles have a hard life, being banged and moved and shaken loose regularly. They are designed to be tough and resilient, without being too heavy for the shepherd to move, and traditional patterns meet this need well.

Hurdles are also used to restrain pigs and bullocks. Patterns are similar to those used for sheep, but are necessarily larger and more robust in their construction. Many third- or quarter-size hurdles are made today for use in gardens to restrain flowers at the borders of paths and to keep pets away from special plants.

Table 2.1 Details of different gate hurdle patterns

Type	Height	Length	Number of rails	Braces	Foot	Other points
Kent	1219mm (48in)	2438mm (96in)	5	Strop + 2 braces – not full width	381mm (15in)	Ferrule at top of heads
Suffolk	1219mm (48in)	1829mm (72in)	6	Strop + 2 braces for full width	152mm (6in)	Metal hoop to fix to post
Hampshire	1067mm (39in)	1829mm (72in)	7	Strop + 2 braces – not full width	152mm (6in)	–
Warwickshire	1219mm (48in)	1829mm (72in)	4	Strop + 2 braces – not full width	152mm (6in)	Base of strop pointed like the feet
Pig	1219mm (48in)	1829mm (72in)	7	Strop + 2 braces for full width	152mm (6in)	Thicker 51mm (2in) rails and braces
Bullock	1820m (72in)	2438mm (96in)	6 or 8	Strop + 2 braces – not full width	381mm (15in)	Thicker 51mm (2in) rails and braces
Garden	457mm (18in)	609mm (24in)	4 or 5	As regional pattern	152 (6in)	Parts slimmer 19–38mm (¾–1½in)

Tips

- Ash, chestnut and willow are the best woods for gate hurdles, although chestnut will last longest.
- Drill rails before nailing to prevent ends splitting.
- Chamfer the tops of the heads to avoid them flaking when hammered.
- Remove any 'spears' from the clefts so they do not injure the animals.
- Chamfer the tops of the strop and braces so they do not catch the hands of anyone who is using the hurdle.
- Sharpened feet should retain a small square at the tip to make them less likely to turn in the ground.

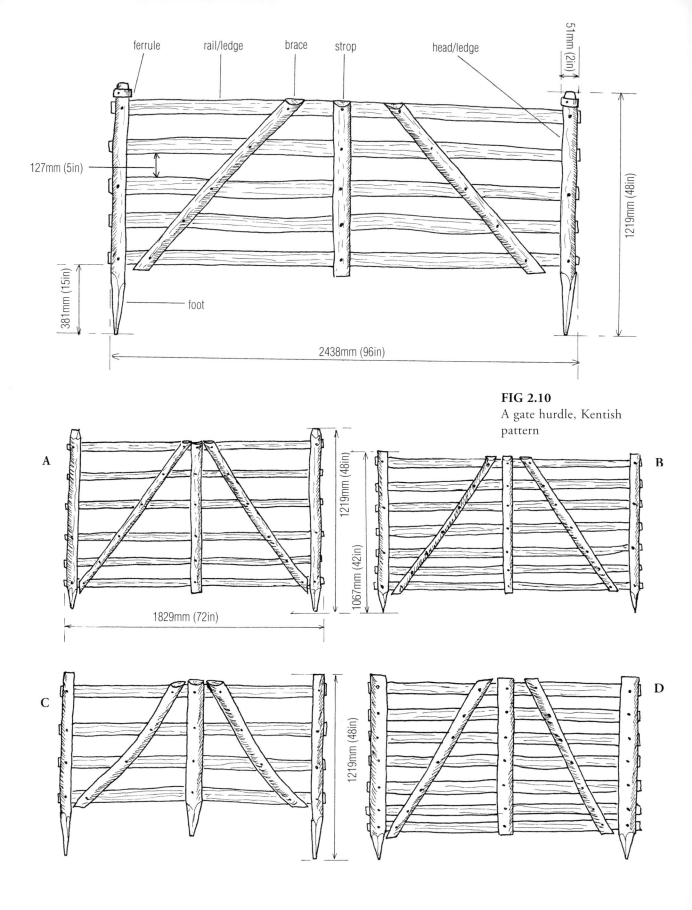

ferrule rail/ledge brace strop head/ledge

51mm (2in)

127mm (5in)

1219mm (48in)

381mm (15in)

foot

2438mm (96in)

FIG 2.10
A gate hurdle, Kentish
pattern

A

B

1219mm (48in)

1067mm (42in)

1829mm (72in)

C

1219mm (48in)

D

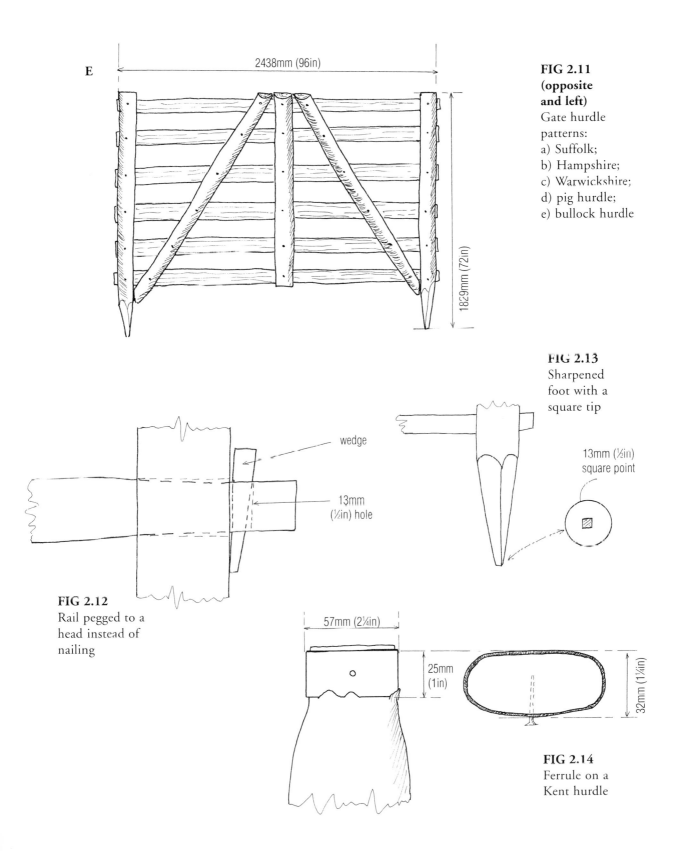

E

2438mm (96in)

1829mm (72in)

FIG 2.11 (opposite and left)
Gate hurdle patterns:
a) Suffolk;
b) Hampshire;
c) Warwickshire;
d) pig hurdle;
e) bullock hurdle

FIG 2.13
Sharpened foot with a square tip

13mm (½in) square point

wedge

13mm (½in) hole

FIG 2.12
Rail pegged to a head instead of nailing

57mm (2¼in)

25mm (1in)

32mm (1¼in)

FIG 2.14
Ferrule on a Kent hurdle

Wattle Fencing

Wattle sheep hurdles represent one of the pinnacles of green woodworking. With only a billhook and his manual skills, a hurdle maker can produce a robust fence capable of restraining animals. Sheep hurdles are 1.8m (6ft) long by 1.2m (4ft) high. They comprise ten upright rods or clefts known as 'zales' (sails) into which horizontal round and cleft rods are woven (**fig 2.15**). These 'weavers' are twisted and taken around the end zales in order to tie them in. A very specific weave is used to 'pick up' the bottom of the hurdle, and to tie in the top in order to prevent the weavers coming out when the hurdle is moved (**figs 2.16** and **2.17**). Exactly the same pattern of weaving has been found in the remains of a hurdle found in the mud of the River Thames in London. The hurdle has been dated to the 18th century, confirming that these weaving patterns have stood the test of time. Simple wattling is an even older craft, a fact that has been demonstrated by the Neolithic track-ways recovered from the Somerset Levels.

Although some key elements of the hurdle pattern are fixed, weaving patterns do vary, reflecting differing uses or regional preferences (**fig 2.18**). Wattle hurdles used with sheep, for example, have their two end zales extended at the top of the hurdle so that it can be fixed to a post. It is also common to have a 'twilly' hole in the middle of the hurdle to make it easier for the shepherd to lift and carry (**fig 2.19**). Lamb 'creep' hurdles (**fig 2.15**) have larger holes that allow lambs to jump through and get to the fresh grazing. Panels for use in gardens need none of these refinements and are plainly woven up to 1.8m (6ft) high. Some regional differences in the pattern of weaving the rods and the use of round and cleft rods can still be found, but have no great functional significance.

What can be done for garden fencing in hazel can be done in willow. However, due to the small size of one-year-old willow rods, it is usual to weave groups of six to eight rods at a time, producing a dense and very windproof fence (**fig 2.20**). Continuous wattle fencing can be made *in situ*, and has the advantage over panels that it will follow the natural contours of the ground. Modern workers such as Stephanie Bunn and Jon Warnes are producing spectacular designs for this type of fencing, a small sample of which is shown in **fig 2.21**. Wattle gates for these fences are usually framed with solid wood to give them extra rigidity.

Tips

- Use hazel, willow or ash for zales, and hazel or willow for weavers.
- Use wood within a few weeks of felling so that it can be twisted to go round the end zales without breaking, and use cleft rods the day they are split.
- Use a measuring rod regularly to make sure the end zales remain parallel and are not pulled in at the top of the panel.
- End zales are best made of round rods, the others from cleft rods.
- Hurdles are made slightly curved so that the weave tightens when the hurdle is flattened.
- Make sure cleft weavers are evenly split along their length so they produce an even weave and do not distort the zales.
- Trim back the ends of the weavers so there are no snags sticking out from the hurdle.

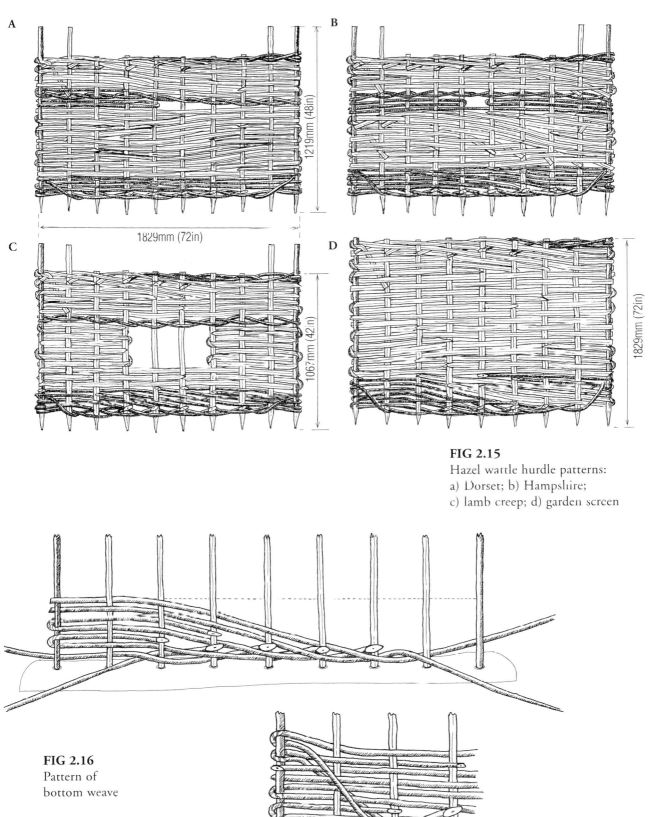

A 1219mm (48in) 1829mm (72in)

B

C 1067mm (42in)

D 1829mm (72in)

FIG 2.15
Hazel wattle hurdle patterns:
a) Dorset; b) Hampshire;
c) lamb creep; d) garden screen

FIG 2.16
Pattern of
bottom weave

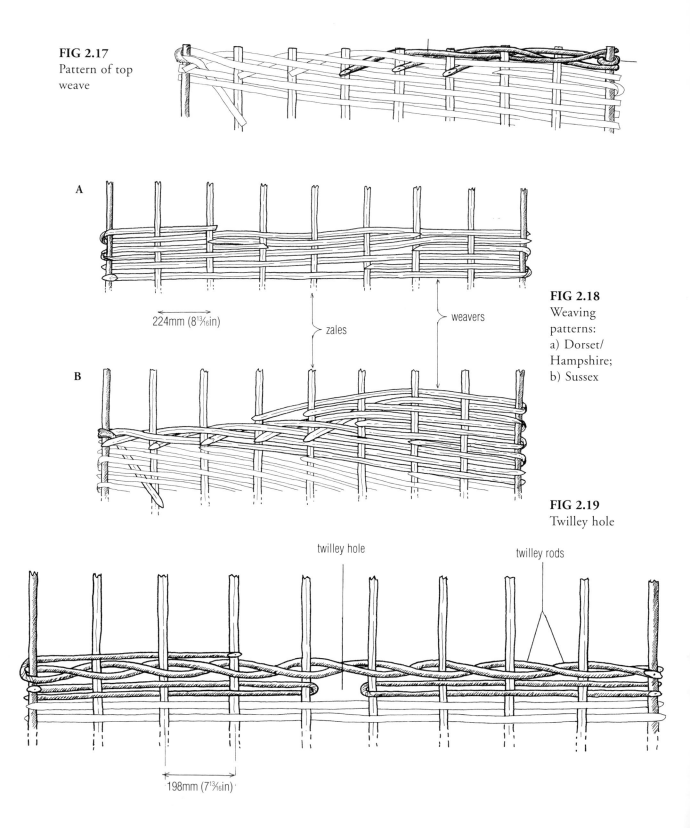

FIG 2.17
Pattern of top weave

A

224mm (8¹³⁄₁₆in)

zales

weavers

FIG 2.18
Weaving patterns:
a) Dorset/ Hampshire;
b) Sussex

B

FIG 2.19
Twilley hole

twilley hole

twilley rods

198mm (7¹³⁄₁₆in)

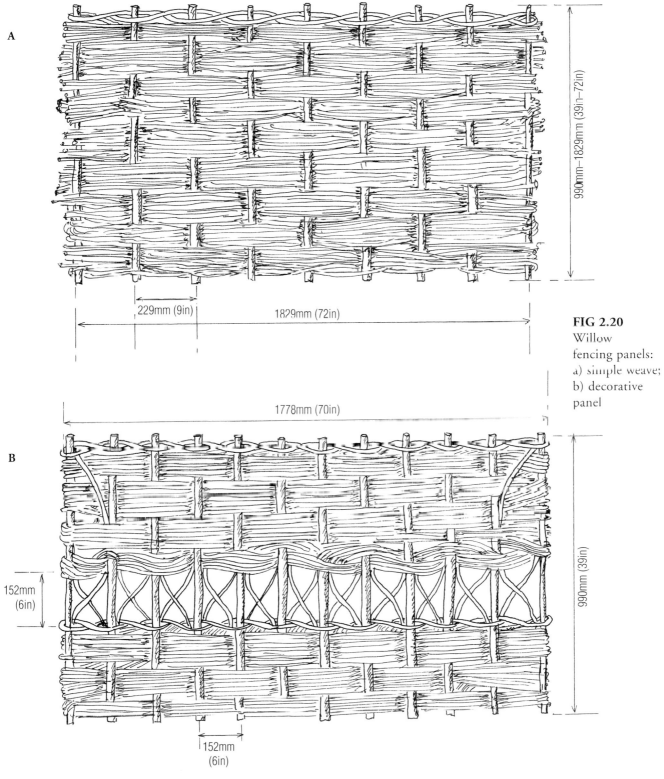

FIG 2.20
Willow
fencing panels:
a) simple weave;
b) decorative
panel

A

990mm–1829mm (39in–72in)

229mm (9in)

1829mm (72in)

B

1778mm (70in)

152mm
(6in)

990mm (39in)

152mm
(6in)

FIG 2.21
A modern *in
situ* woven fence,
Wakehurst Place,
Sussex

Gates

When animals were present on almost every farm
and when cottage gardens were fenced, there was
a tremendous demand for gates. Field gates were
normally 2.7m (9ft) wide by 1.4m (4ft 6in) high.
The basic pattern consists of a vertical stile at
each end (the hanging stile at the hinge end and
the slamming stile at the other) joined by five
horizontal rails and various combinations of
vertical and, most importantly, diagonal braces
(**fig 2.22**). These braces are designed to stop

the gate from 'dropping' at the slamming end.
Different patterns owe more to regional
preferences than to function (**figs 2.23** and **2.24**).
Both stiles are mortised to accommodate the ends
of the rails and these joints are carefully designed
to reduce the tendency for the gate to drop (**figs
24–28** inclusive). This is further assisted by
tapering the heavier top rail so that it is thinner
and lighter at its slamming end. The problem
of a gate dropping is eliminated by the hingeless
gate, which is supported on hooks on both gate
posts, but which has to be lifted both off and
back into place.

Table 2.2 Details of some different gate patterns

Type	Size	Head stile	Tail stile	Rails	Braces	Other points
Basic field gate	2143mm x 1372mm (108in x 54in)	127mm x 76mm (5in x 3in)	89mm x 76mm (3½in x 3in)	4 to 7 rails	1 vertical + 2 diagonal	Many different patterns
Sussex gate	2743mm x 1372mm (108 x 54in)	127mm x 76mm (5in x 3in)	89mm x 76mm (3½in x 3in)	5 rails + 1 diagonal	3 vertical + 1 diagonal	Top rail tapered
Hingeless gate	As field gate but rails 508mm (20in) longer	89mm x 76mm (3½in x 3in)	76mm x 51mm (3in x 2in)	2 rails	2 diagonal	No hinge
Light ash gate	2438mm x 1219mm (96in x 48in)	76mm x 51mm (3in x 2in)	76mm x 51mm (3in x 2in)	5 rails	1 vertical + 2 diagonal	All joints bolted
Horse gate	1524mm x 1371mm (60in x 54in)	127mm x 76mm (5in x 3in)	89mm x 76mm (3½in x 3in)	5 or 6 rails	1 vertical + 2 diagonal	
Cottage/ wicket gate	914mm x 914mm (36in x 36in)	63mm x 38mm (2½in x 1½in)	51mm x 32mm (2in x 1¼in)	2 or 3 rails	1 diagonal	Size can be as required

Greenwood gates are made with cleft, not sawn, wood. This produces a lighter, more water-resistant product, which, when made from butts of oak or chestnut, will last for 70 years. The joints of good gates are held together by wooden pegs in the same wood. Less substantial gates were often made from cleft ash, which was bolted together rather than using mortices. These gates will only last about 15 years.

Heavy gates require equally large posts from which to hang, and it was common practice for the bottom of these posts to be left in the round in order to give more support. Small cottage and wicket gates have a wide range of patterns (**fig 2.28**), but again are designed not to drop at the slamming end.

Tips

- Ensure the tenons on top and bottom rails and braces are designed to be self-supporting.
- Braces should be jointed into both the harr and top rail so the latter cannot drop.
- Holes drilled through mortices and tenons should be drilled slightly off-centre so that as the retaining pegs are driven home they tighten the joint.
- Bevel all edges and shave off any spears so the gate is safe and comfortable to use.
- Mortices for alternate rails are traditionally not taken right through the harr.

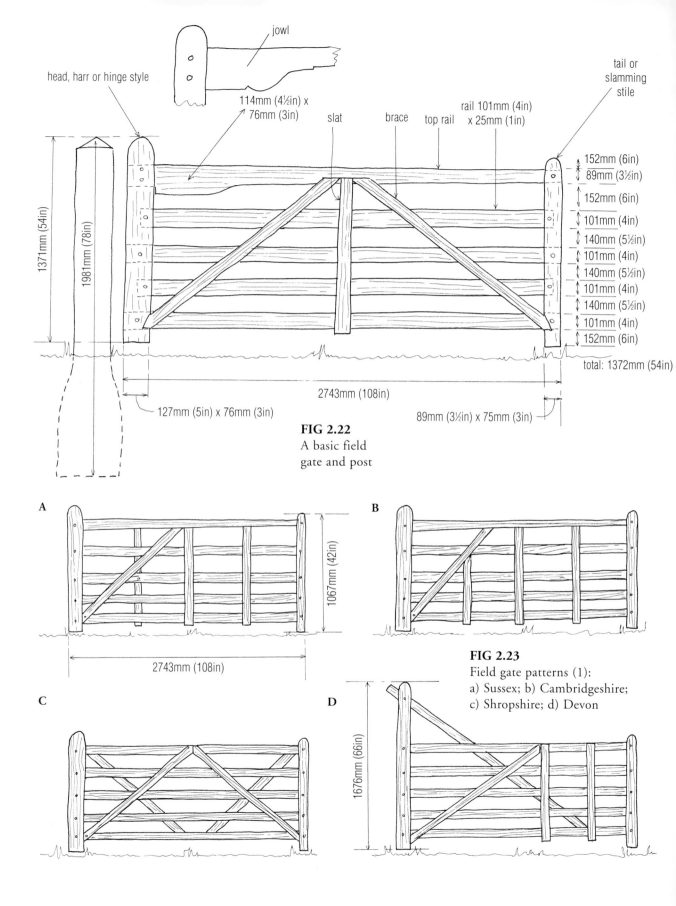

jowl

head, harr or hinge style

114mm (4½in) x 76mm (3in)

slat

brace

top rail

rail 101mm (4in) x 25mm (1in)

tail or slamming stile

152mm (6in)
89mm (3½in)
152mm (6in)
101mm (4in)
140mm (5½in)
101mm (4in)
140mm (5½in)
101mm (4in)
140mm (5½in)
101mm (4in)
152mm (6in)

total: 1372mm (54in)

1371mm (54in)

1981mm (78in)

2743mm (108in)

127mm (5in) x 76mm (3in)

89mm (3½in) x 75mm (3in)

FIG 2.22
A basic field
gate and post

A

1067mm (42in)

2743mm (108in)

B

FIG 2.23

Field gate patterns (1):
a) Sussex; b) Cambridgeshire;
c) Shropshire; d) Devon

C

D

1676mm (66in)

FIG 2.24
Field gate patterns (2): a) Welsh
pole gate; b) light ash gate;
c) Sussex hinge-less gate (lifts
onto hooks); d) horse gate

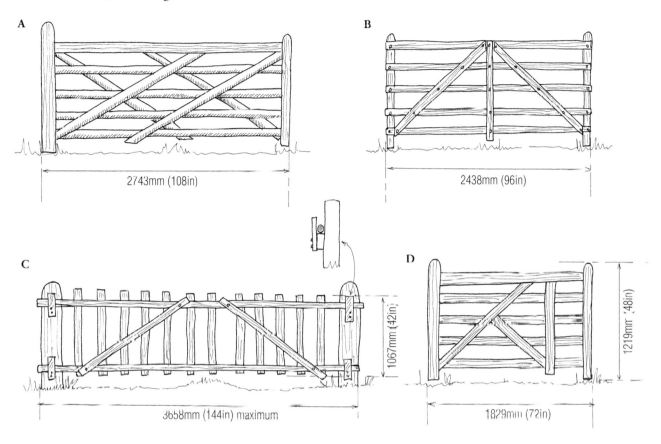

A

2743mm (108in)

B

2438mm (96in)

C

3658mm (144in) maximum

1067mm (42in)

D

1219mm (48in)

1829mm (72in)

FIG 2.25
Modified harr to stop the top
rail dropping: a) and b) top
rail enlarged at mortice to
increase support

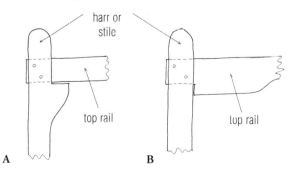

harr or
stile

top rail

top rail

A

B

FIG 2.26
Detail of joint between
braces and top rail

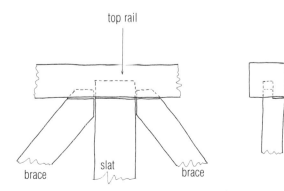

top rail

brace

slat

brace

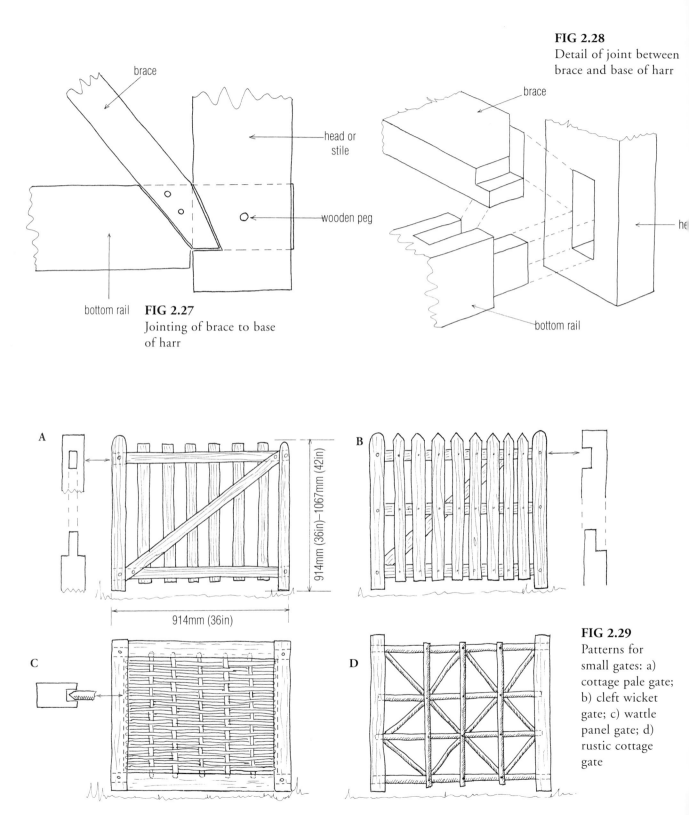

brace

head or
stile

wooden peg

bottom rail

FIG 2.27
Jointing of brace to base
of harr

FIG 2.28
Detail of joint between
brace and base of harr

brace

he

bottom rail

A

B

914mm (36in)–1067mm (42in)

914mm (36in)

C

D

FIG 2.29
Patterns for
small gates: a)
cottage pale gate;
b) cleft wicket
gate; c) wattle
panel gate; d)
rustic cottage
gate

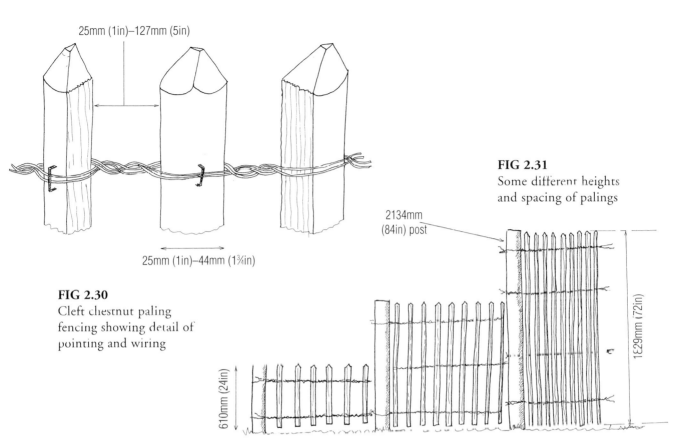

25mm (1in)–127mm (5in)

25mm (1in)–44mm (1¾in)

FIG 2.30
Cleft chestnut paling
fencing showing detail of
pointing and wiring

FIG 2.31
Some different heights
and spacing of palings

2134mm
(84in) post

1829mm (72in)

610mm (24in)

Pale and Wire Fencing

Made from small, usually triangular, clefts of sweet
chestnut wood, this type of fencing was developed
at the end of the 19th century as mass produced
cheap wire began to make all-wire fencing an
attractive alternative to all-wood products. It is
mainly produced in Kent and Sussex. The pales,
which are 25–44mm (1–1¾in) across their face and
between 0.6 and 1.8m (2ft and 6ft) long are held
together by two double strands of 14 gauge,
galvanized wire (**fig 2.30**). These are twisted in
alternate directions between each pale in order to
provide a tight loop around each one and to
provide an even spacing. Two, three, or four
lengths of these multiple strands of wire,
depending on the height of the fence, (**fig 2.31**)
are used to hold the palings, each of which is
stapled once or twice to the wire. Gaps between
the pales are between 25–125mm (1–5in)

depending on the final use for the fence. Each
paling is bluntly sharpened at its top end with
three cuts, providing a surface that sheds water.
Finished fencing is rolled for transport, the length
in each roll depending on the spacing of the pales
(smaller gaps between pales means more weight per
metre). The wires are left about 203mm (8in) long
at the ends of each length so they can be tied to
both the finished roll and to join adjacent lengths
in the finished fence. It is usual to supply pale and
wire fencing with sharpened stakes 457mm (18in)
taller than the fencing.

Tips

• Since pale and wire fencing is the only
green-wood product covered by a British
Standard (BS 1722 part 4), serious fencing
makers should refer to this document for detail.

Chapter 3 Green Wood in the House and Garden

Introduction

Local coppices and hedgerows have always been a source of wood for use in the fabric of local houses and their gardens, and even today remain major markets for green woodworkers. Apart from the effectiveness of small wood for many of these jobs, the products described provide a valuable market for material that would otherwise go on the fire or be left to rot. This material is not solely the preserve of the countryman's cottage and garden. Small wood can be found in the fabric of many grand houses, and in the hundreds of sticks and stakes in walled vegetable gardens and flower beds.

Timber-framed buildings are common in the English landscape and the oak, elm, ash and poplar timber used in their structure usually came from local woods. The design of a particular house not only incorporated traditional wisdom, but also accommodated the size and nature of the raw material available. This is a subject in its own right and is not covered here. But panel filling between the timber framework used large numbers of wattle rods and cleft lathes to hold the daub or plaster that formed the finished wall or ceiling. Similarly, thatched roofs required thousands of hazel spars to hold the straw and reed, while shingles nailed to strong lathes provided an entire wooden roof.

Peas, beans, dahlias, tomatoes, fruit trees and many, many other plants require sticks or stakes to support their growth. A large Victorian garden was a treasure house of effective, attractive and discreet uses for small wood, none of it imported and all from the local wood.

Roofing

Small, usually cleft, wood has been used to secure vegetation to the roof, and to provide the discreet decoration we see on the outside of the roof, since thatch was first used. As many as 12,000 short rods, known as 'spars', 'broches' or 'springles' (**fig 3.1**), can be used on an average-sized roof. Sharpened at each end, they are twisted by the thatcher to make a hairpin, which is driven into the thatch. Rick pegs, less used today, are longer, around 1.05m (3ft 6in), and are used with twine to secure the thatch to a rick. Liggers, which are 1.5m (5ft) long and 13mm (½in) thick, are bluntly sharpened at each end (**fig 3.2**) and are used on top of the thatch at the ridge and eaves of the roof. Longer clefts called 'sways' or 'binders' may be 2.4m (8ft) long and 25mm (1in) thick, and are used within the thatch to hold the straw in place.

Clapboards are radial tapered clefts 1.8m (6ft) long and shaped at either end to overlap adjacent boards (**fig 3.3**) by 75mm (3in). They are feather edged, being no thicker than 13mm (½in) at the thinner end. Each row overlaps its predecessor by about 127mm (5in), providing a surface waterproof to all but the strongest gales. Clapboards are commonly used on roofs in the United States, but are more often seen in England as a wall cladding.

Shingles are also radial clefts from large logs, but are less tapered than clapboards, and resemble a slate (**fig 3.4**). They are produced in standard lengths of 406 (16in), 457 (18in) and 610mm (24in), but there is a tolerance on the width.

American shingles have a curved bottom edge, which is said to throw off water more readily. Larger shingles are more difficult to produce and have names such as 'perfection' and 'royals'.

Tips

- The best thatching wood is hazel – it lasts longer than willow.
- Spars should be trimmed to a sharp point using just three cuts.
- Rick pegs can be made of any wood.
- Where possible leave the outer (weather surface) of clapboards and shingles as riven – it is more waterproof than if shaven.
- Wood for clapboards (usually oak) must be straight grained and free from knots.
- Clapboards shed water better if chamfered at their outer edge.

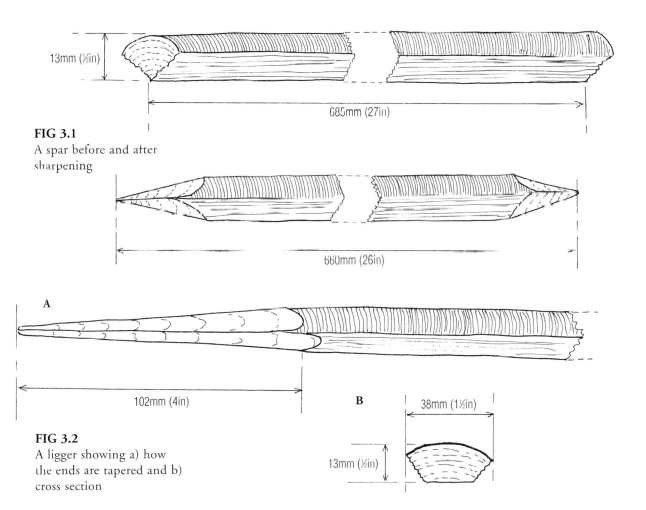

13mm (½in)

685mm (27in)

FIG 3.1
A spar before and after sharpening

660mm (26in)

A

102mm (4in)

FIG 3.2
A ligger showing a) how the ends are tapered and b) cross section

B

38mm (1½in)

13mm (½in)

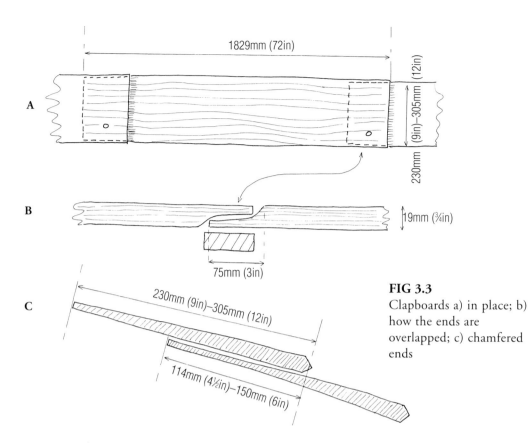

FIG 3.3
Clapboards a) in place; b) how the ends are overlapped; c) chamfered ends

FIG 3.4
Shingles: a–c) standard, American and Royal patterns; d) cross section; e) how a cleft is trimmed

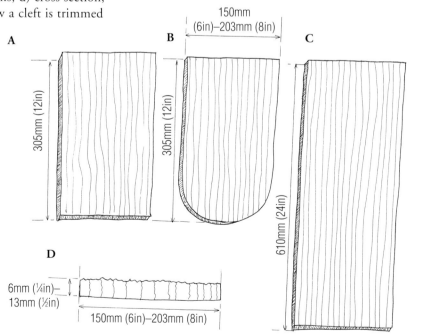

Wattles and Lathes

Wattles and lathes are designed to provide a surface and matrix that walling material, such as plaster, can permeate and lock to while also being worked to a smooth finish. Wattle and daub walling using round hazel rods and mud, dung and straw daub is at least as old as the Iron Age, and reconstructed buildings have shown the effectiveness of the system. This is further underlined by the thousands of houses up to the Victorian period that use variations of this system.

Wattles are simply round bark-on rods of 13–19mm (½–¾in) that are used to create a simple woven panel between the structural beams of a house (**fig 3.5a**). They are woven between thicker rods (**fig 3.6**) and sometimes tied to these. Cut to any length required by the builder up to 1.8m (6ft), little preparation is required by the woodman unless they are cut to specific lengths and shaped or sharpened to fit specific holes or slots in the main frame (**fig 3.7**).

Lathes can either be nailed directly to wall frames or ceiling joists, or be woven into the panel of a wall frame (**fig 3.8**). Most lathes are about 6mm (¼in) thick but 'slater's lathes', to which slates or shingles are directly nailed, are thicker (**fig 3.8**).

Tips

- Oak and chestnut make the best lathes, but any species can be used for wattle rods.
- Wattle rods are easier to weave in short lengths if 19mm (¾in) or less in diameter.
- It is better to leave the cleft surfaces of lathes unshaven as this will give a better purchase for the plaster.
- Lathes for weaving can be of different widths.
- Wood that has seasoned for about six weeks will rive more easily into thin clefts – splits in very green wood runs out more easily.

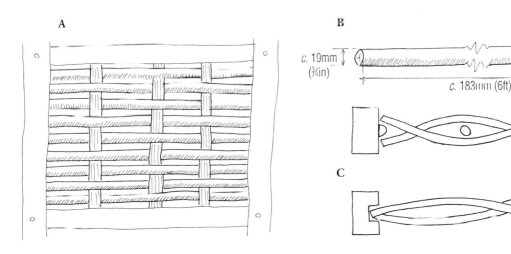

FIG 3.5
Wattles: a) wattle panel in place;
b) wattle rod; c) how rods are
connected to the main frame

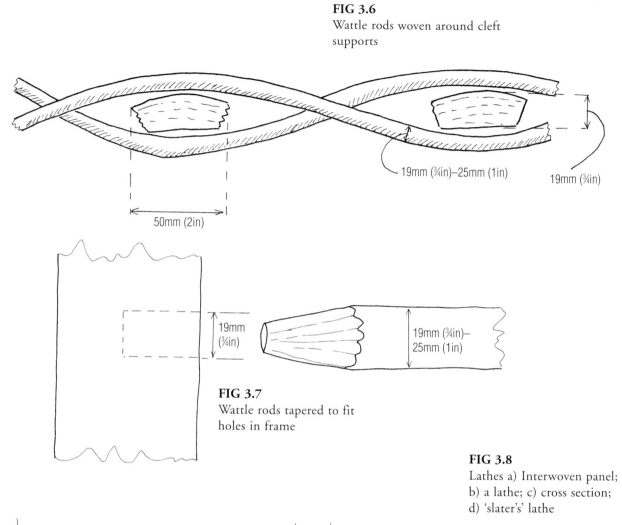

FIG 3.6
Wattle rods woven around cleft supports

19mm (¾in)–25mm (1in)

19mm (¾in)

50mm (2in)

19mm (¾in)

19mm (¾in)–25mm (1in)

FIG 3.7
Wattle rods tapered to fit holes in frame

FIG 3.8
Lathes a) Interwoven panel;
b) a lathe; c) cross section;
d) 'slater's' lathe

A

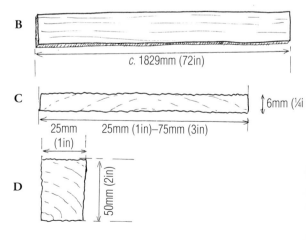

B

c. 1829mm (72in)

C

6mm (¼i

25mm (1in)–75mm (3in)

25mm (1in)

D

50mm (2in)

Sticks and Stakes

A whole variety of different sticks and stakes are used in the well-tended garden. Pea sticks are extremely versatile and look natural. Cut from flat, fan-shaped boughs up to 1.8m (6ft) tall (**fig 3.9**), they are used to support both edible and sweet peas. Laid flat, they protect seed beds from birds and, with their tops folded horizontally supply a supporting frame for tall flowers, such as delphiniums, to grow through.

Bean rods are long, reasonably straight and stout. They are best sharpened at the butt end and have the buds removed to save the user's hands. Other sticks come in a variety of lengths and diameters depending on the job they have to perform and are normally sharpened at the butt end (**fig 3.10**). It is also usual for sticks to be cut to a 'V' at the top so that when hit with a mallet the stick does not split. Thicker stakes are used to support fruit trees and other shrubs, and are usually sharpened to a blunt point. Forked stakes, or 'lugs', are particularly useful to support fruit-laden boughs of fruit trees, and of course thinner longer ones still find use as props for the clothes line (**fig 3.11**). The most massive 'stakes' are used for hop poles, and are still used in some areas.

Table 3.1 Details of the patterns of common sticks and stakes for the garden

Product	Length	Diameter	Other Points
Pea stick	1219–1829mm (48–72in)	20mm (¾in) at butt	Flat- and fan-shaped with angled butt
Bean rod	2134–2438mm (84–96in)	25–38mm (1–1½in) at butt	Bluntly sharpened
Flower stake	914–1371mm (36–54in)	25mm (1in) at butt	Cut to a 'V' at the top and bluntly sharpened
Tomato stake	1524–1829mm (60–72in)	19mm (¾in) at butt	None
Pot sticks	As required	12mm (½in) at butt	None
Clothes prop	2438mm (96in)	38mm (1½in) at butt	Crotch top, sharpened butt, top 610mm (24in) of bark removed
Raspberry stakes	2134mm (84in)	75mm (3in) at butt	Needs socket for bracing post
Tree stake	1676mm (66in)	89mm (3½in) at butt	Sharpened
Hop pole	4800–6000mm (192–240in)	Minimum 75mm (3in) at butt	Bark removed and pole treated

Tips

- Hazel and elm make the best pea sticks if less than ten years old; any species will do for other sticks.
- All sticks and stakes are better if bluntly sharpened; for pea sticks a single angled cut is sufficient.
- Remove the bark from the top 0.6m (2ft) of a clothes prop to avoid staining clothes.
- Cut the top of flower stakes to a 'V' so they will not split when hammered.

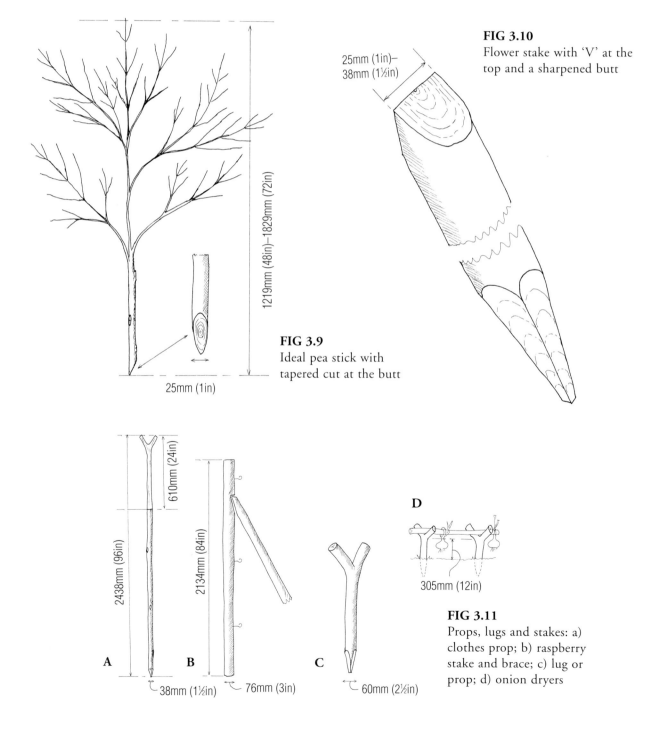

FIG 3.9
Ideal pea stick with tapered cut at the butt

25mm (1in)

1219mm (48in)–1829mm (72in)

FIG 3.10
Flower stake with 'V' at the top and a sharpened butt

25mm (1in)–
38mm (1½in)

A 2438mm (96in)
610mm (24in)
38mm (1½in)

B 2134mm (84in)
76mm (3in)

C 60mm (2½in)

D
305mm (12in)

FIG 3.11
Props, lugs and stakes: a) clothes prop; b) raspberry stake and brace; c) lug or prop; d) onion dryers

Trellis, arches and climbing frames

Trellis is a wooden framework, using open panels, narrow rods and lathes to form a lattice-work (**fig 3.12**). It is very popular in gardens as a framework to support climbing plants. Most commonly used as a barrier, as a support for climbers against a building and to provide arches over a path, trellis offers plenty of scope for the maker's imagination. Trellis comes in panels, usually 1.8m (6ft) long and up to a similar height. It requires posts or a building to support it and is invariably treated with preservative to give it a longer life. Where round poles are used, it is often better to remove the bark so the preservative can penetrate the wood, and the trellis can avoid that unsightly stage of loosing its bark. Where used at a boundary and privacy is required it is possible for the bottom of the panel to be faced in clapboards.

Rose arches designed to go over paths are made of long, narrow, trellis panels with a variety of straight or curved panels forming the arch (**fig 3.13**). Climbing frames fixed to a wall consist of one flat panel of trellis (**figs 3.14** and **3.15**). Within flower beds conical or pyramidal structures are frequently used, the former using woven rods rather than nails to hold the structure together (**figs 3.16** and **3.17**).

Tips

- If treating trellis with normal wood preservative, remove the bark first; to retain the bark, use a highly impervious gloss finish.
- Thin clefts may need holes drilling before nailing to avoid the cleft splitting.
- Provide posts that are 300mm–450mm (12in–18in) taller than the trellis panel.
- Leave sufficient length, at least 150mm (6in), on the vertical members of climbing frames to go into the ground to make the frame self supporting.

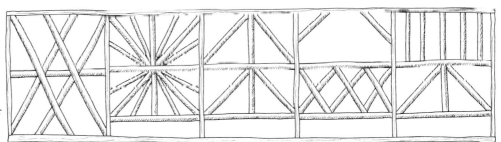

FIG 3.12
Trellis – a variety of patterns for panels

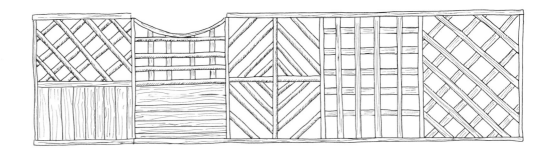

FIG 3.13

Trellis/Rose arches: a variety of patterns

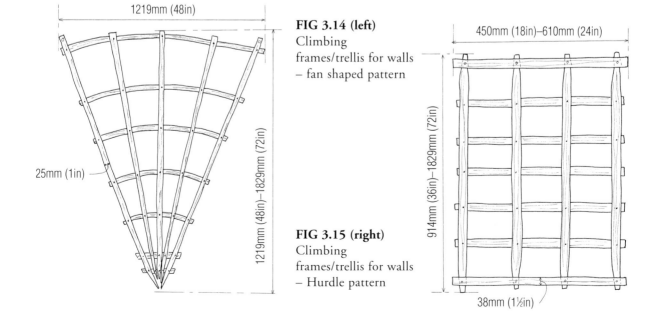

FIG 3.14 (left)

Climbing frames/trellis for walls – fan shaped pattern

FIG 3.15 (right)

Climbing frames/trellis for walls – Hurdle pattern

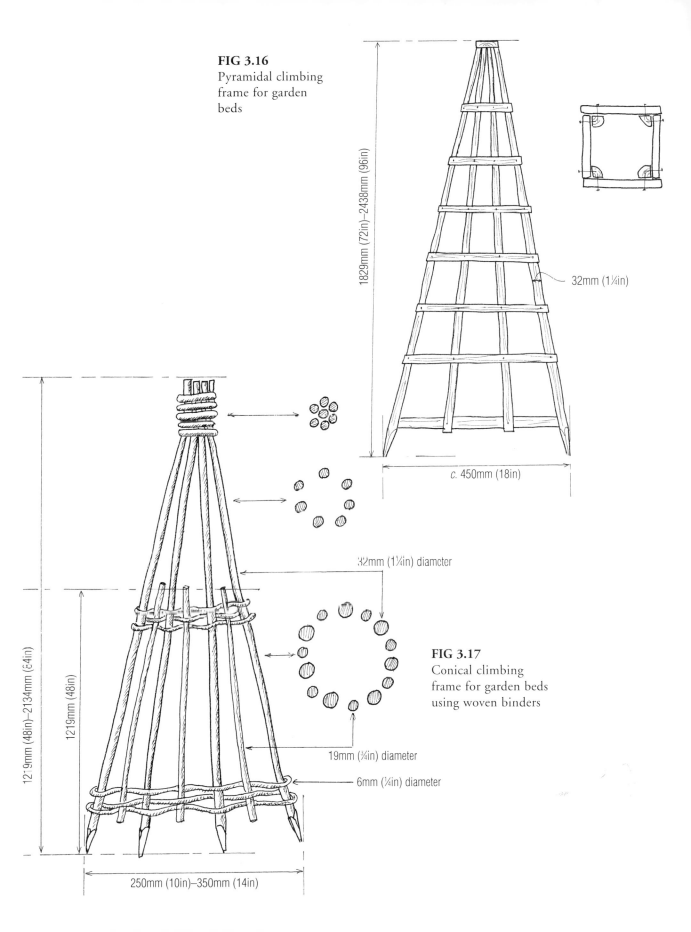

FIG 3.16
Pyramidal climbing frame for garden beds

1829mm (72in)–2438mm (96in)

32mm (1¼in)

c. 450mm (18in)

32mm (1¼in) diameter

FIG 3.17
Conical climbing frame for garden beds using woven binders

19mm (¾in) diameter

6mm (¼in) diameter

1219mm (48in)–2134mm (84in)

1219mm (48in)

250mm (10in)–350mm (14in)

Arbours, Pergolas and Bowers

These are seats, usually enclosed in trellis panels, which, once covered by climbing vegetation, provide a quiet corner on a sunny day. The simplest arbours are based on the arches already described (**fig 3.18**). To make an arch into an arbour, the back is filled in with suitable trellis work and a seat is fitted *c.* 450mm (18in) from the ground and to the full depth of the arbour. A width of 1.2m (4ft) will seat two people. One or more horizontal members can be added to the back to make a back rest, while the bottom 1.4m (4ft 6in) of both sides and back can be filled in with clapboards or rustic panels to give a cosier feel. More complex pergolas can be made from round poles, and a hexagonal pattern is illustrated (**fig 3.19**). Again, the lower panels can be filled in, and permanently-fixed seating installed.

The most rustic bower I have seen is made from woven hazel rods shaped in the form of a half dome (**fig 3.20**). It is made *in situ* with the nine main rods inserted into the ground. The open front is 1.5m (5ft) wide, and about the same height. It is difficult to get much higher than this – but it is great for children!

Tips

- For longevity use oak or chestnut in contact with the ground and hazel for woven work – otherwise use what is to hand.
- Remove the bark from the members if ordinary preservative is used; use a special outdoor finish if you want to leave the bark on.
- Make sure that the bottom members are stout enough to be pegged to the ground and restrain the whole structure in a wind.
- Slightly angle any seat down at the back for more comfort and, in a shallow arbour, ensure that it comes right to the front to give sufficient depth to be comfortable.
- Joint the members together where added strength is required.

FIG 3.18
An arbour based on a rose arch

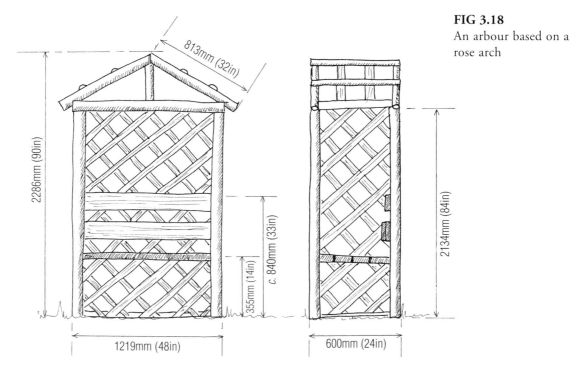

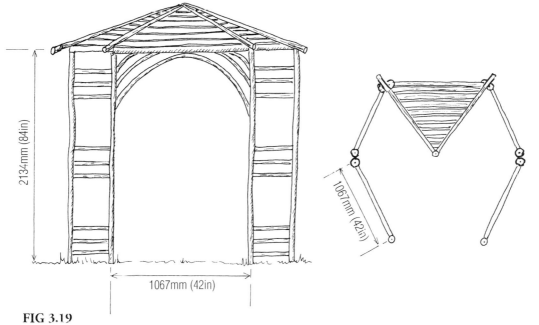

FIG 3.19
A Pergola

2134mm (84in)

1067mm (42in)

1067mm (42in)

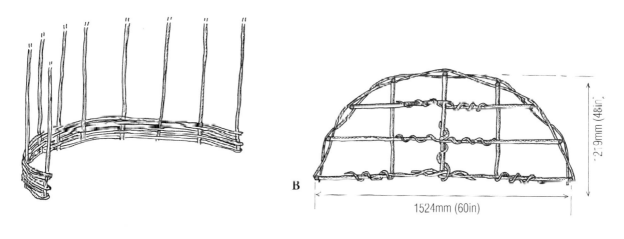

A

B

1524mm (60in)

2;9mm (48in)

FIG 3.20
A wattle bower
a) base; b) frame;
c) finished bower

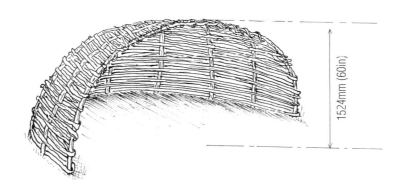

C

1524mm (60in)

Hanging Baskets and Bird Feeders

These are not items with a long tradition. The patterns we see today reflect a combination of the visually attractive with some knowledge of bird behaviour.

Rustic hanging baskets are made from small round rods built up in pairs at right angles to each previous pair (**fig 3.21**). Three or four additional rods form the base, and the whole is held together by cords threaded through holes at either end of each rod. The cords are also the means of suspending the basket.

Patio planters can be made that appear rather similar, but for these it is best if the rods are nailed to a frame of cleft members so they can be fitted more tightly together to avoid excessive leakage of the contents (**fig 3.22**).

Rustic bird feeders come in various patterns. The most basic is a flat tray, with a rim to retain the loose feed, and holes at each corner to allow it to be suspended (**fig 3.23**). Gaps in the rim allow water to drain away. Hanging feeders can be fitted with simple roofs (**fig 3.24**). Alternatively the tray can be supported on a post and fitted with a roof to provide some protection (**fig 3.25**). Cleft wood is used to produce the base of the tray and the roof.

Fat feeders consist of posts (**fig 3.26**) or hanging logs (**fig 3.27**) with holes drilled in them and into which fatty food can be forced. More birds can be encouraged to these by inserting small rods for them to stand on while feeding. Any combination of these ideas can be put together to make an original feeder.

Tips

- Use chafe-resistant cord where possible.
- Use a non-toxic preservative where wood is in contact with the ground or exposed to the weather.
- Ensure the design allows water to drain from the surface of the table.
- The bark remains longer on cleft wood if it has been split and allowed to season protected from direct sunlight.
- Almost any wood can be used, but oak and chestnut will last longer.

FIG 3.21
A hanging basket

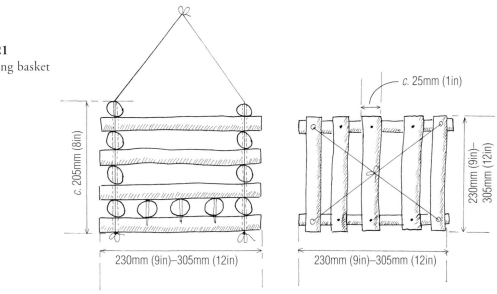

c. 205mm (8in)

230mm (9in)–305mm (12in)

c. 25mm (1in)

230mm (9in)–305mm (12in)

230mm (9in)–305mm (12in)

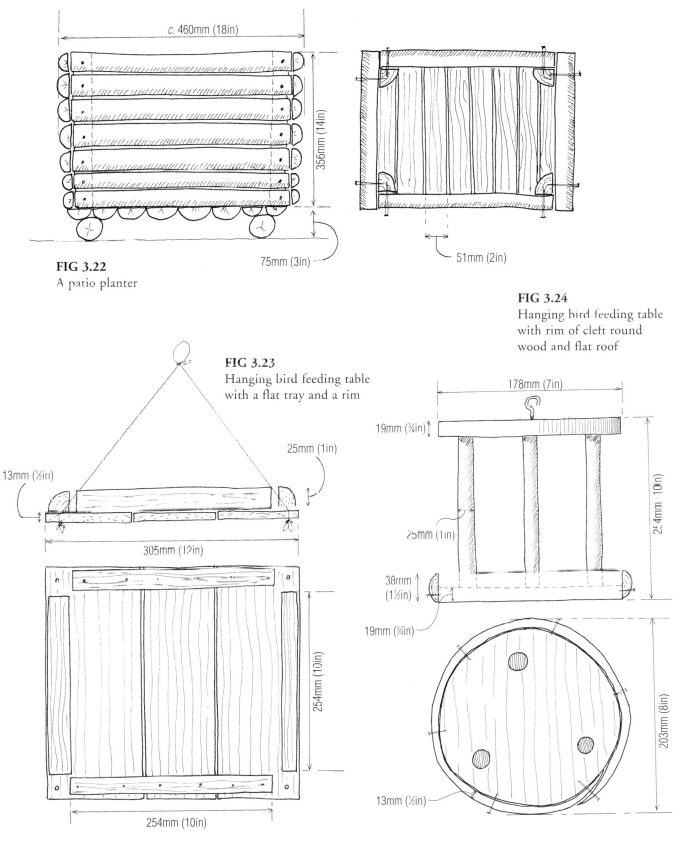

c. 460mm (18in)

356mm (14in)

75mm (3in)

51mm (2in)

FIG 3.22
A patio planter

FIG 3.24
Hanging bird feeding table
with rim of cleft round
wood and flat roof

FIG 3.23
Hanging bird feeding table
with a flat tray and a rim

25mm (1in)

13mm (½in)

305mm (12in)

254mm (10in)

254mm (10in)

178mm (7in)

19mm (¾in)

254mm (10in)

25mm (1in)

38mm (1½in)

19mm (¾in)

203mm (8in)

13mm (½in)

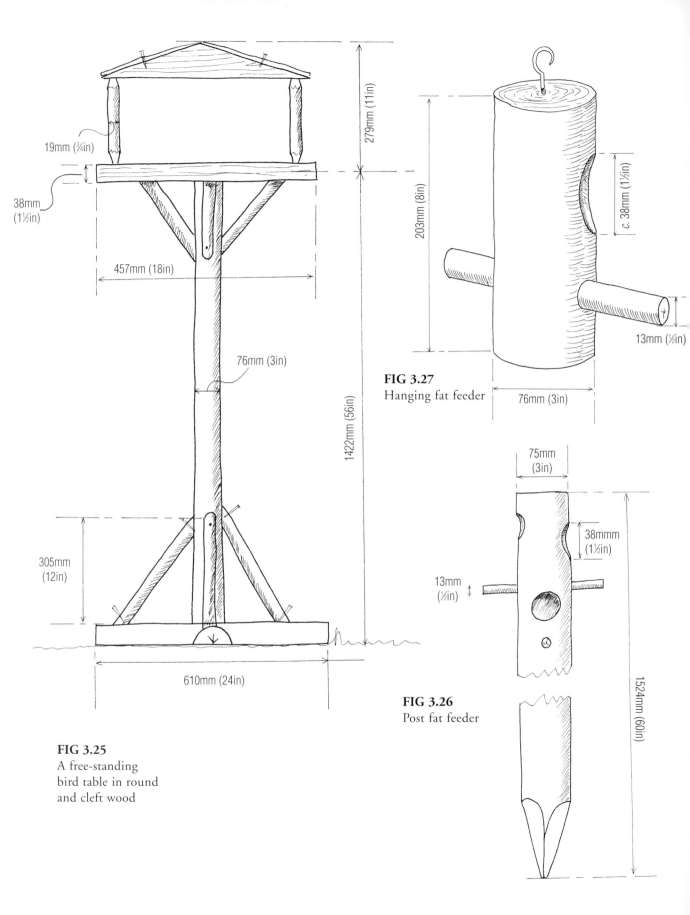

279mm (11in)

19mm (¾in)

38mm (1½in)

457mm (18in)

76mm (3in)

1422mm (56in)

305mm (12in)

610mm (24in)

FIG 3.25
A free-standing
bird table in round
and cleft wood

203mm (8in)

c. 38mm (1½in)

13mm (½in)

76mm (3in)

FIG 3.27
Hanging fat feeder

75mm (3in)

38mmm (1½in)

13mm (½in)

1524mm (60in)

FIG 3.26
Post fat feeder

Borders and bins

Green wood can be used to good effect in making borders for raised flower and vegetable beds, in providing composting bins, and in making tree guards.

Borders are made from long cleft poles that are nailed to short stakes driven into the ground (**fig 3.28**). These must be shaped to fit closely together to retain the soil. Wattled borders are very attractive and are woven in place around short stakes already driven into the ground. If not treated they do not have a long life. Very short posts held together by wire stapled to them are popular, but must be treated and require additional stakes in the ground to support them; these are best for beds with tight or frequent curves.

Compost bins can be made of woven hazel (**fig 3.29**). These use a circle of stakes driven into the ground around which small hazel rods are woven. The top rods are 'twillied' so that the weave does not lift off the stakes. A square bin is produced by making four separate panels, each made by nailing cleft pales to a frame (**fig 3.30**). The panels can be tied to each other at the corners or fixed to posts

driven into the ground. These have a longer life than wattles.

Tree guards, suitable for protecting young trees from browsing by large animals, are similar to bins, but generally smaller. If wattle is used (**fig 3.31**) the smallest diameter is about 1m (3ft 6in). Square or triangular tree guards can have sides as short as 0.6m (2ft), with either vertical or horizontal members to make a framework. In parkland it is common to use guards 1.2m (4ft) square (**fig 3.32**) made with four sharpened corner posts and three horizontal bars on each face.

Tips

- Oak and chestnut are the best material for products that are kept outside or are touching the ground, but hazel is an essential wood for woven products.
- Most of these products are better if treated with preservative, although this is difficult with round bark on hazel rods.
- Woven products are best made *in situ*.
- Where long clefts are butted together to retain soil, shape them to fit fairly tight, or use wider clefts and overlap them.

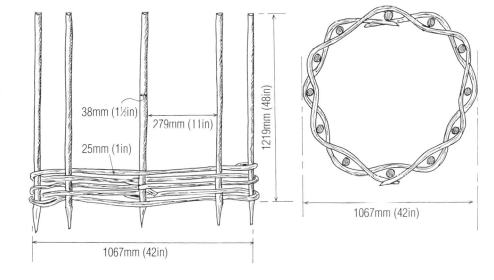

FIG 3.29
Wattle composting bin (weaving not yet completed to the top of the bin)

38mm (1½in)

279mm (11in)

25mm (1in)

1219mm (48in)

1067mm (42in)

1067mm (42in)

A

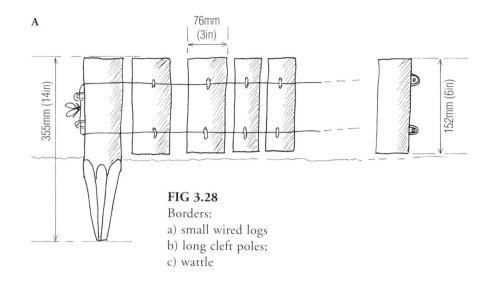

76mm
(3in)

355mm (14in)

152mm (6in)

FIG 3.28
Borders:
a) small wired logs
b) long cleft poles;
c) wattle

B

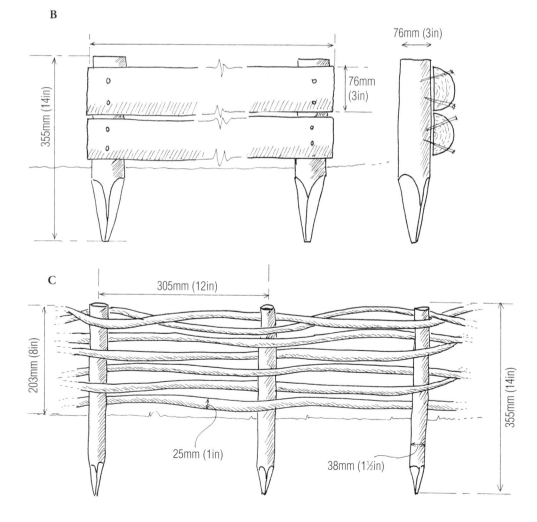

355mm (14in)

76mm
(3in)

76mm (3in)

C

305mm (12in)

203mm (8in)

355mm (14in)

25mm (1in)

38mm (1½in)

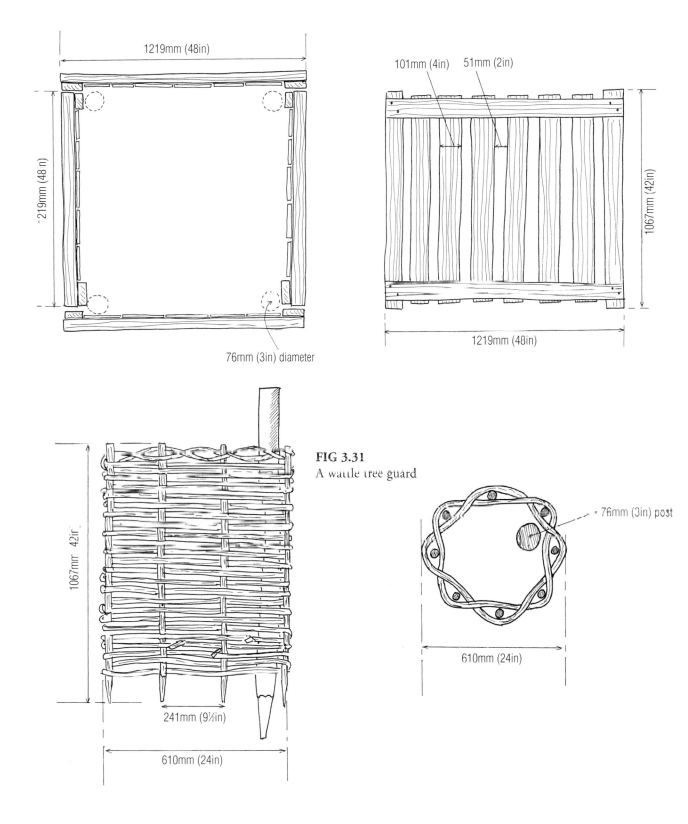

FIG 3.30
Composting bin of
framed lathes

1219mm (48in)

1219mm (48in)

76mm (3in) diameter

101mm (4in)   51mm (2in)

1067mm (42in)

1219mm (48in)

FIG 3.31
A wattle tree guard

76mm (3in) post

610mm (24in)

1067mm 42in

241mm (9½in)

610mm (24in)

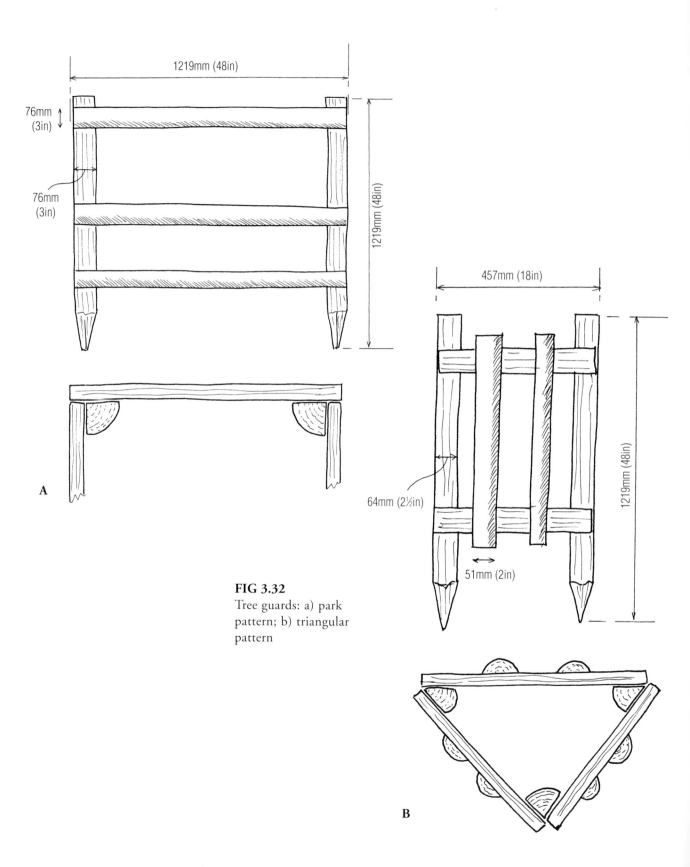

FIG 3.32
Tree guards: a) park pattern; b) triangular pattern

Chapter 4 Household Treen

Introduction

It is perhaps hard for us today, living in a society based on metal, ceramics and plastics, to realize the extent to which our forebears relied on wooden products in their day-to-day lives. This chapter concentrates on patterns for a whole range of wooden products that are used in the home, with many of which our ancestors would be familiar. In addition there are some designs and concepts that are entirely modern, and which confirm that good functional design skills have not been lost.

Treen literally means 'made of wood' – a word derived from the Anglo-Saxon. Here I use it to mean a whole range of small wooden objects regularly used in the home. Ornaments are excluded. Wood, of course, does not last well in the long term, so we have hardly any examples of products that our ancestors used prior to the 16th century. For these early times we are very dependent on illustrations, such as those in the Bayeaux Tapestry. For later periods we are very lucky to have finds such as the Tudor warship *Mary Rose*. In this case the waters of the Solent have preserved all of the wooden products that were on the ship when it went down. There are examples of spoons, scales, candle-holders, tankards, whistles, bowls and other everyday treen of Tudor times. In this chapter we will look at these items and more, a number of which are still made and used in the home.

Many of the patterns shown are traditional and have a long history. They include a range of artefacts that are still popular, and more importantly, all of which are useful and useable in today's kitchens. We do not still use them simply because we like their appearance. There are very good reasons for using wood where it comes into contact with the food we eat. It has been scientifically proven that there are substances within the wood itself that help to suppress the growth of bacteria in a way that plastic cannot. As a result, even when they are scored or slightly damaged, wooden utensils and cutting boards, if kept clean, can be safer than plastic ones.

Lastly, this is an area of products where you can give full reign to your imagination in terms of design and function. By exploring the properties of wood it is possible to make completely new artefacts or new patterns of old favourites. This is an area where you really can make beautiful, desirable products.

Patterns of turnery shapes

As with many areas of art and design, the pattern and form of the objects we make are not randomly arrived at. They are often the result of centuries of development and subtle change, so that at any point in time there is a set of patterns in use that represent the distillation of good taste during that era. This is the case with turnery that is used to either embellish or improve the functionality of many of the products in this section. But this turnery is done within certain rules or guidelines. Some of the shapes, and the terms used to describe them, come from the patterns of classical architecture. So cyma reversa and cyma recta are descriptive of types of moulding found in the buildings of antiquity.

A variety of these shapes, ranging from the simple taper to the more complex curves of an 'inverted cup', are shown in **figs 4.1** and **4.2**. The first ones show combinations of the earlier patterns that result in attractive patterns, some of which you will be familiar with, particularly in the legs of chairs. The later illustrations are of individual items. The beauty of this approach is that an individual worker can put together combinations to suit the particular artefact he or she is making. However, good taste should always prevail and tell the worker which combinations work well together and which appear overly fussy. Turning shapes for their own sake has little merit; turning them where they add a touch of beauty or make the artefact easier to use is a target we should all aspire to.

The complexity of some of these shapes is the very reason for keeping a record of the patterns used. It is worth keeping patterns on record so that you can repeat them, as discussed in Chapter 1.

Spoons

Some of the points in this section are inspired by Eric Rogers' splendid booklet on spoons (see bibliography, page 236). Although very few ancient spoons survive, we do know that they have a long history. The oldest examples were little more than flattened spatulas with no bowl. Welsh caul spoons can be traced back over 1,000 years, and there are occasional examples of medieval and Tudor spoons available to us. **Fig 4.3** shows some patterns of early spoons, whose round deep bowls and simple handles were the most common pattern. The handle could either join the bowl flush at its rim, or be slightly lower. It was not uncommon for

better-quality examples of these spoons to have turned handles with a decorative knob at the end.

Wooden kitchen spoons: used during cooking, these are well known and used by most of us. Many examples are still made today, albeit by machine and not by hand. These are typically long-handled and with a very shallow bowl (**fig 4.4**) and because they are machine-made they have no angle between bowl and the stem of the handle, which makes them difficult to use for tasting the contents of the pot. Some have a straight edge at the end of the bowl to allow the pot to be scraped. I particularly like the long-handled 'tasting spoon' (**fig 4.4**), which performs its function exactly and without dripping.

Strainers: these are particularly useful and come in different patterns (**fig 4.5**). Examples with a deep bowl and a short-angled handle are used to get items such as olives out of jars, while leaving the liquor. Larger versions have a straighter handle, and sometimes holes on only one side of the bowl.

Caddy spoons: these seem to have originated in the United States. They have a medium-sized round bowl and a very short flat handle (**fig 4.6**) so they fit easily into a caddy. The shape and length of the handle can be changed to make a more attractive or functional spoon.

Dessert, tea and soup spoons: these are sized according to their task and designed to be effective and comfortable to use (**fig 4.7**). The key points to making a spoon effective when used, are: an angle between the handle and bowl; slightly cutting away the rim of the bowl adjacent to the handle; and a comfortable curve at the end of the handle (**fig 4.8**). A selection of different ends to handles is shown in **fig 4.9**.

Handed spoons: these were made for right- or left-handed users, accounting for their unusual shape (**fig 4.10**).

Mustard spoons: these are not really spoons but are more reminiscent of a blunt knife. The handle is usually turned (**fig 4.11**).

Honey drizzlers: again, not really a spoon, but performing the function of transferring honey from pot to bread more effectively, and a nice piece of turnery to have in the kitchen (**fig 4.12**).

Tips

- Although any wood can be used for a spoon, close grained varieties are best (fruit wood, beech, spindle, maple, yew, box etc).
- If the spoon is to be used, make sure it is trimmed to be comfortable and effective (**fig 4.8**).
- Spoons last longer in use if treated with an oil (sunflower or walnut are good), but be aware of problems resulting from a users allergy.
- Use a fine garnet paper to get a very smooth finish if required (our ancestors didn't bother), and wet the spoon between each sanding in order to raise the grain.

FIG 4.2
Turnery patterns: a) bead, coves and astragal; b) bead and cove; c) vase; d) cove and inverted cup; e) cove and cyma reversa; f) cyma reversa

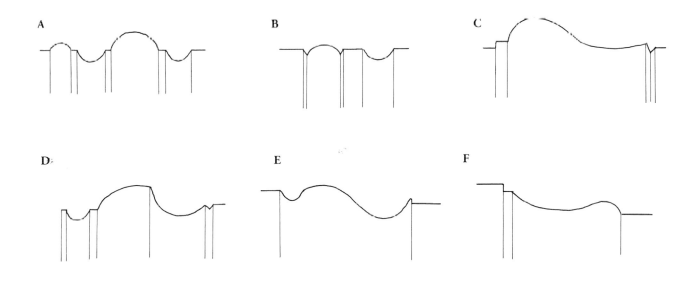

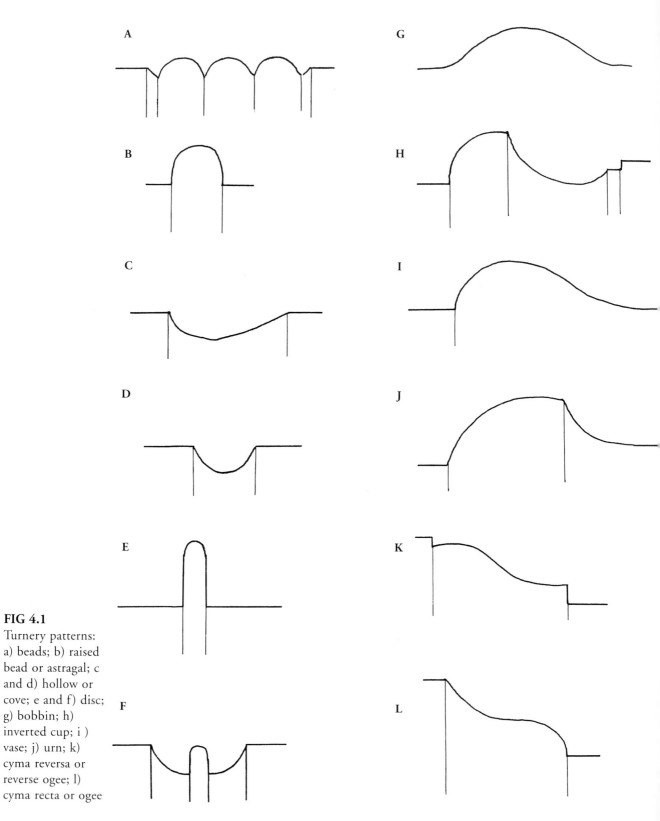

FIG 4.1
Turnery patterns:
a) beads; b) raised
bead or astragal; c
and d) hollow or
cove; e and f) disc;
g) bobbin; h)
inverted cup; i)
vase; j) urn; k)
cyma reversa or
reverse ogee; l)
cyma recta or ogee

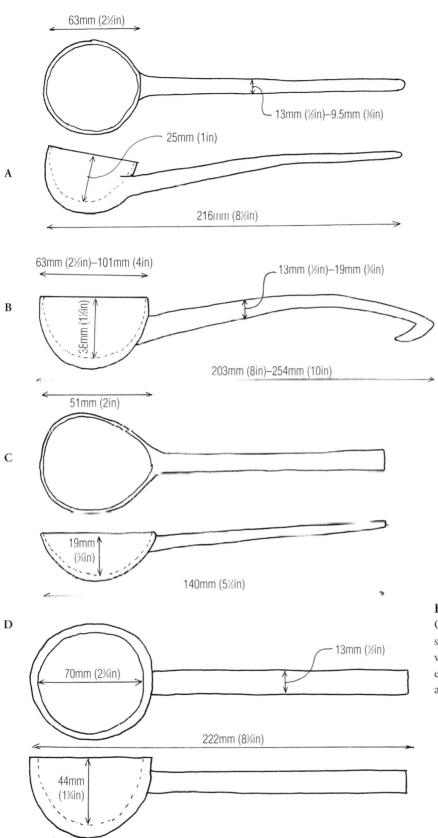

63mm (2½in)

13mm (½in)–9.5mm (⅜in)

25mm (1in)

A

216mm (8½in)

63mm (2½in)–101mm (4in)

13mm (½in)–19mm (¾in)

B

38mm (1½in)

203mm (8in)–254mm (10in)

51mm (2in)

C

19mm (¾in)

140mm (5½in)

D

70mm (2¾in)

13mm (½in)

222mm (8¾in)

44mm (1¾in)

FIG 4.3
Old spoon patterns: a) Welsh caul spoon; b) traditional Welsh spoon with hooked handle; c) Tudor eating spoon; d) Tudor ladle (c and d from *Mary Rose* collection)

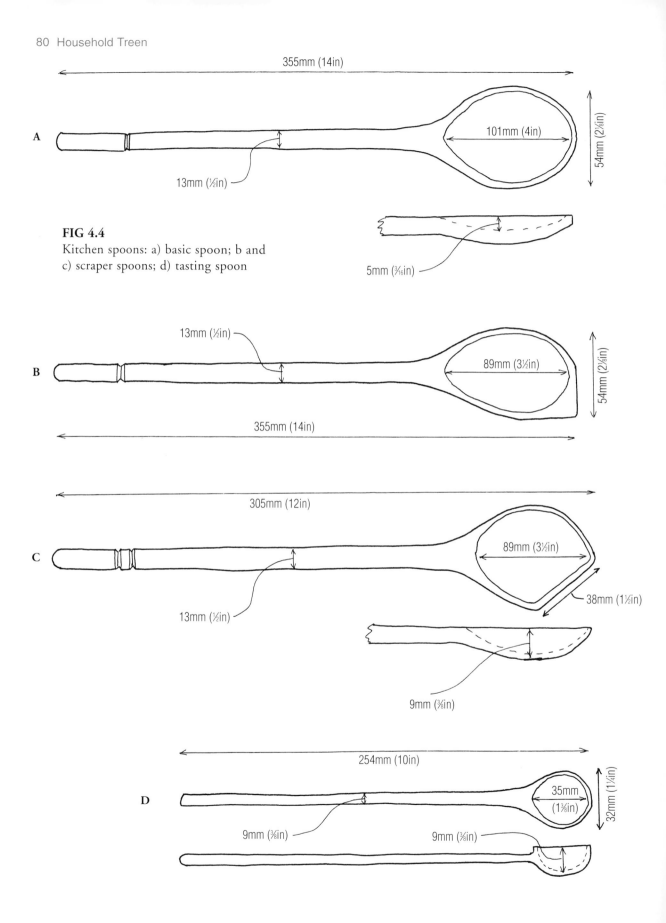

FIG 4.4
Kitchen spoons: a) basic spoon; b and
c) scraper spoons; d) tasting spoon

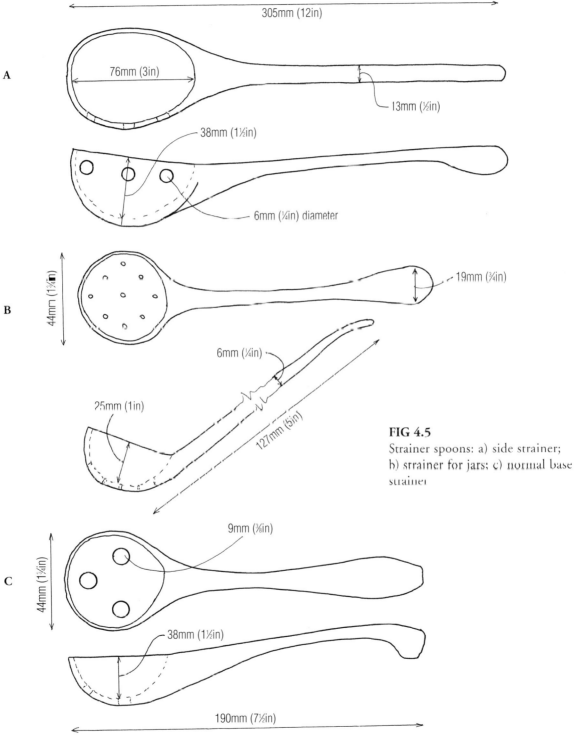

305mm (12in)

A

76mm (3in)

13mm (½in)

38mm (1½in)

6mm (¼in) diameter

B

44mm (1¾in)

19mm (¾in)

6mm (¼in)

25mm (1in)

127mm (5in)

FIG 4.5
Strainer spoons: a) side strainer;
b) strainer for jars; c) normal base
strainer

9mm (⅜in)

C

44mm (1¾in)

38mm (1½in)

190mm (7½in)

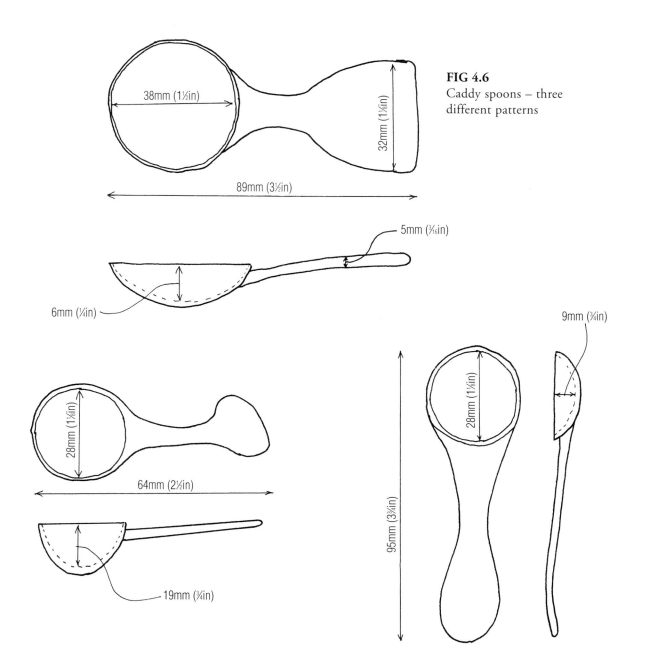

FIG 4.6
Caddy spoons – three different patterns

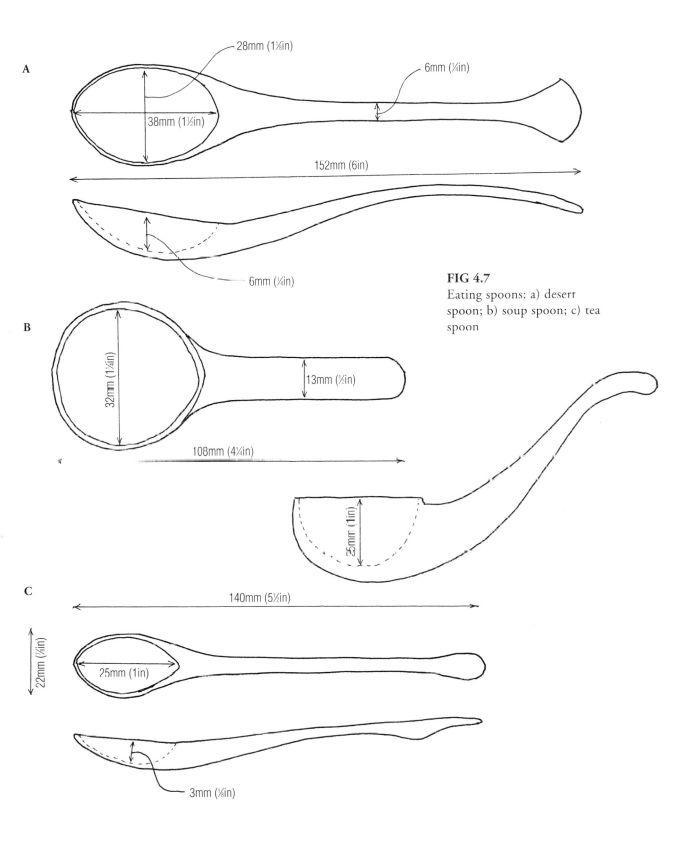

A

28mm (1⅛in)

6mm (¼in)

38mm (1½in)

152mm (6in)

6mm (¼in)

FIG 4.7
Eating spoons: a) desert
spoon; b) soup spoon; c) tea
spoon

B

32mm (1¼in)

13mm (½in)

108mm (4¼in)

25mm (1in)

C

140mm (5½in)

22mm (⅞in)

25mm (1in)

3mm (⅛in)

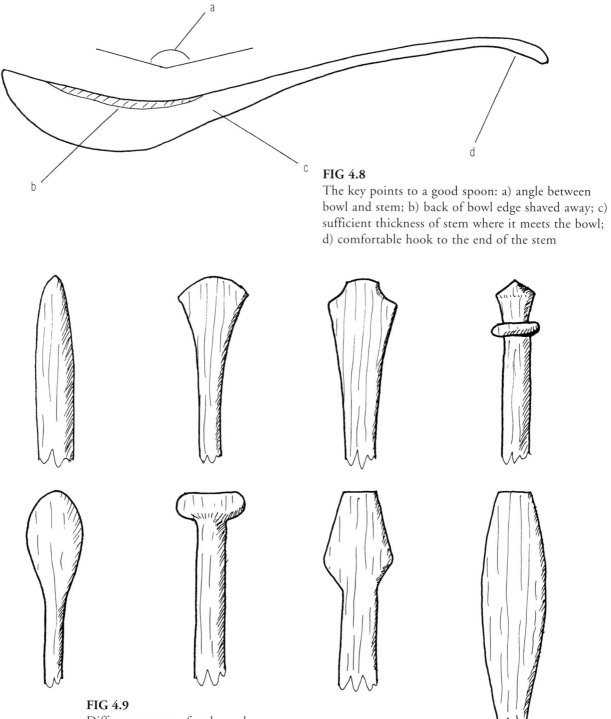

FIG 4.8
The key points to a good spoon: a) angle between bowl and stem; b) back of bowl edge shaved away; c) sufficient thickness of stem where it meets the bowl; d) comfortable hook to the end of the stem

FIG 4.9
Different patterns for the end of a spoon handle

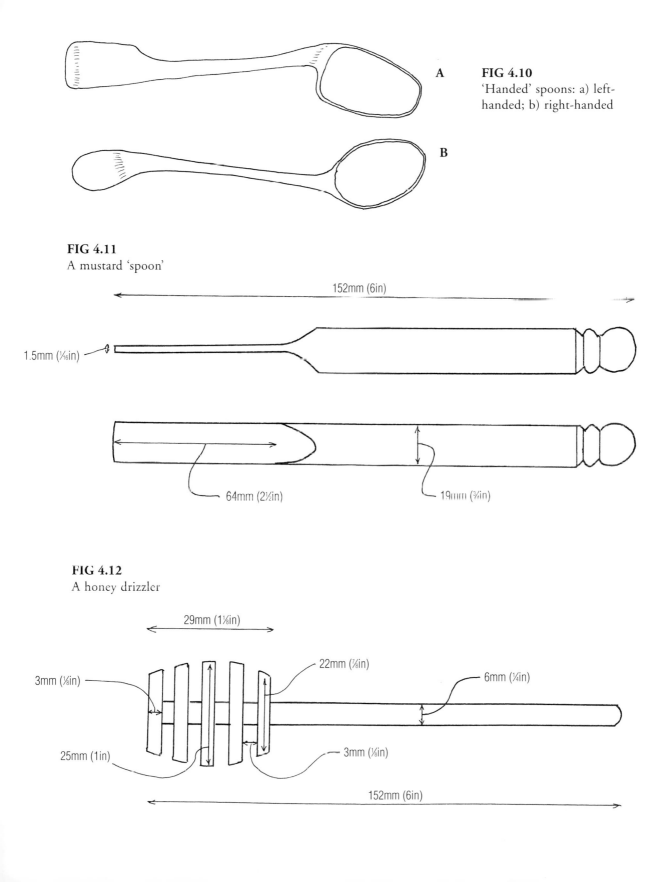

A

B

FIG 4.10
'Handed' spoons: a) left-handed; b) right-handed

FIG 4.11
A mustard 'spoon'

152mm (6in)

1.5mm (¹⁄₁₆in)

64mm (2½in)

19mm (¾in)

FIG 4.12
A honey drizzler

29mm (1⅛in)

3mm (⅛in)

22mm (⅞in)

6mm (¼in)

25mm (1in)

3mm (⅛in)

152mm (6in)

Kitchen implements

There is a whole range of wooden tools, both useful and attractive, that are used in the kitchen.

Scrapers, spatulas and strainers are flat, thin clefts of wood, shaped to perform their particular function (**fig 4.13**). The normal pattern is of a handle and a blade, the latter being shaped as required. Shaping of the blade should be designed to fit the pots with which they will be used. The strainer, which is held to the rim of a pan as it is tipped, has holes along its bottom edge to release water; it is used in place of a straining bowl. One pattern of strainer is more like a scoop (**fig 4.14**), while another comes as a small bowl with two arms to support it over a pan (**fig 4.15**) – a precursor to the modern colander.

Spurtles are of Scottish origin and are round, smooth sticks (**fig 4.16**) with which to stir porridge. The top may be turned to make it easier to hold (**fig 4.16b**).

Lemon reamers or juicers are beautiful and work really well. The earliest juicers were a simple lever, similar to a nut cracker, which squeezed the lemon from the sides. But the best consist of a handle attached to a round or conical section that is strongly ridged, and which is twisted into the cut face of a half fruit (**fig 4.17**). These need to be made in a hard wood.

Vegetable mashers (**fig 4.18**) are simple to make and are a good example of brute force doing the job! Less violent are cabbage presses, designed to get surplus water from the cooked vegetable (**fig 4.18**).

Rolling pins are in every kitchen. They can be a perfectly straight cylinder with no adornments, or can have long or short handles at either end (**fig 4.19**). I have seen rolling pins that are tapered to either end from the middle, but these must be an acquired taste!

Toast tongs originated in the United States for those with tender fingers. There are two patterns. The first is simply a piece of wood, carved to a shape like a tuning fork, and which holds items when the sides are pushed together (**fig 4.20**). A more sophisticated pattern is hinged and uses the natural springiness of the wood to stay open. These need occasional oiling to maintain their springiness.

Salad tongs are similar in principle to toast tongs (**fig 4.21**) and is, of course, used for serving salad.

The pie server is a beautiful tool. It has a flat triangular blade leading to a curved handle (**4.23**). It is shaved to a fine thickness and with chamfered edges so it slips under the pie with ease.

Wooden forks are really like spoons with larger or smaller segments removed to make the prongs (**fig 4.23**). These are usually fairly thick in both directions to give them sufficient strength. They are curved and may be angled to the handle, like a spoon, to make the fork effective and comfortable to use.

Apple corers/cheese samplers are elegant tools that have a pointed end and a half round blade. They are inserted into the product and rotated to cut out an apple core or remove a cylinder of cheese (**fig 4.22**).

Dish slopes are simply stepped wedges used to tilt a heavy, hot dish to make it possible to remove the gravy. Two are required for a large dish (**fig 4.24**).

Mortars were made of the densest woods in order to resist excessive wear when grinding. They have a curved base to the mortar and the pestle to avoid any corners in which food could be trapped and not ground (**fig 4.25**).

Bottle corkers were much used when home-made wines were more common. They are based on a metal-lined conical funnel that compresses the cork to a slightly smaller diameter than the bottle opening. The cork is forced into the bottle by hammering on the rammer (**fig 4.26**).

Holders for the ubiquitous roll of kitchen towel are simple and easy to make (they are good starter projects for youngsters). Horizontal and vertical patterns are shown (**fig 4.27**).

Tips

- Use fine garnet paper to achieve a smooth finish and, like spoons, wet between each sanding to raise the grain.
- These items are best treated with hot oil, but beware of allergy products.
- Take care with the direction of the grain when producing very fine artefacts; the grain must go along the length of the piece, rather than across, so that it does not snap.
- To keep these tools working well they should be kept dry and oiled occasionally.

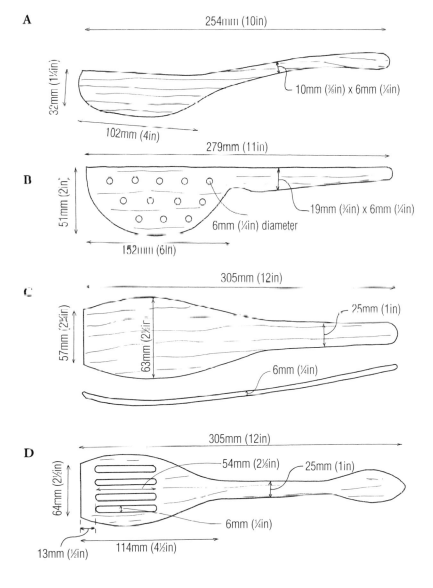

A
254mm (10in)
32mm (1¼in)
10mm (⅜in) x 6mm (¼in)
102mm (4in)

B
279mm (11in)
51mm (2in)
19mm (¾in) x 6mm (¼in)
6mm (¼in) diameter
152mm (6in)

C
305mm (12in)
57mm (2¼in)
63mm (2½in)
25mm (1in)
6mm (¼in)

D
305mm (12in)
64mm (2½in)
54mm (2⅛in)
25mm (1in)
6mm (¼in)
13mm (½in)
114mm (4½in)

FIG 4.13
Kitchen tools: a) pot scraper; b) strainer; c) pan scraper; d) scraper/strainer

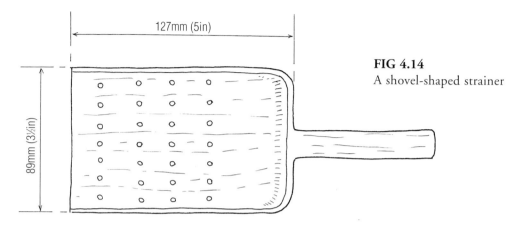

127mm (5in)

89mm (3½in)

FIG 4.14
A shovel-shaped strainer

32mm (1¼in)

FIG 4.15
A strainer designed to rest
across the top of a pan

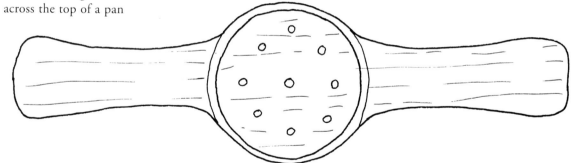

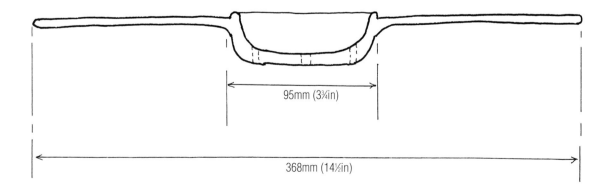

95mm (3¾in)

368mm (14½in)

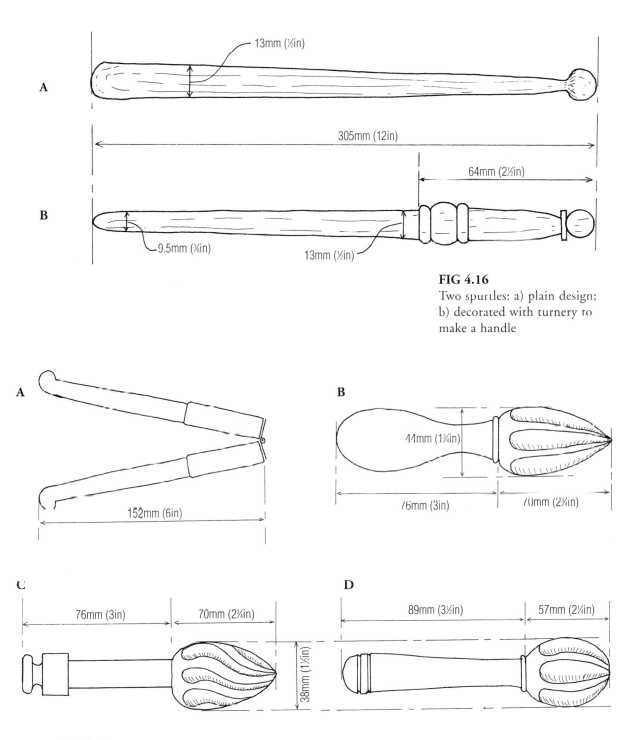

FIG 4.16
Two spurtles: a) plain design;
b) decorated with turnery to
make a handle

FIG 4.17
Lemon juicers/reamers: a) an
early pattern that squeezes a
small lemon; b, c and d)
different patterns of reamers

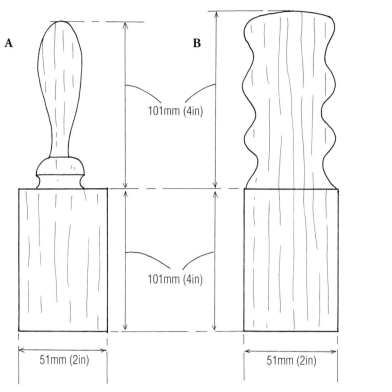

A

B

101mm (4in)

101mm (4in)

51mm (2in)

51mm (2in)

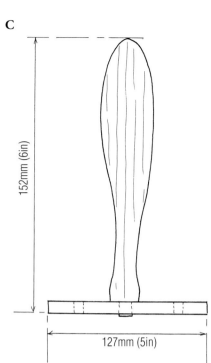

C

152mm (6in)

127mm (5in)

FIG 4.18
Vegetable mashers: a and b)
potato/root vegetable mashers;
c) a cabbage press to remove
water from the cooked
produce

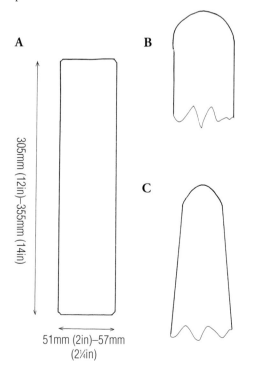

A

B

C

305mm (12in)–355mm (14in)

51mm (2in)–57mm
(2¼in)

FIG 4.19
Rolling pins: a) plain rolling
pin; b) curved end on a
normal pin; c) curved end on
a tapered pin; d) bead on the
end of a pin; e) handle on the
end of a pin

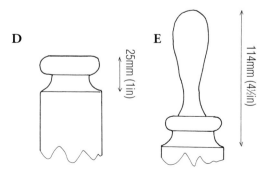

D

E

25mm (1in)

114mm (4½in)

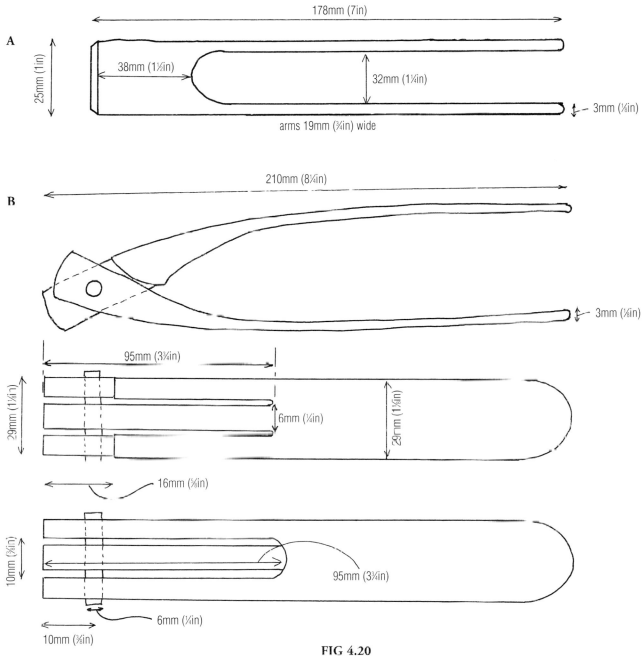

178mm (7in)

A

25mm (1in)

38mm (1½in)

32mm (1¼in)

3mm (⅛in)

arms 19mm (¾in) wide

210mm (8¼in)

B

3mm (⅛in)

95mm (3¾in)

29mm (1⅛in)

6mm (¼in)

29mm (1⅛in)

16mm (⅝in)

10mm (⅜in)

95mm (3¾in)

6mm (¼in)

10mm (⅜in)

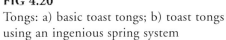

FIG 4.20
Tongs: a) basic toast tongs; b) toast tongs
using an ingenious spring system

FIG 4.21
Salad tongs

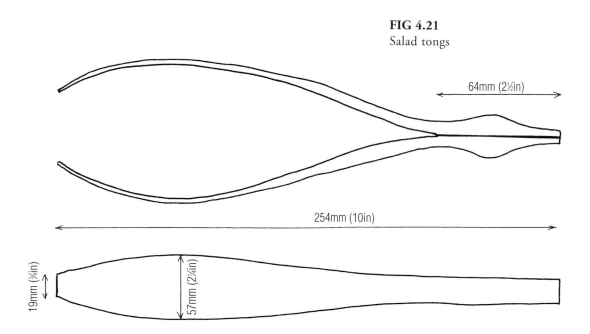

64mm (2½in)

254mm (10in)

19mm (¾in)

57mm (2¼in)

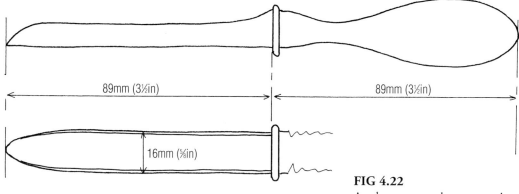

89mm (3½in)

89mm (3½in)

16mm (⅝in)

FIG 4.22
Apple corer or cheese sampler

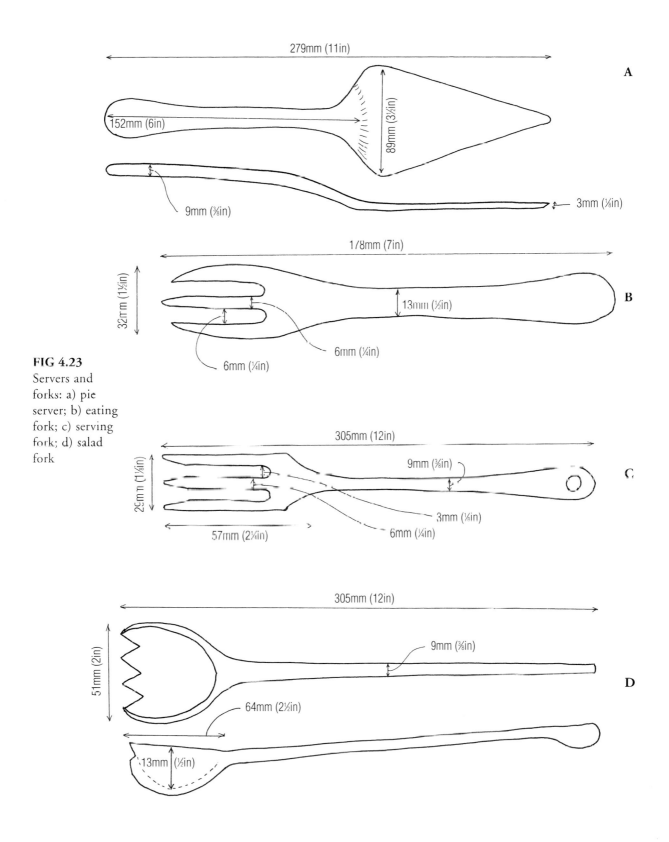

FIG 4.23
Servers and forks: a) pie server; b) eating fork; c) serving fork; d) salad fork

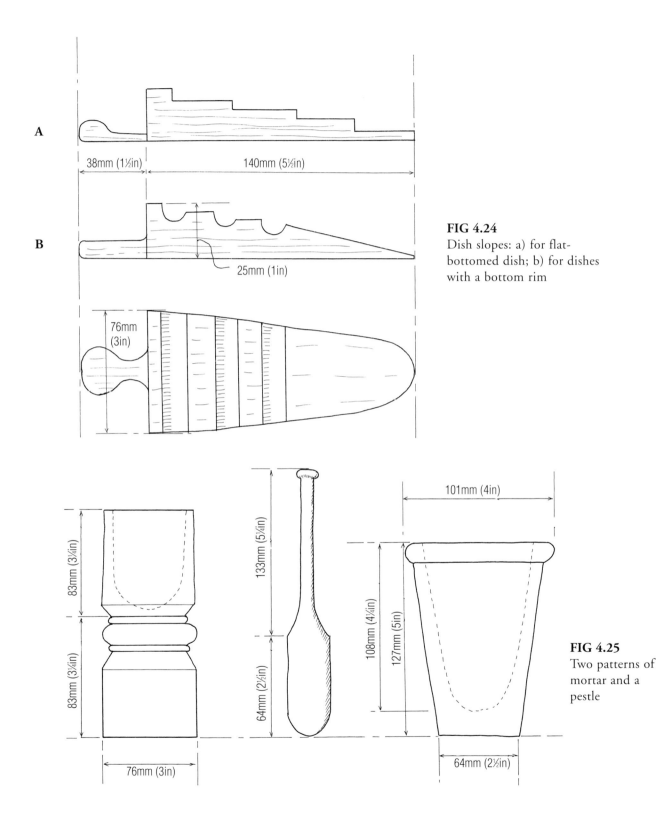

A

38mm (1½in)   140mm (5½in)

B

25mm (1in)

FIG 4.24
Dish slopes: a) for flat-bottomed dish; b) for dishes with a bottom rim

76mm (3in)

83mm (3¼in)

83mm (3¼in)

76mm (3in)

133mm (5¼in)

64mm (2½in)

101mm (4in)

108mm (4¼in)

127mm (5in)

64mm (2½in)

FIG 4.25
Two patterns of mortar and a pestle

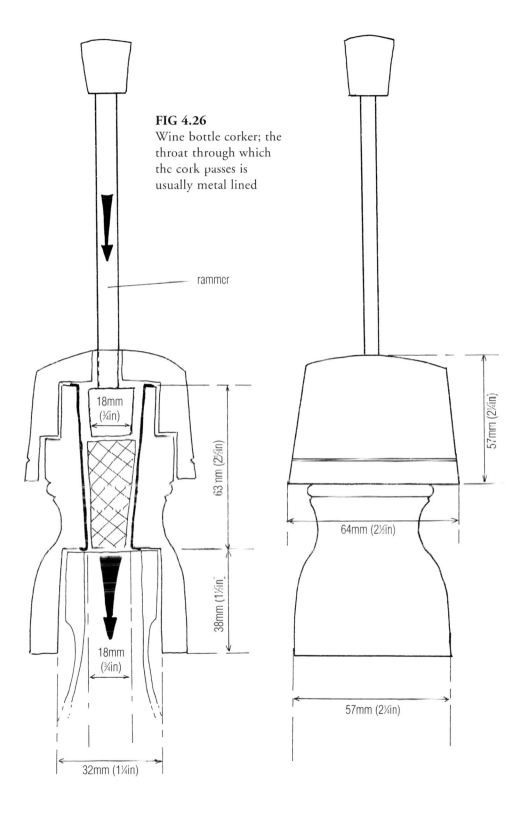

FIG 4.26
Wine bottle corker; the
throat through which
the cork passes is
usually metal lined

rammer

18mm
(¾in)

63 mm (2½in)

38mm (1½in)

18mm
(¾in)

32mm (1¼in)

57mm (2¼in)

64mm (2½in)

57mm (2¼in)

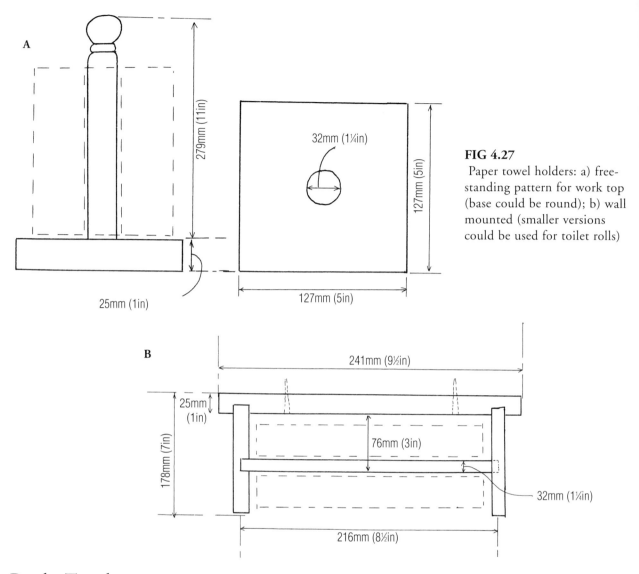

FIG 4.27
Paper towel holders: a) free-standing pattern for work top (base could be round); b) wall mounted (smaller versions could be used for toilet rolls)

Bowls, Trenchers, Platters and Egg Cups

The patterns of some of the oldest dishes discovered originate from Iron Age excavations, although their first production probably predates this. The earliest 'bowls' were oblong, hollow troughs, probably hollowed by flint or knife, rather in the way that dough troughs are still made today. The Egyptians had lathes and metal cutting tools, so all that was required was the craftsman with the skill to make hollow bowls. Making hollowed bowls was a great step forward, and civilized the process of eating and drinking considerably. Treen for the table was widely used until the Tudor period after which it was increasingly replaced by pewter and china. There seems to have been a longer-lived tradition of using wooden products in both Wales and Scotland. In Wales salad bowls and implements, dinner sets, egg cups and drinking cups were still made in some numbers up to the middle of the 20th century, as were porridge bowls in Scotland.

Bowls come in an almost infinite variety of shapes and sizes. Apart from differences in the diameter of the bowl, the main factors that change are the shape and angle of the wall, the curve to the wall,

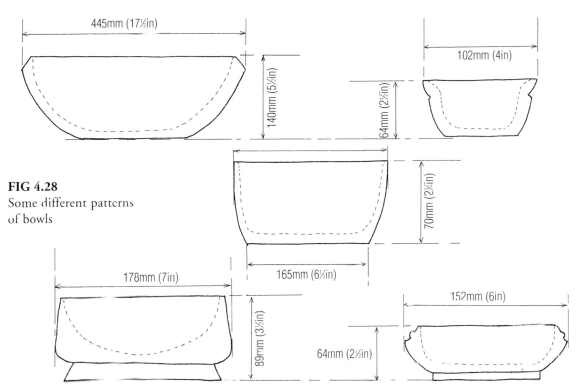

FIG 4.28
Some different patterns
of bowls

whether there is a distinct base, and whether any
decoration is applied to the bowl (**fig 4.28**).

Trenchers are perhaps the earliest treen 'plates'.
Their name comes from the French *tranche*, which
was a square of thin dry bread upon which meat
was served. In time the bread was dispensed with
and a square board or trencher was used. They have
a round depression in the centre to hold the food
and frequently another much smaller one to hold
salt (**fig 4.29**). Some patterns had a deep peripheral
groove to contain meat juices, while others had a
raised bead mimicking the edge of a modern plate.

Platters developed from trenchers. They are round,
with the classic appearance of a plate. The earliest
appear to have a wide, low peripheral ridge, and
were often almost completely flat inside this (**fig
4.30**). Later platters became more dish-like in
profile and included decoration in the form of
turned mouldings such as grooves and beads,
applied as the platter was turned. These resemble
our current plates and are every bit as effective.
Many of the thinner platters and bowls have
warped with use over many years.

Egg cups of all types have one thing in common –
the internal cavity is always virtually the same
diameter since chickens are very consistent! They
frequently come in sets of four or six (**fig 4.31**),
and individual cups had a wide range of shapes
(**fig 4.32**).

Salts are simple small open bowls used to hold
salt on the table (**fig 4.33**). It was removed in the
fingers – hence pinch of salt!

Tips

- The best bowls are made of sycamore, maple and
  elm. Ash is satisfactory for drier uses, having a
  coarser finish.
- Bowls that are to be used for food are best
  treated as described for spoons. Some bowl
  makers use teak oil.
- Take care to fill any holes in the base created by
  the holding system on the lathe to prevent water
  getting into the wood and becoming a problem.

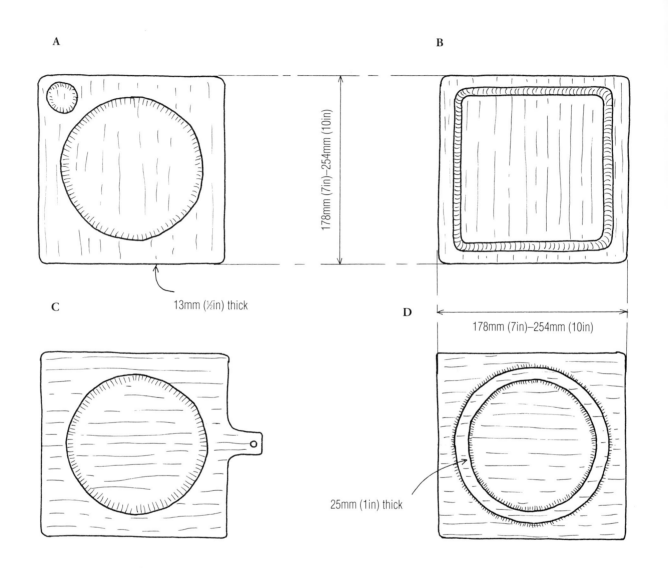

FIG 4.29
Trenchers: a) has a depression for salt; b) has a trough to retain meat juices; c) has a small handle or tag for hanging the trencher up; d) has a raised circular rim to retain meat juices

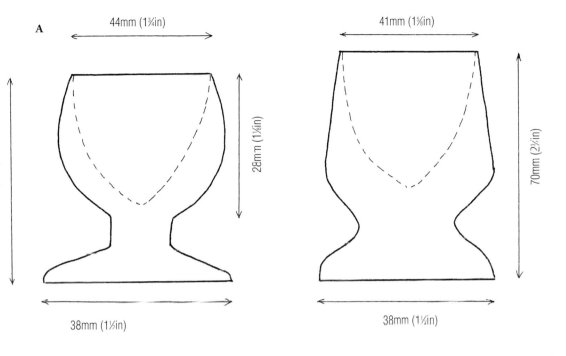

A

44mm (1¾in)

41mm (1⅝in)

64mm (2½in)

28mm (1⅛in)

70mm (2¾in)

38mm (1½in)

38mm (1½in)

FIG 4.31
Egg cups: a) two basic
patterns of cup; b) a turned
round stand for bringing
four eggs to the table

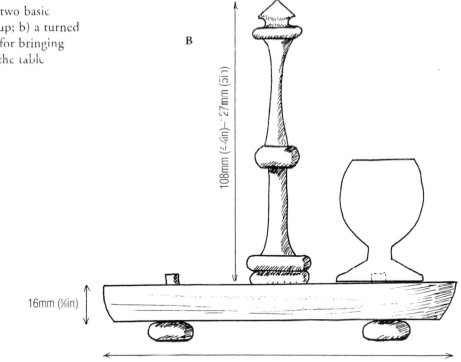

B

108mm (4in) – 127mm (5in)

16mm (⅝in)

127mm (5in)

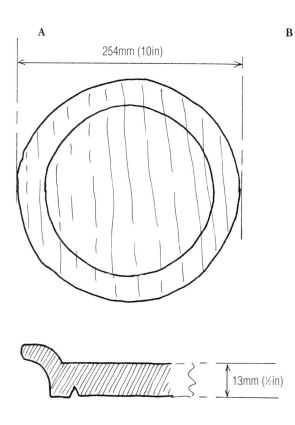

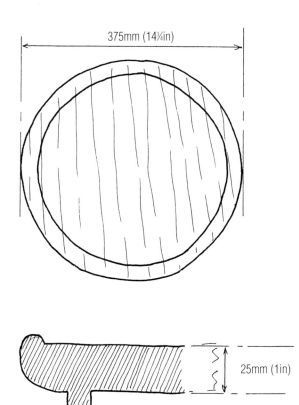

FIG 4.30
Platters: a and b) very
flat platters with simple
rims; c) A range of more
complex rims giving a
deeper platter

C

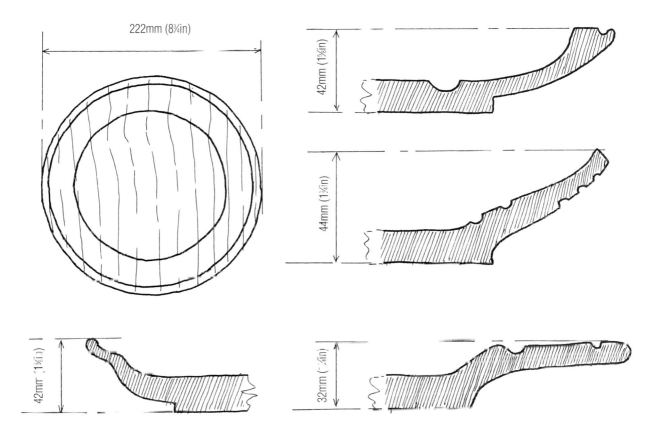

222mm (8¾in)

42mm (1⅝in)

44mm (1¾in)

42mm (1⅝in)

32mm (1¼in)

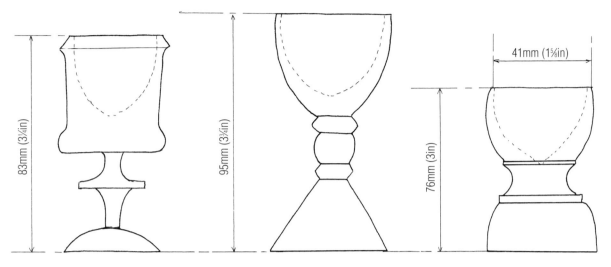

FIG 4.32
More egg cup patterns (there
are hundreds!)

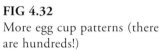

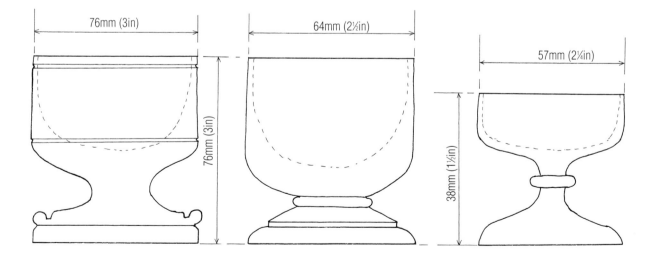

FIG 4.33
Salt bowls

Drinking vessels

The earliest drinking vessels were entirely natural, using items such as scallop shells and coconut shells. Wooden drinking vessels probably date from the Iron-Age when metal knives were available to hollow out primitive bowls. By the Middle Ages, well after the introduction of the pole lathe, a sophisticated range of products was being produced, some of which were made from staves (like a barrel), rather than being turned. This wooden tableware was gradually replaced by pewter and china products, in the same way as plates and platters.

Bowls: the earliest drinking bowls are quite small and shallow (**fig 4.34**). They were frequently personalized by the owner by marking them on the base, a process that never occurred with platters.

Mazers were prized drinking bowls with metal ornamentation and rims. Originally they may have been made exclusively of burr maple, from which the name mazer was derived. They were common in institutions such as monasteries between the 13th and 16th centuries, but are now very scarce. A few were staved rather than whole (**fig 4.35**). Research by Robin Wood (see bibliography page 236) has suggested that much simpler, undecorated mazers, made in a range of woods, were in fact common in the Middle Ages.

Bickers and Quaiches are Scottish, staved two-handled bowls made with two different woods to produce a black and white striped appearance (**fig 4.36**).

Beakers are the simplest of the turned drinking vessels, being plain, deep and straight-sided (**fig 4.37**).

Goblets are more decorated than beakers and have a bowl supported by a turned and decorated stem arising from a flat foot (**fig 4.38**). They are the wooden equivalent of a wine glass.

Tankards are staved ale mugs. The staves are rebated at the bottom to hold the base in place, while the staves are held tight by a binding of willow or hazel bonds (**fig 4.39**). A wooden handle and lid are commonly fitted, and pitch is sometimes used to seal the inside. The oldest tankard discovered is reputedly Celtic and dated to 50 BC (Pinto, 1969, see bibliography page 236). A few tankards were turned (**fig 4.39**).

Piggins are straight-sided, staved vessels with willow bindings. One stave is left long to act as a handle. They are used, not only for drinking, but also to ladle liquids from larger containers (**fig 4.40**). Turned ladles with a handle at one side were also commonly made (**fig 4.41**), fulfilling the same role as a piggin. Making these on the pole lathe requires considerable skill.

Tips

- Close grained wood is preferable for good drinking vessels, and cross-grained wood-like burrs is more resistant to warping.
- For light coloured wood use sycamore or maple; for a dark colour use laburnum or alder.
- Oak or possibly pine will make good staves for tankards, with hazel, ash or willow for the bindings.
- Staves need to be precisely shaped on their edges in order to be watertight – exactly as in barrel making.
- The base of a tankard is best turned in order to fit the staves.

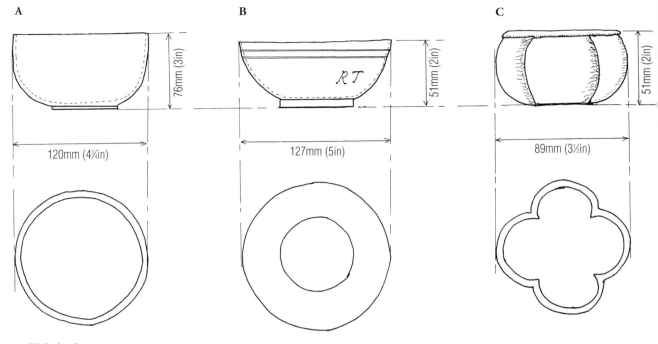

FIG 4.34
Drinking bowls: a) basic bowl; b) shallow bowl with owner's initials; c) an unusual quatrefoil bowl

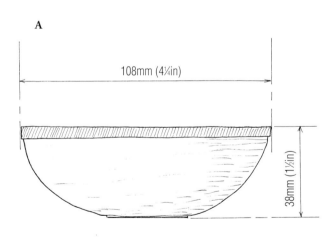

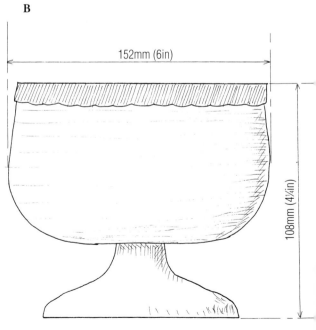

FIG 4.35
Mazers: a) shallow bowl with metal (silver) rim; b) an unusual mazer bowl with a foot and a silver rim

FIG 4.36
Quaiches: a and b) are staved,
bound with willow, and have two
handles; c) is a turned bowl with
four lugs/handles

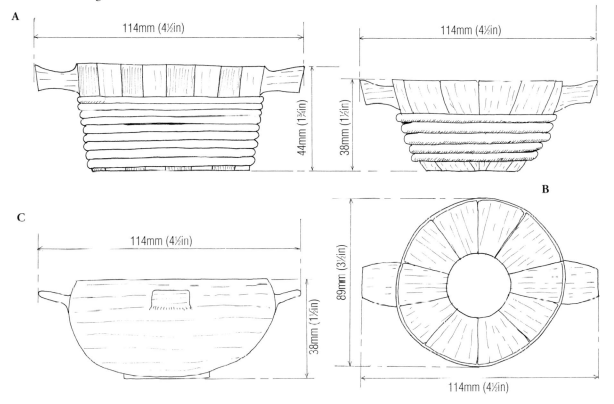

A

114mm (4½in)

114mm (4½in)

44mm (1¾in)

38mm (1½in)

B

C

114mm (4½in)

38mm (1½in)

89mm (3½in)

114mm (4½in)

FIG 4.37
Beakers: a range of three
different patterns

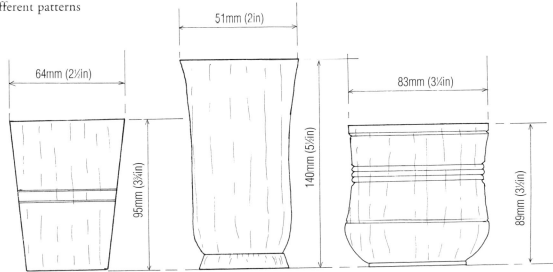

64mm (2½in)

51mm (2in)

83mm (3¼in)

95mm (3¾in)

140mm (5½in)

89mm (3½in)

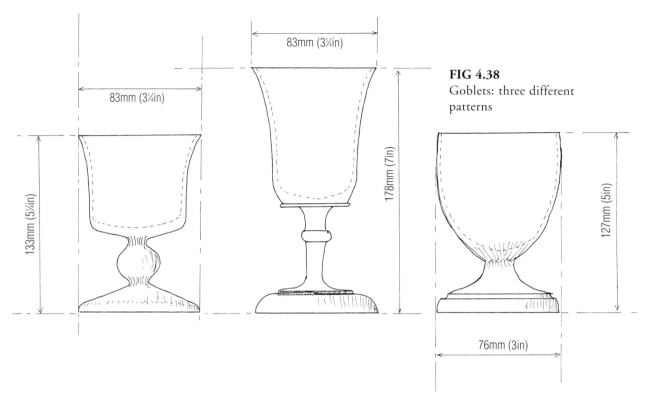

FIG 4.38
Goblets: three different patterns

83mm (3¼in)

83mm (3¼in)

133mm (5¼in)

178mm (7in)

127mm (5in)

76mm (3in)

FIG 4.39
Tankards: a) staved tankard with willow bindings; b) staved tankard with ash bindings and a lid; c) a turned one piece tankard with applied handle

A

B

C

165mm (6½in)

165mm (6½in)

114mm (4½in)

120mm (4¾in)

114mm (4½in)

FIG 4.40
Piggins: A staved piggin with ash bindings and one stave extended to provide a handle

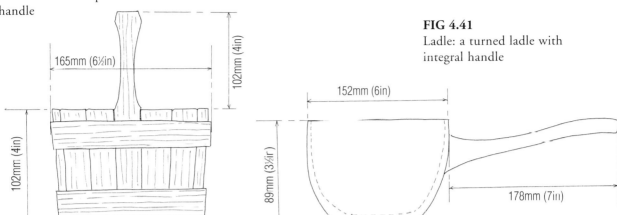

FIG 4.41
Ladle: a turned ladle with integral handle

Items in the house

There is a whole range of small turned or shaped items that are useful, attractive and fun to make.

Door stops and porters at their most basic are simply a wooden wedge, sized to the type of door you have and the gap underneath it. But this is a good example of an area where a bit of turnery adds not only to the appearance, but also to the function of the artefact. It is a lot easier to get hold of the turned end than it is to grasp the plain wedge (**fig 4.42**). Porters are heavily-weighted door stops; they can be combined with a wedge for more effect (**fig 4.43**).

Candle holders in wood are common. The most basic is a simple upright holder, wide enough at the base, and low enough, to be stable (**fig 4.44**). They can be produced with a wider, saucer-like base, but, because this would waste a lot of wood, it is better to make the holder in two pieces and join them together afterwards (**fig 4.44**). The most basic candle holder can be found on the *Mary Rose* – a small cone with a hole in the top and a handle on one side (**fig 4.44**). A squat, round piece of wood, nicely turned and with a suitable hole, makes a safe night light holder (**fig 4.45**). A travelling candle is shown in **fig 4.46**.

Paper knives are great for presents until all the relatives have one. The handle is turned and the blade shaped afterwards with a draw-knife. The blade is thin enough to flex without breaking and the turning pattern is up to the maker (**fig 4.47**).

Light pulls fit on the end of cords to the switch and are fairly small. They have two sizes of hole – one for the cord and a larger one to take the knot at the end of the cord. The patterns that you can use are endless – four are shown in **fig 4.48**.

Bag carriers: how often have you had your fingers numbed by carrying heavy carrier bags? These simple handles solve the problem (**fig 4.49**).

Tips

- Make the hollows at the end of bag carriers deep enough to avoid the plastic carrier bag handle slipping off.
- All candle-holders must have a metal lining to the socket to avoid risk of fire.
- Paper knives should have a suitable point to get under the sealed flap of a letter.
- Door stops should not be too thick; they must fit under the door.
- Porters can be weighted by placing lead in a cavity in the base.

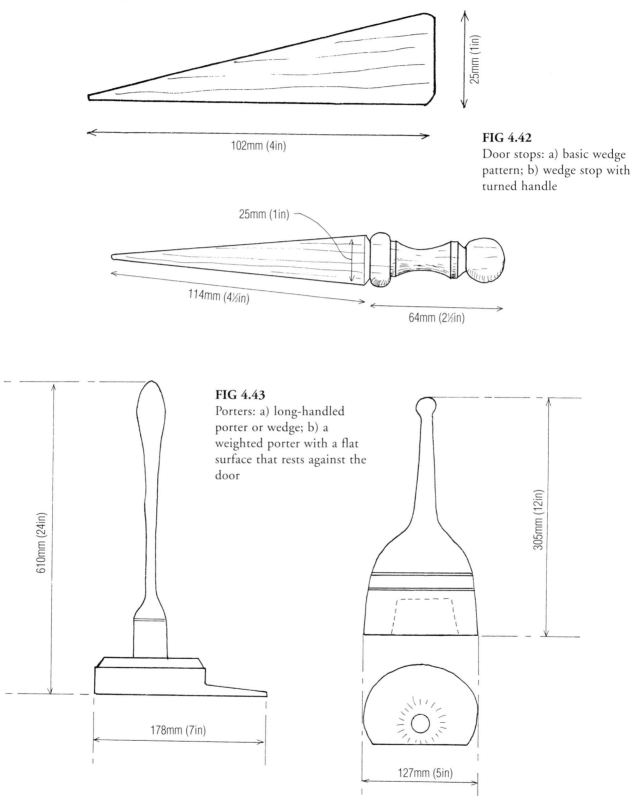

25mm (1in)

102mm (4in)

FIG 4.42
Door stops: a) basic wedge
pattern; b) wedge stop with
turned handle

25mm (1in)

114mm (4⅛in)

64mm (2½in)

FIG 4.43
Porters: a) long-handled
porter or wedge; b) a
weighted porter with a flat
surface that rests against the
door

610mm (24in)

305mm (12in)

178mm (7in)

127mm (5in)

A

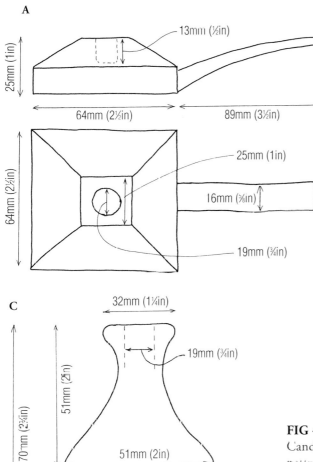

13mm (½in)

25mm (1in)

64mm (2½in)

89mm (3½in)

64mm (2½in)

25mm (1in)

16mm (⅝in)

19mm (¾in)

B

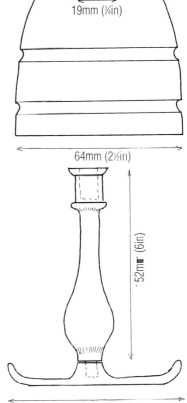

44mm (1¾in)

13mm (½in)

19mm (¾in)

89mm (3½in)

64mm (2½in)

C

32mm (1¼in)

19mm (¾in)

51mm (2in)

70mm (2¾in)

51mm (2in)

76mm (3in)

D

52mm (6in)

127mm (5in)

FIG 4.44
Candle holders: a) Tudor
pattern (from *Mary Rose*);
b) simple turned holder; c)
turned holder with saucer
base; d) two piece
candlestick

FIG 4.45
Turned night light holder

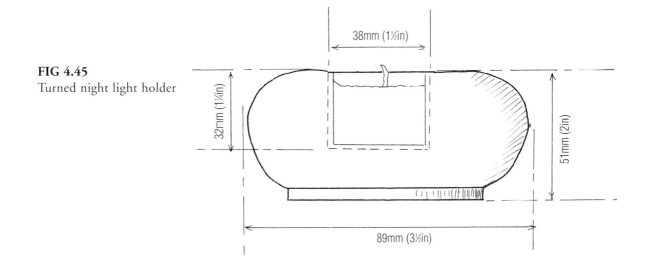

38mm (1½in)

32mm (1¼in)

51mm (2in)

89mm (3½in)

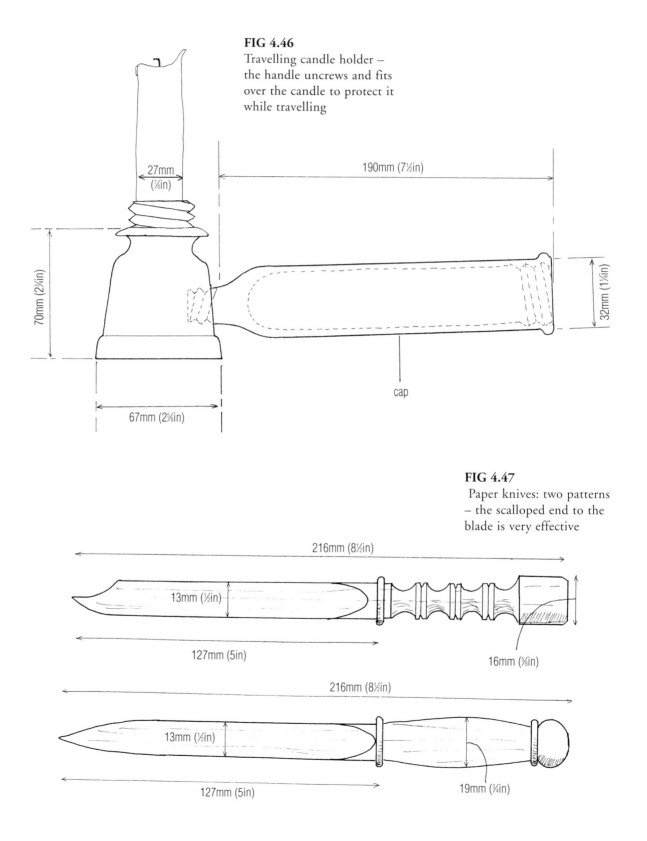

FIG 4.46
Travelling candle holder –
the handle uncrews and fits
over the candle to protect it
while travelling

27mm
(⅛in)

190mm (7½in)

70mm (2¾in)

32mm (1¼in)

cap

67mm (2⅝in)

FIG 4.47
Paper knives: two patterns
– the scalloped end to the
blade is very effective

216mm (8½in)

13mm (½in)

127mm (5in)

16mm (⅝in)

216mm (8½in)

13mm (½in)

127mm (5in)

19mm (¾in)

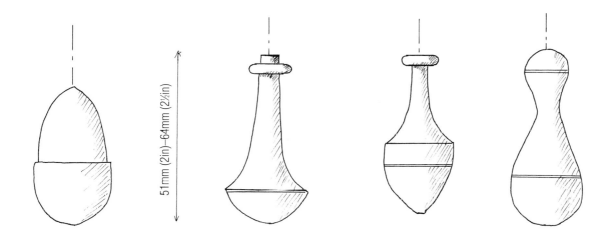

FIG 4.48
A variety of light pulls

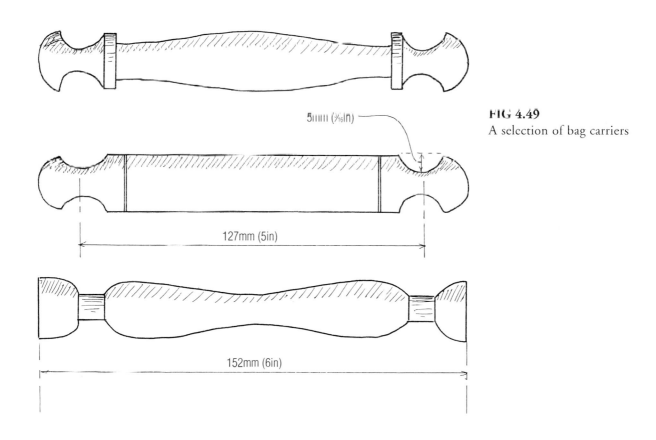

FIG 4.49
A selection of bag carriers

Chapter 5 Wooden Tools and Tool Handles

Introduction

Since prehistoric times man, has used wood to make many of his tools and weapons. Our ancestors soon understood the differing nature of the various woods that grew in the forest and how their properties could be best used. For example, resilient ash is best for handles that will need to absorb sudden shocks, such as for axes or spears, whereas elm, which is often difficult to split, is ideal for mallet heads. Over the centuries this wisdom has been refined so that the tools described here all perform their task efficiently and are a pleasure to use. The sizes and patterns described are those most commonly used today, although many tools or handles are 'made to measure' in order to best fit the user. So if a customer wants an axe helve to have a specific length, it presents no problem. This reflects the situation that existed during the 19th century, when green woodworking was an important trade and toolmakers had to offer a wide range of tool sizes in order to guarantee their business.

Wooden Rakes

Before the mechanization of most manual work on the land, thousands of rakes were made every year in small rural workshops. Used to gather hay into rows, to rake the soil in the vegetable garden, to gather leaves or to rake up cornfields, every use and region had a particular pattern honed by years of use. The classic hay rake is composed entirely of wood barring three nails and a tin band (**fig 5.1a**). The 2m (6½ft) handle is split so it fits to the head in two places and is thus more secure. The wooden teeth are driven into their sockets and part sharpened so as not to split in use (**fig 5.1c**). The whole head is slightly angled (**fig 5.1b**) to give the best compromise between collecting the product efficiently and the teeth not digging into the ground.

Other uses demanded a more rugged construction and some of the patterns illustrated (**fig 5.2**) use metal teeth, metal braces and additional bow stays to achieve the greater strength required. Details are given in table 5.1. Large rakes were used in the lowlands where hay was lush, but smaller rakes with angled heads worked better on hilly ground with a sparser crop. All of the patterns described here are the product of years of use. A good rake is light in weight, well balanced, and a joy to use all day.

Tips

- Ash or Hickory are the best woods for all parts of the rake, but sallow can be used for handles and birch for the heads.
- Metal rings for split-handled rakes can be made from tinplate.
- The end of the handle can be bluntly sharpened (often called a Dunmow pattern) so the rake can be stood up in the ground – they don't get lost or stepped on that way!
- Part-pointing the teeth (tines) is essential so they do not split in use.
- A 75 to 80 degree angle between head and stail will stop the teeth digging into the ground and gather up the hay or leaves more efficiently.
- Always use seasoned, dry ash for the teeth – they will not shrink and come loose.

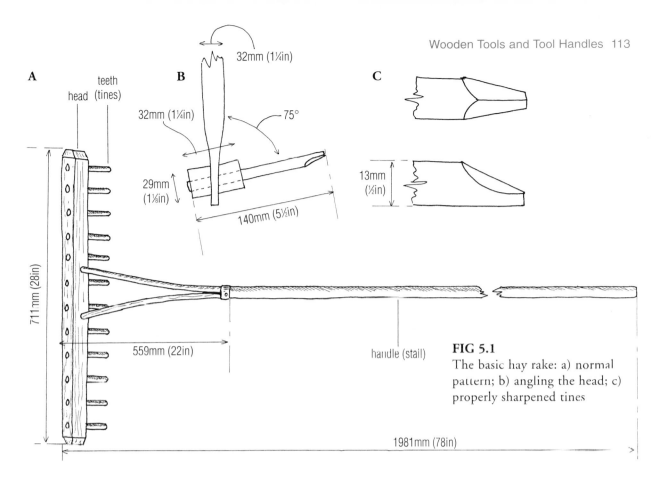

FIG 5.1
The basic hay rake: a) normal pattern; b) angling the head; c) properly sharpened tines

Table 5.1 Details of different rake patterns

Type of rake	Width of head	Length of handle	Number of teeth	Type of teeth	Type of handle
Hay/Old English	710mm (28in)	1081mm (70in)	12–19	wooden	Split (crotch)
Seed	710mm (28in)	1981mm (78in)	12	wooden	Split
Twitch	710mm (28in)	1829mm (72in)	12	rose head nails	Split
Garden	450mm (18in)	1524mm (60in)	7–13	rose head nails	Split
Wire tooth + stay	710mm (28in)	1981mm (78in)	12	steel nails	Unsplit + stay
Drag	2134mm (84in)	1981mm (78in)	23 per 1200mm	wooden	Split + brace
Bow stay	710mm (28in)	1829mm (72in)	12	wooden	Unsplit, bow + stay
Corn	710mm (28in)	1981mm (78in)	11	wooden	Split
Leaf	710mm (28in)	1829mm (72in)	17	wooden	Split
Welsh hill	450mm (18in)	1829mm (72in)	7–13	wooden	Unsplit + 1 or 2 bows

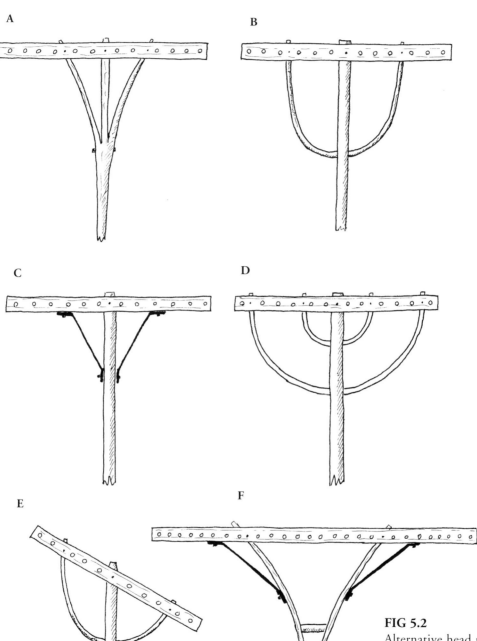

FIG 5.2
Alternative head patterns: a) a split stail style from the United States; b) bow stay; c) unsplit handle with metal stays; d) double bow stay; e) Welsh pattern; f) drag rake (buck rake in United States)

Besoms

Besom brooms were common in almost every house, garden and workplace before the arrival of the 'wail bone' broom. A basic besom comprises a 'head' of twigs about 914mm (36in) long, bound to a 254mm (10in) circumference at their butt ends by bonds of ash, bramble, or wire (**fig 5.3**). This is fixed to a 1067mm (42in) handle or 'tail' by a wooden peg, making the classic 'witches' broomstick'. Fortunately besoms still enjoy a steady sale, since they are hard to beat for sweeping up autumn leaves, clearing light snow, and, when they are worn, for removing moss from the lawn. If made with the right material, kept dry, and stored with the head uppermost, besoms can last up to ten years of regular use.

A normal garden broom has a 254mm (10in) circumference at the point where it is bound (**fig 5.4**). A tougher pattern for heavier use has a 305mm (12in) circumference and three bindings (**fig 5.4**). An American pattern made with a head of 'broomcorn' (a member of the Sorghum plant family) tied with willow withes is shown in **fig 5.5**.

Swales, which are besoms without a handle, were used in iron works to remove slag from the metal during the manufacture of high-quality steel, the alchemy between birch twigs and the steel giving a very pure end product.

Tips

- Birch makes the best heads, having the fine, tough, flexible twigs that are required. In some areas heather (ling) is used in its place and 'broomcorn', split bamboo and millet straw are also good alternative materials for the head.
- For the best results, harvest material for brooms during the winter when there is no leaf on the trees (and no flowers on the ling) – it will last much longer in use.
- Bindings can be made from split ash, small hazel rods, bramble, or wire. The latter has no 'give', and can break the smaller twigs if it is tightened too much. In the United States hickory or lime bast are often used for the bindings.
- Natural bindings should be prepared and used immediately before they dry and become brittle.

FIG 5.3

Besoms: a basic besom

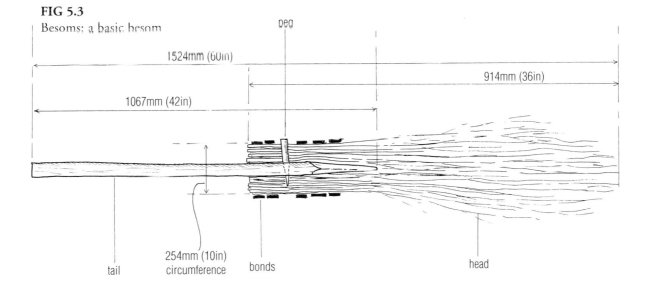

peg

1524mm (60in)

914mm (36in)

1067mm (42in)

254mm (10in) circumference

tail

bonds

head

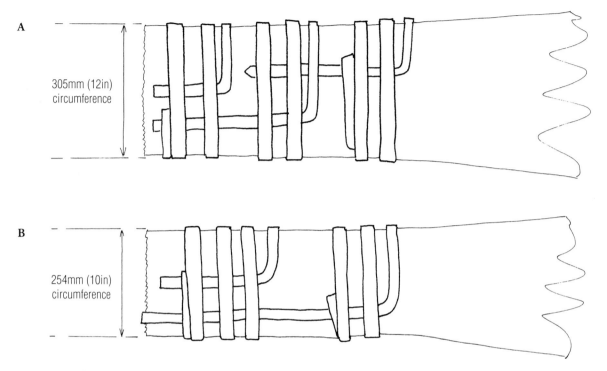

A

305mm (12in)
circumference

B

254mm (10in)
circumference

FIG 5.4
Different bindings: a) three
bindings on a 305mm (12in)
besom; b) two on a 254mm
(10in) besom

FIG 5.5
An American broom with a
'broomcorn' head bound
with willow withes.

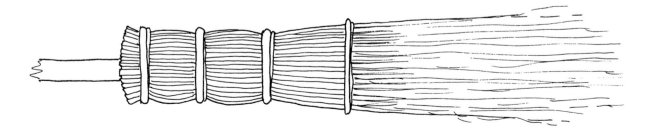

Mallets

Mallets are based on cylindrical or octagonal heads made from a material resistant to splitting. To these are fitted handles that are most commonly tapered at the head end, so that they pull tight into the head when used, and cannot fly off (**fig 5.6**). This loose fitting requires no wedge and is simpler and safer. Heavy mallets have metal bands fitted around the ends of the heads to prevent splinters coming away from the side of the head during use. Mallets and 'beetles' are among the oldest of tools. Indeed, the simple beetle made from the butt of a pole can be little different from the first clubs used by primitive man. Although supplanted by steel-headed sledge hammers for some tasks, there is still a good demand for wooden mallets. And for good reason, for wooden mallets do not damage wooden tools, or tent pegs, nor do they 'turn' steel wedges or froes, which by their very nature have to be hit hard in order to perform their job. This does mean that wooden mallets and beetles suffer a shorter life, but this is good news for those that make these tools! A range of mallets and beetles is illustrated in **fig 5.6**.

Tips

- Ash or hickory are always best for handles, due to their resilience. Elm, fruit wood and hornbeam make the best heads, being resistant to splitting.
- Knots and branches can be used to advantage in heads, since they will not split.
- If a wedge is used to hold the head, it should be driven at right angles to the grain of the head in order to avoid splitting it.
- Metal rings must be applied hot so that as they cool and shrink they tighten onto the head.
- Mallets are best if seasoned before use in order to reduce the risk of splitting.

Table 5.2 Details of different wooden mallet types

Type or name	Handle length	Approximate head weight	Approximate head size	Other features
Camping mallet	308mm (12in)	0.5kg (1lb)	152 x 76mm (6 x 3in)	Round head
Garden mallet	381mm (15in)	0.7kg (1.5lb)	152 x 102mm (6 x 4in)	Round or octagonal
Workshop mallet	533mm (21in)	1.1kg (2.5lb)	203 x 102mm (8 x 4in)	Round or octagonal
Beetle for froe	381mm (15in) overall	1.1kg (2.5lb)	N/A	Shaped butt of ash/elm
Beetle or Commander	1016mm (40in)	2.3kg (5lb)	305 x 152mm (12 x 6in) nailed three times	Round head with iron rings
Maul	965mm (38in)	2.3kg (5lb)	305 x 152mm (12 x 6in)	Hewn from one log

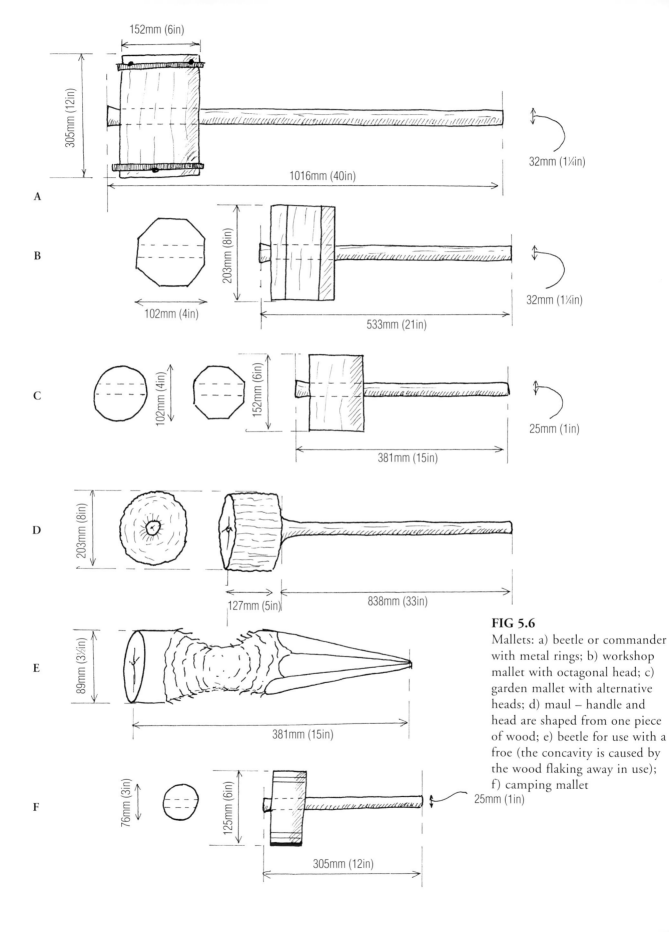

152mm (6in)

305mm (12in)

32mm (1¼in)

1016mm (40in)

A

203mm (8in)

102mm (4in)

32mm (1¼in)

533mm (21in)

B

102mm (4in)

152mm (6in)

25mm (1in)

381mm (15in)

C

203mm (8in)

127mm (5in)

838mm (33in)

D

89mm (3½in)

381mm (15in)

E

76mm (3in)

125mm (6in)

305mm (12in)

25mm (1in)

F

FIG 5.6

Mallets: a) beetle or commander with metal rings; b) workshop mallet with octagonal head; c) garden mallet with alternative heads; d) maul – handle and head are shaped from one piece of wood; e) beetle for use with a froe (the concavity is caused by the wood flaking away in use); f) camping mallet

Stable and Hay Forks

Stable forks are used for mucking out stables. They consist of a stout ash pole, the last 508mm (20in) of which is sawn down the middle and forced apart using a wooden wedge in order to make a simple two-prong fork (**fig 5.7**). They perform much better if the tines are slightly curved. These simple two-prong forks work very well when moving accumulated straw. They have a hard life, but their simplicity makes them cheap and easy to make. The curved tines usually require steaming to shape. The really beautiful hay forks, two of which are illustrated, are North American in design. Like hay rakes, mechanization has rendered them obsolete in large-scale farming, but for smallholders they remain useful for cocking and loading hay. Hay forks can be made with from two to five tines (**fig**

5.8), and the thickness of the fork end of the handle is adjusted accordingly. The curve of the tines can only be achieved by steaming and setting them in a form.

Tips

- Ash and hickory are the best woods for these products.
- Use a small wedge to separate the tines of the stable fork and nail them in place.
- Use round hazel to make the continuous spacer bars of the hay fork, nailing each tine to the bar to give the right spacing.
- Take care to cut the tines to an even thickness – without this they will not spread evenly or may break.

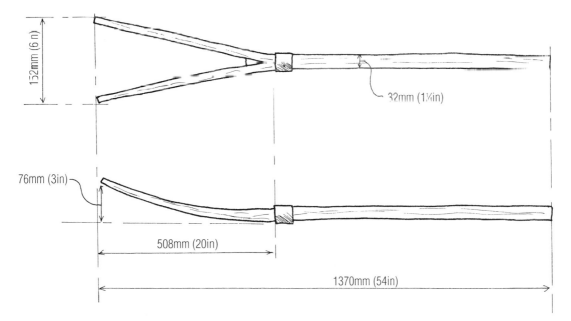

FIG 5.7
Pattern of a basic stable fork

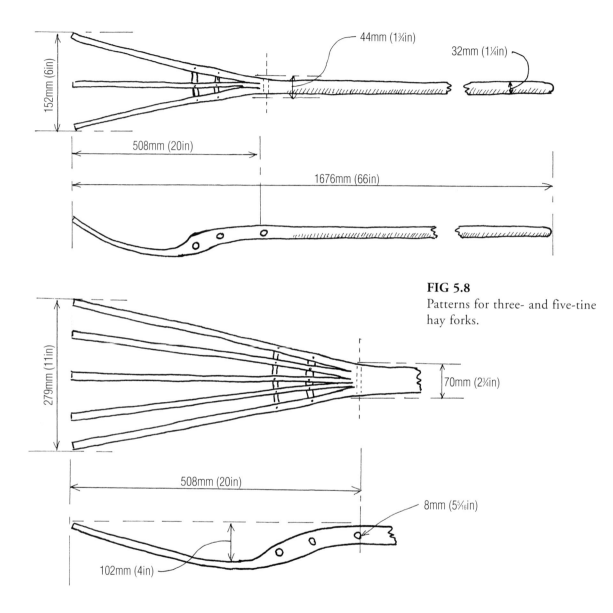

152mm (6in)

44mm (1¾in)

32mm (1¼in)

508mm (20in)

1676mm (66in)

FIG 5.8
Patterns for three- and five-tine hay forks.

279mm (11in)

70mm (2¾in)

508mm (20in)

8mm (5⁄16in)

102mm (4in)

Tool handles

The list of tools that use wooden handles is seemingly endless. As far back as the Stone Age primitive handles were applied to shaped flints in order to make axes, and the process has never stopped, because wood makes the perfect handle. It is warm to the touch and absorbs shocks that are applied to the tool. If not varnished, wooden handles do not slip through the hand (indeed willow absorbs sweat that would otherwise render it slippery), yet develop a patina as a result of regular use which makes the tool comfortable to the touch. The patterns, sizes and materials used in making tool handles have a long history based on developing the most ergonomic tool. Handles must be no only robust but shaped so that the tool is effective and safe to use.

A selection of the handles that are most often requested are illustrated (**figs 5.9** and **5.10**). I am always amazed at the number of favourite old tools that emerge from people's sheds requiring new handles.

Hook and chisel handles: simple round and ovoid handles are made on the lathe, as are parts of those that are sockered and knopped. This allows an accurate fit to be turned for the metal ferrule. Handles made for tools with long tangs (those in **fig 5.9**) must be the right size to allow the tang to project at the butt end so that it can be hammered over and hold the handle tight (**fig 5.11**). Chisel handles, always made of very close-grained wood, must have a hole just long enough to take the tang, which does not protrude at the end of the handle (**fig 5.11**). Both hook and chisel handles are fitted with ferrules at the blade end so that the handle does not split when the tang is driven home. It is also common for the handles of chisels that suffer a lot of heavy use to have a second ferrule at the other end of the handle to prevent it being split by the mallet (**fig 5.10**). Handles for tools with a socket fixing need to be turned to fit the socket accurately (**fig 5.11**).

Sledge, adze and axe handles: These are usually asymmetric and or oval handles (**figs 5.12** and **5.13**) with a swollen head shaped to fit into the socket of the tool. The head is usually sawn to accommodate a wedge that will hold it tight. When being shaped, the handles are held between two centres and shaped using a draw-knife and spoke shave. Village craftsmen always made tool handles exactly to the user's needs. When, during the industrial revolution, larger companies started to supply tools, they listed the wide range of sizes

they offered: axe handles for example were offered in 14, 16, 18, 20, 22, 24, 26, 28, 30, 32, 34, and 36 inches long!

Shovel trees are a mixture of turned, carved and steamed products for which there is a steady demand (**fig 5.14**). The specific size of an individual tree is determined by the sockets into which it must fit.

Scythe handles, or snaiths (**fig 5.15**), must be steamed and set in a frame to obtain the distinctive shape required. Most handle makers turn the small handles (nibs) that go with the snaith, but purchase the metal fittings for these and the blade.

Tips

- Resilient woods such as ash and hickory should be used for long handles where the tool has frequent heavy impact in use. Dense-grained wood such as box and beech are best where the handle will be hit (such as for chisels).
- Use wood seasoned for at least three months when making a handle and use clefts that are no larger than a quarter of the log circumference. This will reduce shrinkage and any tendency to split.
- Most tool tangs are tapered. To accommodate this, drill holes of progressively different diameters to make a tapered channel to fit the tang.
- Ferrules on the handles of tools with a tang are essential to prevent the handle splitting when the tang is forced home.
- Do not varnish handles of tools that are swung when used (such as axes and billhooks) otherwise they may slip in the hand. Rubbing linseed oil into the wood will protect against damp.

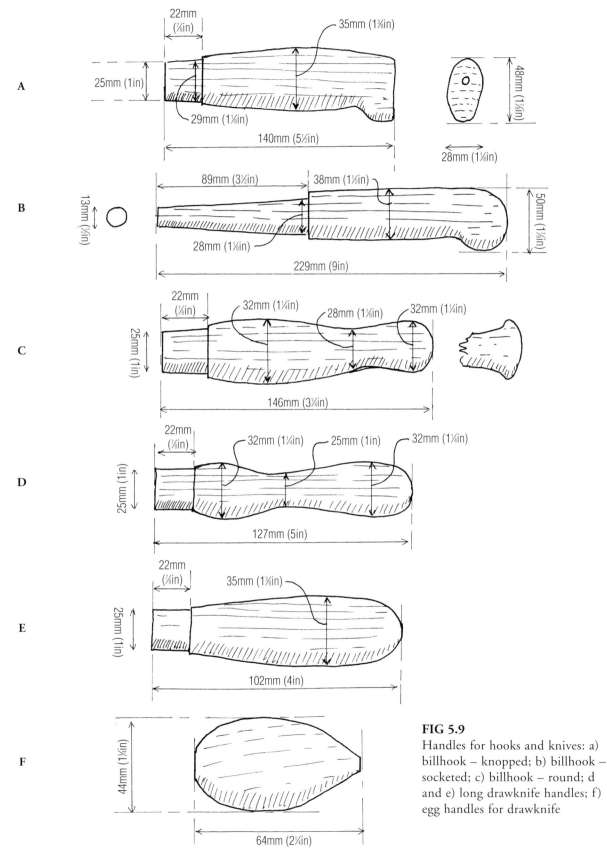

FIG 5.9

Handles for hooks and knives: a) billhook – knopped; b) billhook – socketed; c) billhook – round; d and e) long drawknife handles; f) egg handles for drawknife

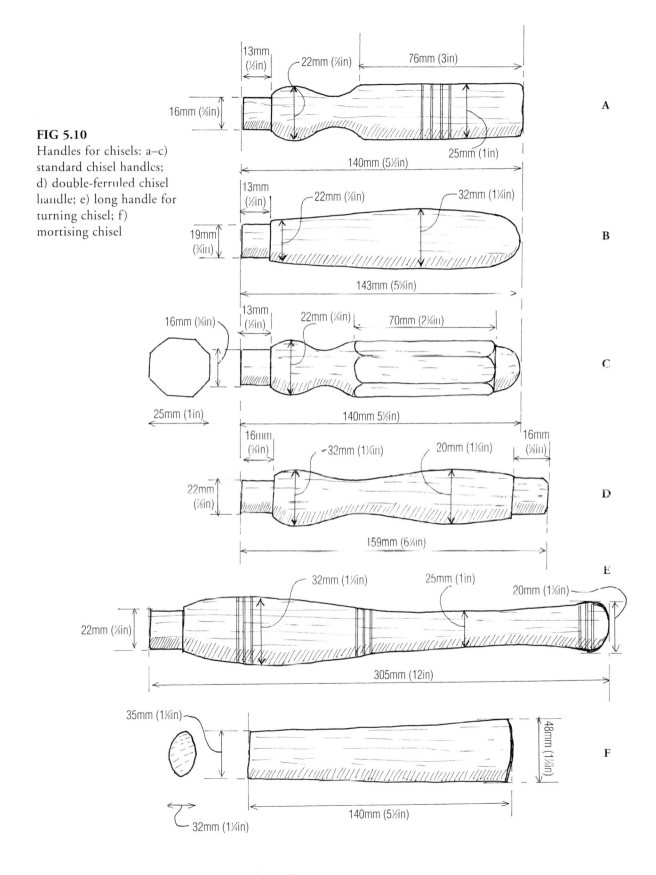

FIG 5.10
Handles for chisels: a–c) standard chisel handles; d) double-ferruled chisel handle; e) long handle for turning chisel; f) mortising chisel

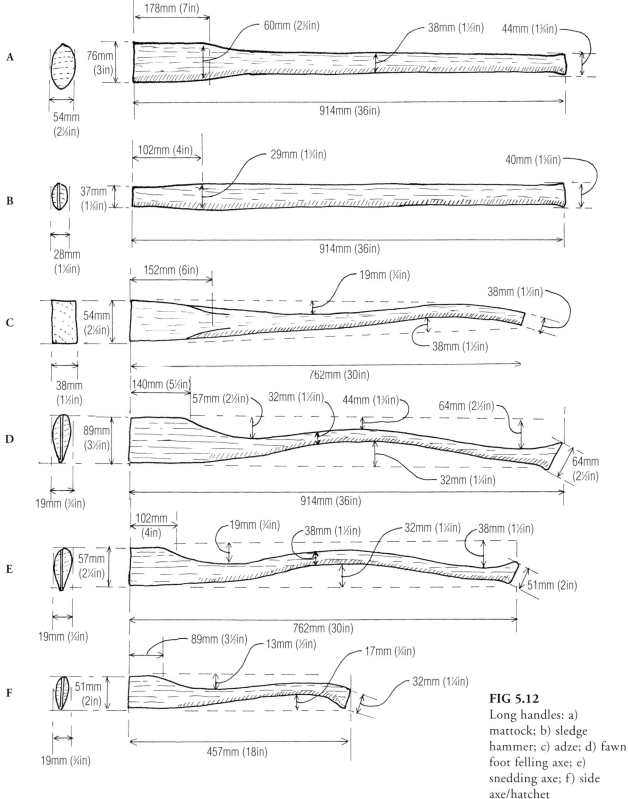

FIG 5.12
Long handles: a) mattock; b) sledge hammer; c) adze; d) fawn foot felling axe; e) snedding axe; f) side axe/hatchet

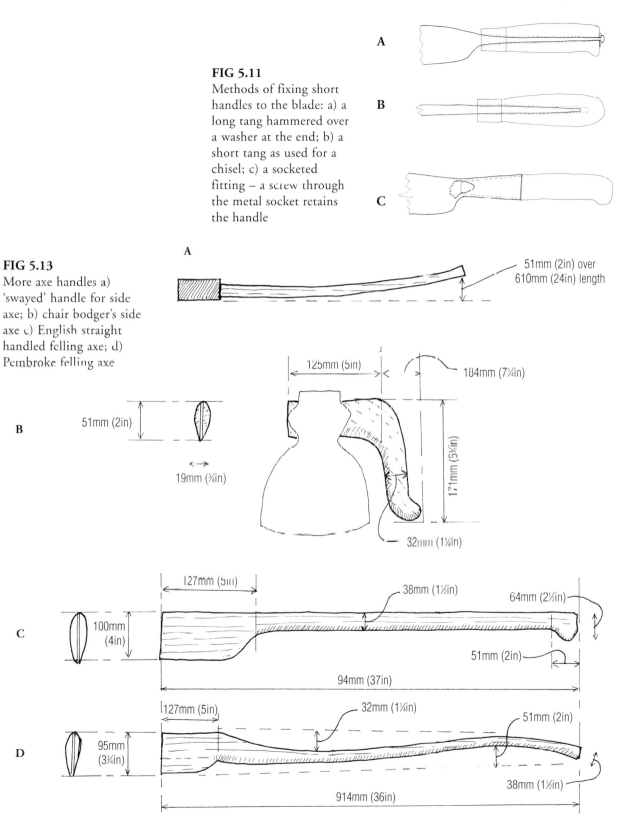

FIG 5.11
Methods of fixing short handles to the blade: a) a long tang hammered over a washer at the end; b) a short tang as used for a chisel; c) a socketed fitting – a screw through the metal socket retains the handle

A

B

C

FIG 5.13
More axe handles a) 'swayed' handle for side axe; b) chair bodger's side axe c) English straight handled felling axe; d) Pembroke felling axe

A

51mm (2in) over
610mm (24in) length

125mm (5in)

184mm (7¼in)

51mm (2in)

B

19mm (¾in)

171mm (5¾in)

32mm (1¼in)

127mm (5in)

38mm (1½in)

64mm (2½in)

C

100mm
(4in)

51mm (2in)

94mm (37in)

127mm (5in)

32mm (1¼in)

51mm (2in)

D

95mm
(3¾in)

38mm (1½in)

914mm (36in)

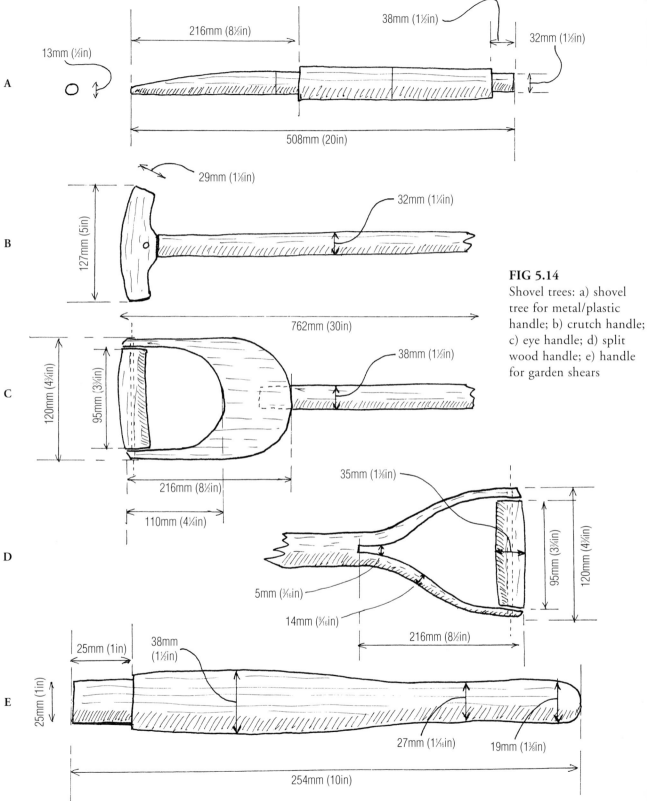

A 13mm (½in)

216mm (8½in)

38mm (1½in)

32mm (1¼in)

508mm (20in)

B 29mm (1⅛in)

127mm (5in)

32mm (1¼in)

762mm (30in)

C 120mm (4¾in)

95mm (3¾in)

38mm (1½in)

216mm (8½in)

110mm (4¼in)

D 35mm (1⅜in)

95mm (3¾in)

120mm (4¾in)

5mm (³⁄₁₆in)

14mm (⁹⁄₁₆in)

216mm (8½in)

E 25mm (1in)

38mm (1½in)

25mm (1in)

27mm (1¹⁄₁₆in)

19mm (1⅜in)

254mm (10in)

FIG 5.14
Shovel trees: a) shovel
tree for metal/plastic
handle; b) crutch handle;
c) eye handle; d) split
wood handle; e) handle
for garden shears

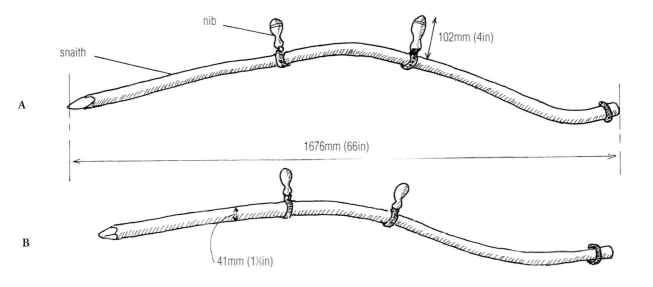

A

nib

snaith

102mm (4in)

1676mm (66in)

B

41mm (1⅝in)

C

FIG 5.15
Scythe 'snaiths': a)
English; b)
Suffolk/Norfolk; c)
Roding; d) American

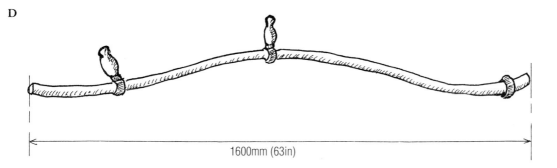

D

1600mm (63in)

Dibbers, shovels and scoops

Dibbers are still much used in gardens, both professional and amateur, to pot on or plant out seedling plants of all sizes. They are turned and comprise a simple handle above a tapered, conical section that is used to make a cylindrical hole in soft soil to accommodate a young plant (**fig 5.16**). It is common for the tapered part of the dibber to be marked with grooves at 25mm (1in) spaces so that a hole of a precise depth can be produced. Diameters of the tool vary with the size of the young plants being worked. An altogether bigger dibber is used for setting out larger plants, and is made with a handle that allows more pressure to be applied (**fig 5.17**).

Garden lines are two turned pegs used to hold either end of a string line to allow a straight line to be marked. The bottoms are tapered to allow them to be easily inserted into the ground while the tops are shaped to allow the string to be wound around them and retained (**fig 5.18**).

Wooden spades are not used for digging where flint and stones will damage the edge of the blade – for this they need to be sheathed in metal. There are some jobs, however that an all-wooden spade does better than a metal one. A less common tool in the countryside was the 'snow spade'. Made from a flat cleft of wood and with a long flat blade (**fig 5.19**), it was rated as the best way to move deep snow, which adhered to the blade less than to one of metal.

Shovels with wide, deep blades are probably best known for their use in shovelling grain or malt (**fig 5.20**). A wooden blade cannot raise a spark whatever it hits, making it much safer to use in grain stores where the risk of dust explosions is ever present. The deep lip in the design of these spades also means that a greater volume of product can be handled.

Wooden scoops were used for a wide variety of jobs in shops, farms and in the house. This means there was a large number of different sizes, although the basic patterns are all very similar (**fig 5.21**).

Tips:

- Dibbers are best made from close-grained wood such as box or fruit wood, but ash and maple will serve.
- Spades are often made of ash in order to get the long, wide straight clefts required.
- Deep shovels are made in two or three pieces. The blade is hollowed from a single piece of wood – maple is very good but hard to find in large enough sizes.

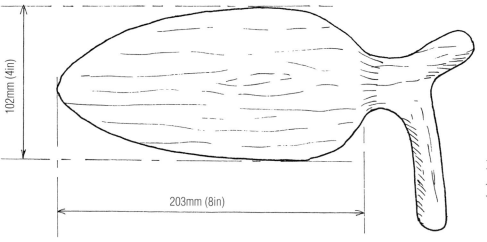

FIG 5.17
A large pattern dibber with an unusual handle

102mm (4in)

203mm (8in)

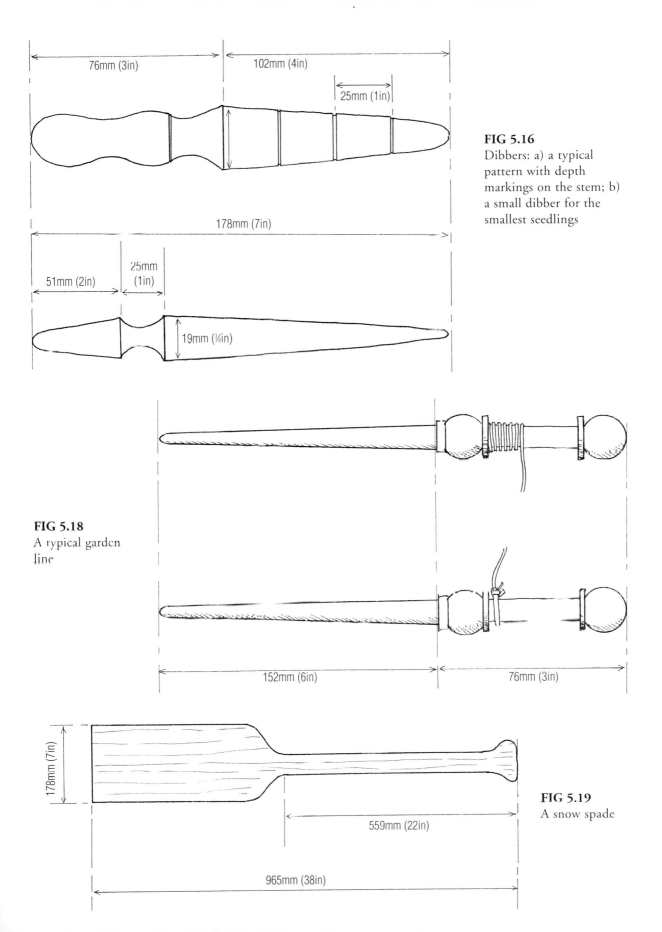

76mm (3in)

102mm (4in)

25mm (1in)

FIG 5.16
Dibbers: a) a typical
pattern with depth
markings on the stem; b)
a small dibber for the
smallest seedlings

178mm (7in)

51mm (2in)

25mm (1in)

19mm (¾in)

FIG 5.18
A typical garden
line

152mm (6in)

76mm (3in)

178mm (7in)

559mm (22in)

FIG 5.19
A snow spade

965mm (38in)

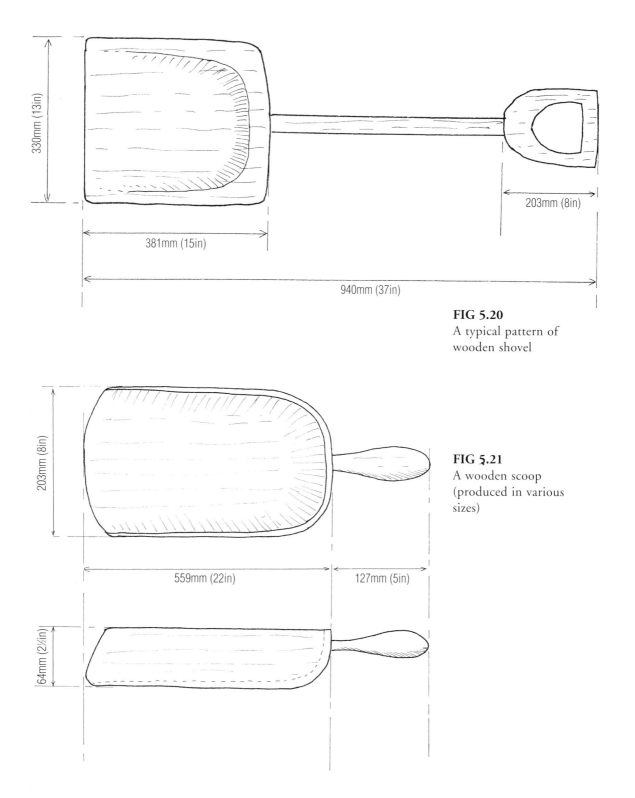

FIG 5.20
A typical pattern of
wooden shovel

FIG 5.21
A wooden scoop
(produced in various
sizes)

Chapter 6 Rustic Furniture and Benches

Introduction

Much of the furniture in this chapter descends from the cottage furniture that our ancestors produced. But, of course, being cheap, expendable and made of wood, there are virtually no examples pre-dating the 18th century remaining for us to see. There is evidence from the United States that rustic furniture was produced by native Americans, and it is described in 18th and 19th century furniture catalogues. After a decline in popularity, recent decades have seen a resurgence in demand for rustic products as an increasingly urbanized population seeks to maintain contact with its natural roots.

Rustic furniture is less commonly the product of factories but rather that of small rural workshops. The description 'hedge carpenters' for those who made these products is both apt and accurate – much of the material used came from hedges and spinneys. And since all of the wood is of small diameter and used in the round, a twisted grain and extra knots does not present a problem – in fact they probably contribute to the character of individual pieces. Rustic furniture has been described as being 'a celebration of natural forms'. This is a good description, as it relies on the craftsman seeing the potential offered by natural features and shapes, and being able to make furniture that is both functional and pleasing to the eye.

An advantage to rustic work in many of its forms is that it can be faster than other types of furniture to make. There is rarely a rigid plan to which the craftsman works – he has mental picture of how the finished product will both look and perform. But the detail emerges as the project progresses and each item of raw material is gauged for its suitability for the final product. This furniture is also rather more forgiving of the craftsman, since many of the components do not have to be an exact size to perform their task, though this does not detract from the skill and sense of good design that is required. The result is that each piece is truly individual, expressing the form and beauty of the wood from which it is made. The other side of this coin is that there are fewer fixed patterns than with the other products described in this book. This chapter can only give the reader an idea of the principles involved and show examples of some of the imaginative products that makers around the world are producing.

Jointing patterns and methods

It is not the role of this book to explain how to make the artefacts it describes. But with rustic furniture it is often less obvious how the components are jointed. Since these techniques are essential to achieving some of the patterns illustrated, particularly in round wood, it is important that they are described and understood.

Traditional square-sided mortice and tenon joints are used in rustic furniture, but mainly in the heavier benches where the individual members are large. In these cases the tenons invariably pass right through the mortised member (**fig 6.1**), there being no need for 'fox' (hidden) wedging. For the best benches the tenon may project beyond the mortice and be pegged to prevent it moving (**fig 6.2**). On the smaller forms of rustic furniture, round mortice and tenon joints are regularly used and are extremely efficient. These can be wedged (**fig 6.3**), nailed, or glued. Some workers use a rotary cutter to make a square-shouldered rather than taper-shouldered tenon (**fig 6.4**), but there is nothing to suggest this will result in a stronger joint.

The general principle in jointing is to avoid round-surface to round-surface joints, and this is achieved by the various lap and butt joints shown in **fig 6.5**. The only time that round surfaces together are secure is when the two members are bolted together. If bolts are used, washers are essential to avoid damage to the wood. A principle that particularly applies to stick and twig furniture is to gain strength without weight by using numbers of small members that are properly secured and positioned to brace the main structure (**fig 6.6**). These small members are best mortised into the main frame. If secured by nails they are usually pre-drilled to avoid them splitting. Nails can be allowed to protrude and then be clenched over so that they do not pull out, but the best patterns avoid this where the nail may contact the user of the chair.

Sometimes the number of joints required can be reduced by the judicious use of naturally branched material, and a natural joint will always be stronger for its size than a man-made joint. This is important with twig and stick furniture where the use of diagonal bracing is needed to give the required rigidity to the piece. These methods have stood the test of time, for in a piece from 1858 (Mack, 1996, see bibliography page 236), the writer describes how rustic furniture was put together by boring holes for the main framework and by nailing for the smaller pieces.

Tips

- Use galvanized nails for outside use to reduce rust – they also grip more tightly.
- Tenons should be very dry before assembly – they can then only swell and tighten the joint.
- Remove the bark in any areas where joints are to be glued.
- Very small wood is best seasoned for three months before use – this will reduce its tendency to split when nailed.
- Use an anvil (an old flat iron will do) when clenching nails to make them as tight as possible.
- Flatten the tips of nails before they are used in order to reduce the chance they will split green wood.

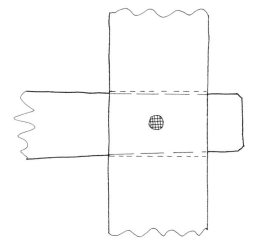
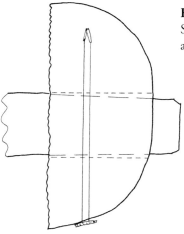

FIG 6.1
Simple nailed mortice
and tenon joint

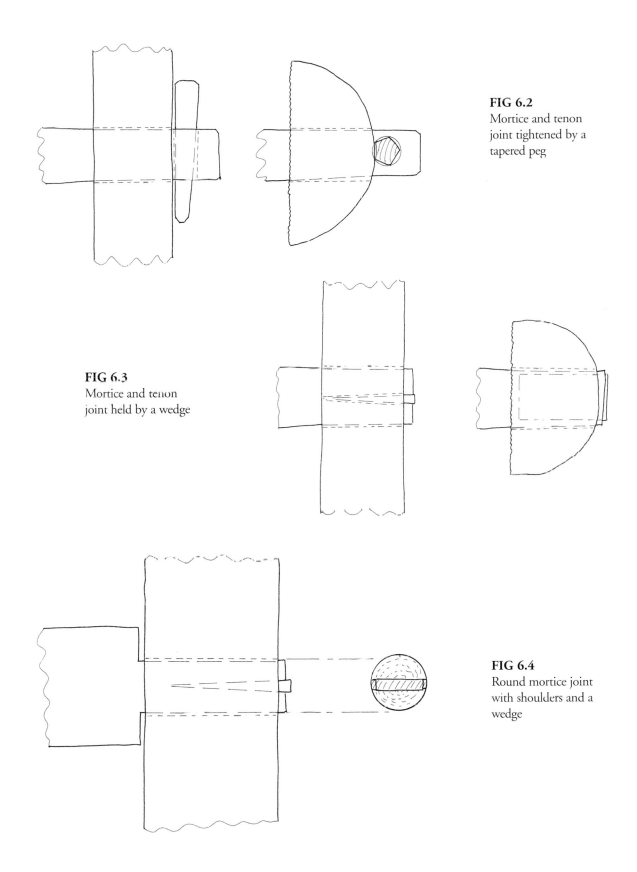

FIG 6.2
Mortice and tenon
joint tightened by a
tapered peg

FIG 6.3
Mortice and tenon
joint held by a wedge

FIG 6.4
Round mortice joint
with shoulders and a
wedge

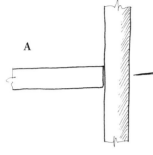

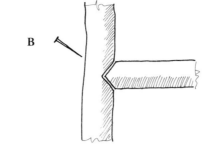

FIG 6.5
Joints for stick furniture: a) butt; b) 'V' butt; c) part lap; d) half lap; e) corner half lap; f) round mortise and tenon with hidden end

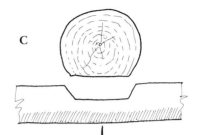

A

B

C

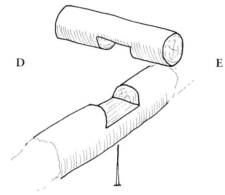

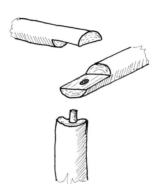

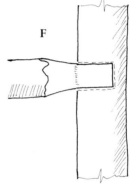

D

E

F

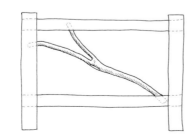

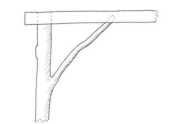

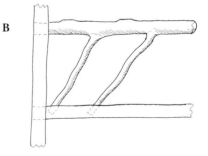

A

B

FIG 6.6
Using natural sticks to brace furniture: a) bracing a simple joint; b) a braced arm for a chair; c) bracing a chair frame; d) bracing a bow back

C

D

Stick Furniture

Stick furniture, as its name suggests, is made from round stick wood (small poles) as it is collected from coppice or hedge. On the smaller material, knots, twists, and side branches may be retained. It is not uncommon for the bark to be left on stick products, so care is required when collecting the raw material. The bark will slow the rate of seasoning considerably, but in larger poles will also reduce the long radial splits that are the result of drying too quickly.

The pattern of stick furniture is very close to post and rail (see Chapter 7), with a main frame based on four upright poles that form the legs. In a stool (fig 6.7), these upright poles are braced by one or two stretchers on each side. Four members form the basic seat frame. In a chair, the rear two posts extend to the full height of the back without joint (fig 6.8c and d). In an armchair, the front two posts are extended to support the arms at the front of the chair (fig 6.8). All of the major joints in these chairs are formed by round mortises and tenons that are either glued or nailed. Settees are made using the same principles (fig 6.9). Stick chairs differ significantly from standard post and rail chairs in that they are made entirely of round wood rather than from clefts. This means that no two members are identical in their curvature, shape, branching or size, and the craftsman must sort his material to find a combination of the best fit, visual appearance and durability. This means that although chairs may be based on 'classical' designs, they do have a rural appearance. The main area of the chair where the craftsman can truly express his individuality is in the back. Here a variety of thinner and more branched sticks can be used, as it can for the bracing under the seat. A range of chair backs is shown in fig 6.10. An interesting pattern, quite common in the country, is the triangular or 'corner' chair (fig 6.11), and it

is believed that these were used back to front to form a circle around a cock fight in the back room of the village pub! A more modern pattern has two back legs instead of one, but set close together.

Seating can come in various patterns. Some are of woven bast or canvas material as described in Chapter 7, but many are made from the sticks available to the craftsman (fig 6.12). Most commonly small diameter rods are used set very close together. These are able to follow a contoured frame and are close enough to be comfortable to sit on for some time. Half clefts of larger poles are often used, but when used round-side up are less comfortable; although this is improved if they are nailed round-side down, they may rock when fixed this way. This problem is reduced if the clefts are made narrower and nailed tightly together. Flat clefts or pales avoid these issues, and when shaved smooth make a fine seat that can also be slightly shaped. A final option is to weave small rods and make a wattle seat.

The principles of using small sticks can be applied to other articles of furniture as well as chairs. Picture frames, shelving, standard lamps and tables are shown in figs 6.13 and 6.14.

Tips

- Remove any knots and spears from wood to be used for seating.
- Use forked sticks to brace the chair and provide a good appearance.
- Almost any wood can be used for indoor furniture, but oak, ash, hickory and elm will always make the best.
- Collect 'sticks' in spring when the sap is rising and it is easiest to remove the bark without damaging the still soft wood underneath.
- Finish chairs with wax oil.

A

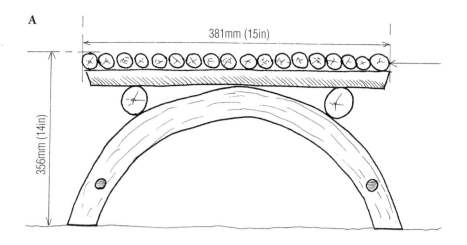

381mm (15in)

356mm (14in)

B

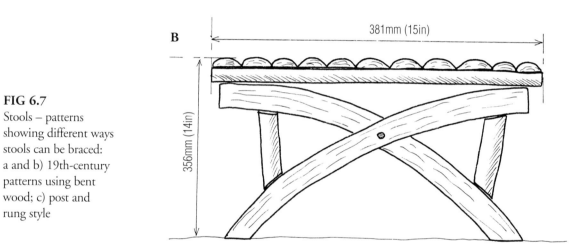

381mm (15in)

356mm (14in)

FIG 6.7
Stools – patterns
showing different ways
stools can be braced:
a and b) 19th-century
patterns using bent
wood; c) post and
rung style

C

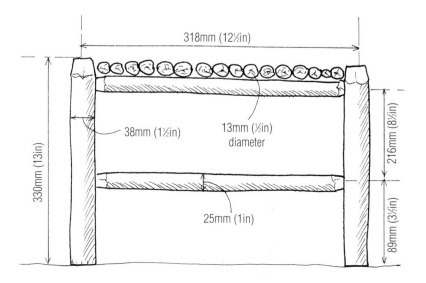

318mm (12½in)

38mm (1½in)

13mm (½in)
diameter

330mm (13in)

216mm (8½in)

25mm (1in)

89mm (3½in)

FIG 6.8

Stick furniture patterns: a) low-backed arm chair (see Mack, 1996, bibliography page 236); b) arm chair using curved members; c) high-backed chair; d) high-backed chair of less formal design (see Mack, 1996, bibliography page 236). Note that a), c) and d) require woven or canvas seats

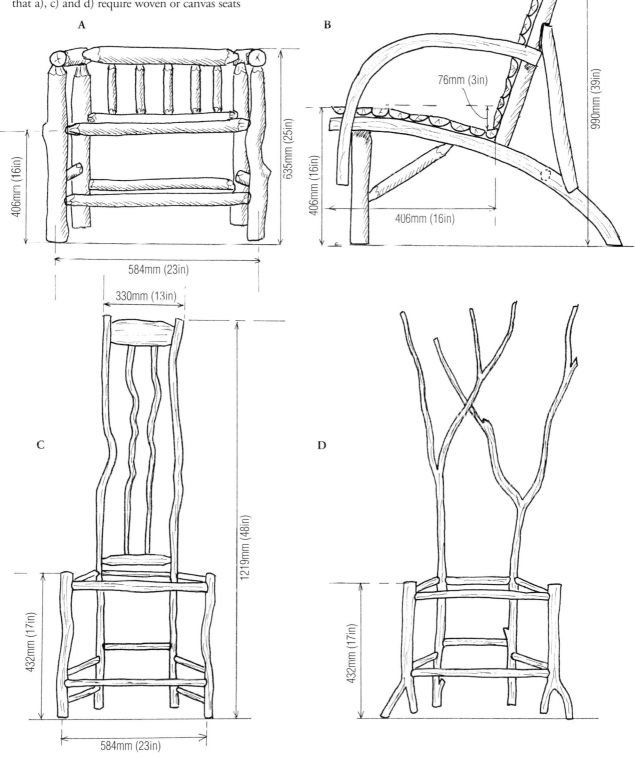

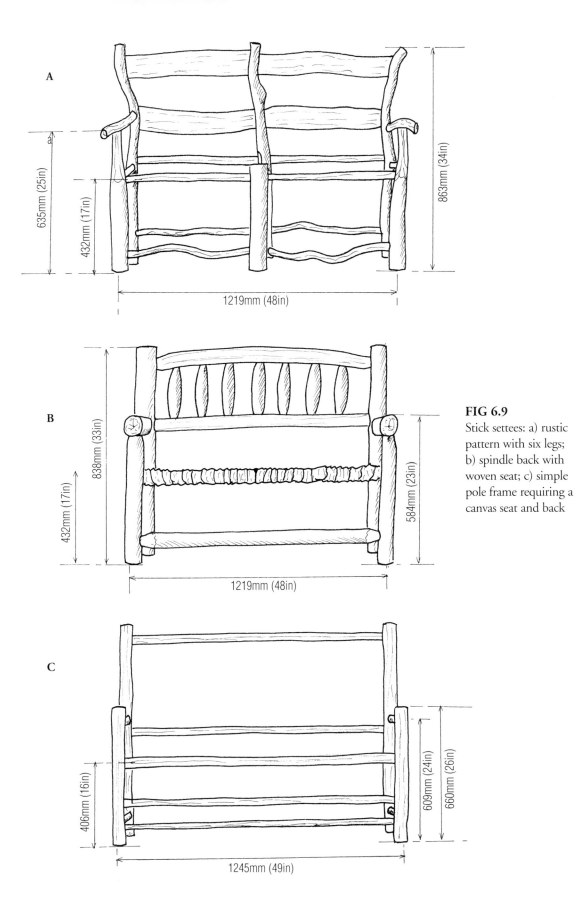

FIG 6.9
Stick settees: a) rustic pattern with six legs; b) spindle back with woven seat; c) simple pole frame requiring a canvas seat and back

A

B

C

D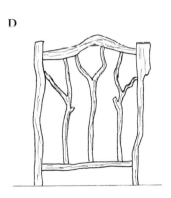

E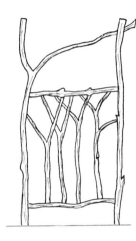

F

FIG 6.10
Stick chairs – a
range of patterns
for the backs from
formal to very
original use of
natural material

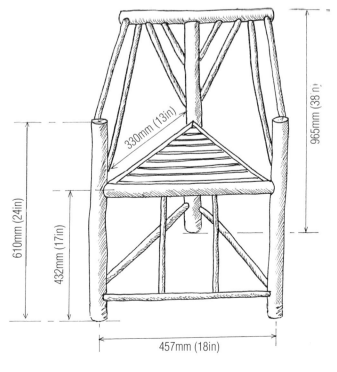

330mm (13in)

965mm (38 in)

610mm (24in)

432mm (17in)

457mm (18in)

FIG 6.11
Corner chair made
from round poles
and with cleft
members for the
seat

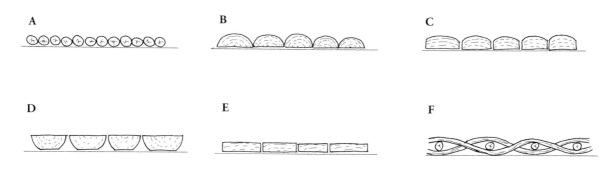

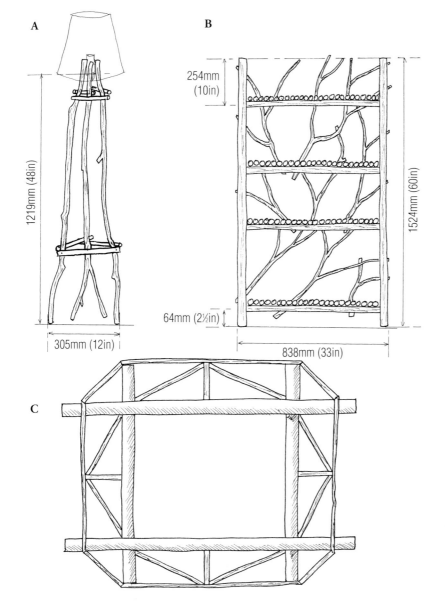

FIG 6.12 (above)
Patterns for wooden seats: a) small round rods; b) half round clefts; c) half round clefts narrowed to reduce the 'valley' between them; d) half round clefts flattened to give a flat surface; e) thick lathes; f) woven (wattled), small, round rods

FIG 6.13 (left)
Stick furniture: a) standard lamp (based on Ruoff); b) shelving; c) mirror or picture frame

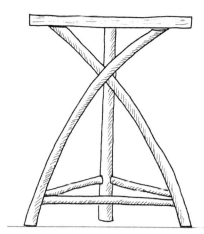

482mm (19in)–610mm (24in)

711mm (28in)

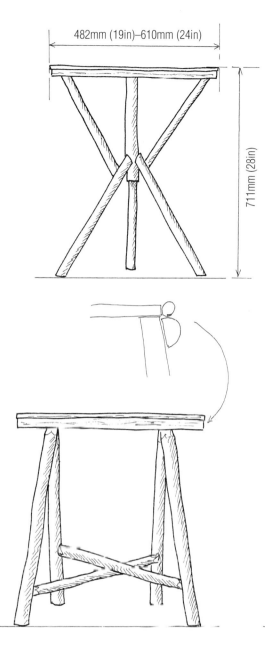

FIG 6.14
Stick tables: various
patterns using three
and four legs.

Twig, willow and bent wood chairs

First some definitions. 'Bent wood' is applied to
furniture made by using long thin green rods that are
bent around and fixed to a solid frame of poles (**fig
6.15**), patterns for which are described here. 'Twig'
furniture is a hybrid between bent wood and stick
furniture. It often uses a solid frame, but uses smaller
sticks and twigs than the stick furniture already
described (**fig 6.16**). Finally 'living willow' describes
furniture and sculptures composed entirely of woven
willow rods, often inserted into the ground so they

may remain alive and sprout leaf. Patterns for this type,
which may be very similar to those of bent wood
furniture, are not described here, but see Warnes,
2001, for detail (see bibliography page 236). Bent
wood furniture requires some planning. The craftsman
needs to have a mental picture of the final shape of the
piece. That shape dictates the frame needed to both
support and shape the curves adopted by the pliable
rods. There are certain patterns of frames that are
regularly used (**fig 6.17**), and from those illustrated it is
possible to see how they hold the rods and achieve the
bold sweeps in the arms and backs that are typical of

this furniture. Green sticks are used to form the outer rim of the seat back, and a range of patterns for the in-fill is shown in **fig 6.18**. Another feature of this furniture is that the small-diameter sticks are used in bundles of three to five to both strengthen and give the size of arm or back bow that is effective and comfortable. The orientation of the sticks can be altered from one end to the other, producing an elegant twist that is not possible in any other medium (**fig 6.19**).

Frames can be made in a variety of patterns to make chairs, armchairs, loungers, settees and tables (**fig 6.20**). Backs are normally high, but it is possible to make low-back armchairs or settees with lovely flat arms (**fig 6.21**). While small sticks remain pliable they can be used to produce wattle patterns akin to hurdles. Wattling can be used to make both chair-backs and seats, and the ends of the sticks are either left protruding (**fig 6.22b**) or, more neatly, sandwiched between two bow rods (**fig 6.22a**). Small sticks are used to form the seat of bent wood chairs.

For the back, the rods are continuous from the top of the back to the front of the seat, forming a comfortable curve where seat and back join (**fig 6.23**).

It is possible to make a bent wood chair without a frame. A superb example made in the United States is shown in **fig 6.24** revealing how groups of sticks can provide a unique combination of strength and beauty.

Tips

- Small sticks for bent wood work should be willow or hazel.
- Sticks must be used green, although are best held for a few weeks under cover after cutting to toughen.
- Green sticks should be drilled before nailing to avoid splitting.
- For outdoor products use galvanized nails and paint with a protective finish.
- It is normal to leave the bark on this furniture.

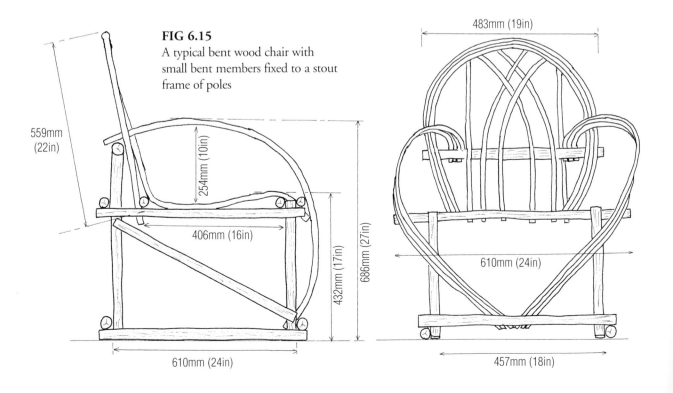

FIG 6.15
A typical bent wood chair with small bent members fixed to a stout frame of poles

559mm (22in)

254mm (10in)

406mm (16in)

432mm (17in)

686mm (27in)

610mm (24in)

483mm (19in)

610mm (24in)

457mm (18in)

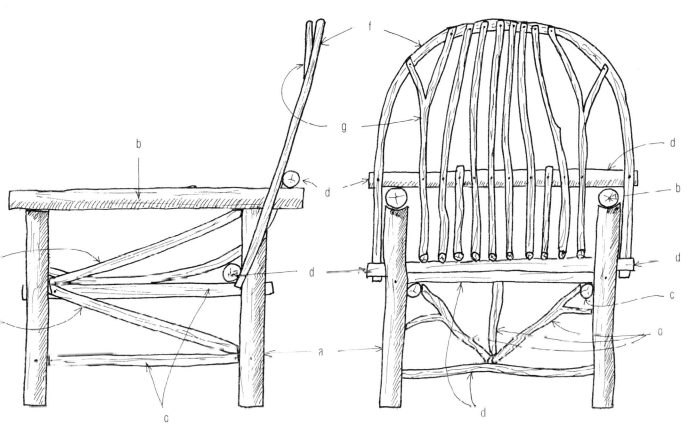

FIG 6.16
Stick furniture, where
small diameter rods are
fixed to a stout pole frame:
a) legs; b) arms; c) braces;
d) horizontal supports; e)
braces; f) bow back; g)
sticks for seat and back

FIG 6.17
Bent wood furniture: the small rods
(dotted lines) are bent around the
pole frame (solid lines) and fixed to it
at the points indicated by the small
arrows

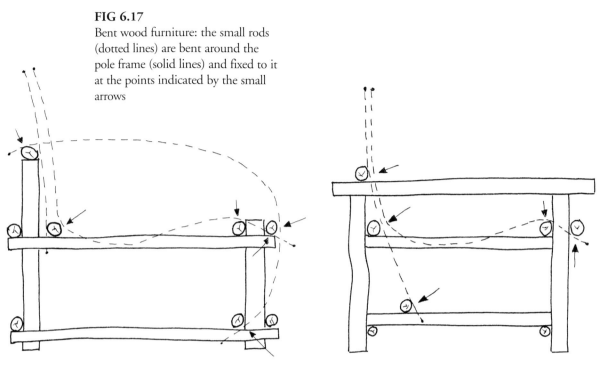

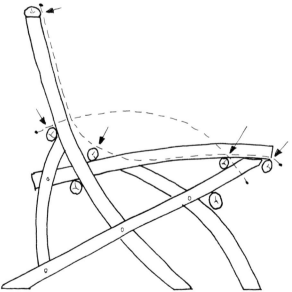

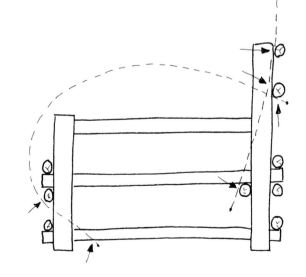

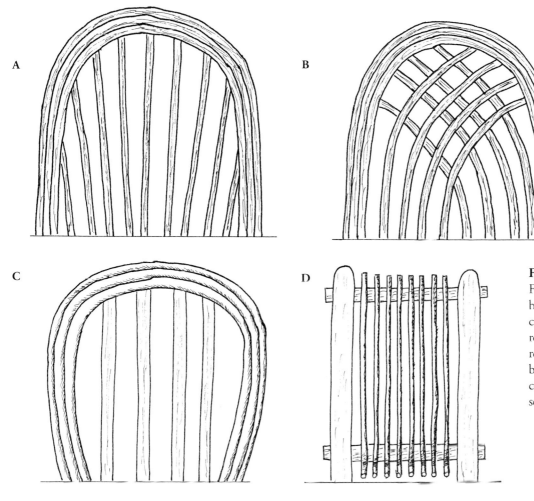

A

B

C

D

FIG 6.18
Filling patterns for the back of bent wood chairs: a and b) round rods; c) lathes; d) round rods bent at the bottom to make a continuous back and seat

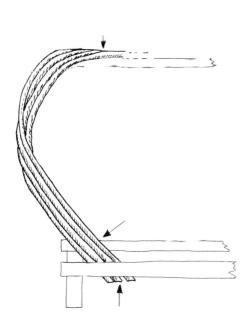

A

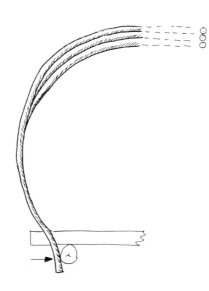

B

FIG 6.19
Curves in bent wood furniture: a) when forming an arm; b) forming the back bow – both viewed from the front of the chair. Arrows show fixing points

FIG 6.20
Other bent wood
patterns: a) a lounger;
b and c) small tables

A

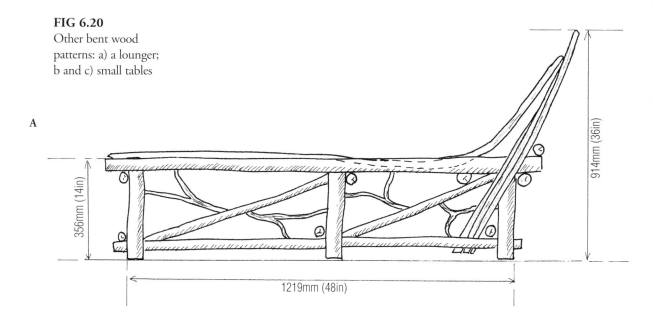

B

C

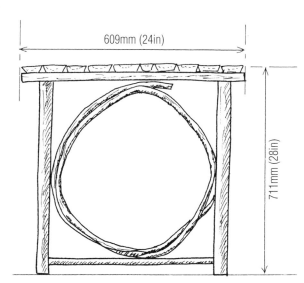

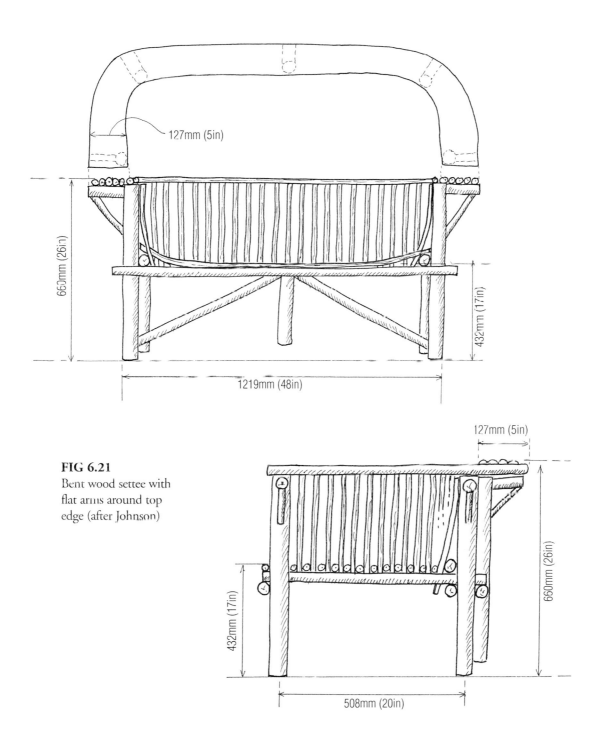

127mm (5in)

660mm (26in)

432mm (17in)

1219mm (48in)

FIG 6.21
Bent wood settee with
flat arms around top
edge (after Johnson)

127mm (5in)

432mm (17in)

660mm (26in)

508mm (20in)

A

B

FIG 6.22
Bent wood chair backs
incorporating wattling

FIG 6.23
Chair with one-piece
bent rods from top of
back to front of seat

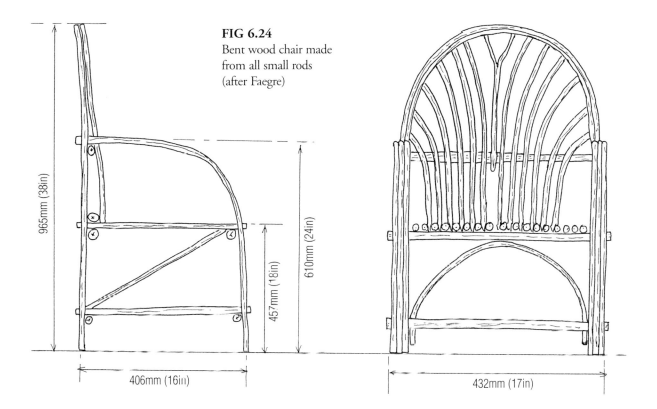

FIG 6.24
Bent wood chair made
from all small rods
(after Faegre)

965mm (38in)

457mm (18in)

610mm (24in)

406mm (16in)

432mm (17in)

Benches

Benches are for outdoor use and are more solid in construction than the settees we have already seen. They come in sizes to accommodate two or three people. Because of their size, most benches have mortice and tenon jointing of their main members, and these can be either round or oblong, and either pegged or nailed (**figs 6.1** to **6.4**). The bark can be left on, or removed, but in either case it is normal for most knots to be removed unless they are required for decorative purposes.

A bench is sized to give comfort (**fig 6.25**). The seat height is much as it would be for a chair, as is its depth, and it normally comes between the two front legs. For comfort the back should lean at an angle to the seat.

Some patterns are made all in round wood (**fig 6.26**). This can make them quite heavy, but this may be a benefit if they are not to be moved frequently. Seats are

mostly from pieces of cleft or round wood, as already described for stick chairs, with the very best being of thick clefts. The most basic bench seat is simply a thick cleft from a large log (**fig 6.27**). The backs of benches can come in any number of patterns that can be a few simple rustic poles, or more complex patterns made from natural sticks (**fig 6.28**). Patterns dating from the 19th century, such as that illustrated in **fig 6.29**, are both formal and complex. All benches have a series of triangulating braces to stop the structure from rocking either sideways or from back to front.

Some of the nicest benches are those made from cleft wood (**fig 6.30**). This method offers the advantage of a very solid structure without excessive weight, and because when wood is cleft it produces two mirror images, a very symmetrical yet rustic product results. Furthermore the use of mirror clefts can produce identically curved members which look so good. In some benches of this type the parallel back members are joined by turned spindles in the same way as a spindle-back chair.

Tips

- Almost any wood can be used to make benches, but hickory, oak and chestnut are the most durable, and ash the easiest to work.
- Benches are best treated with preservative or water repellent to give a longer life.
- When large poles have been barked, store them

under cover so that they season slowly; otherwise they may develop serious radial splits.
- Use galvanized nails or bolts to secure the mortice and tenon joints.
- Bracing is essential to avoid a wobbly seat.
- Remove all knots and splinters where they will be a nuisance or risk to users.

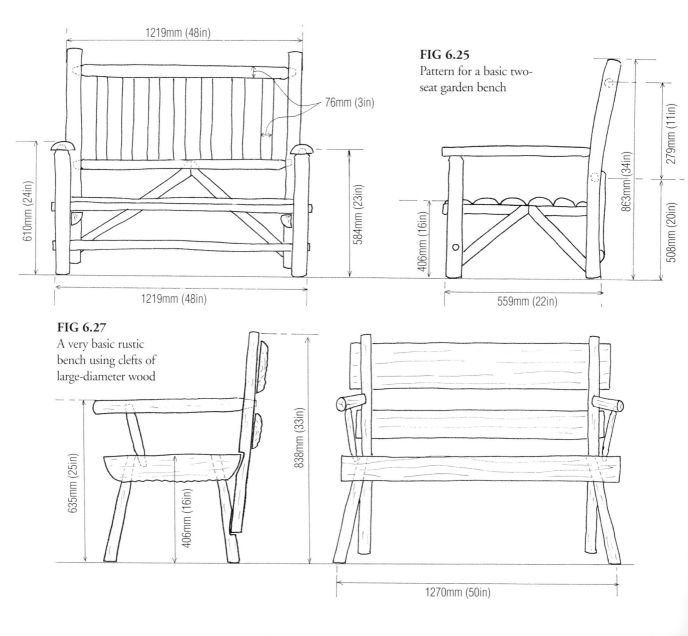

FIG 6.25
Pattern for a basic two-seat garden bench

FIG 6.27
A very basic rustic bench using clefts of large-diameter wood

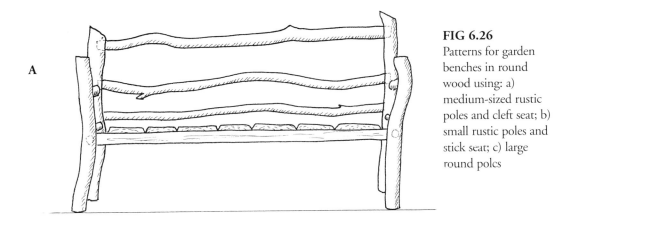

A

FIG 6.26
Patterns for garden benches in round wood using: a) medium-sized rustic poles and cleft seat; b) small rustic poles and stick seat; c) large round poles

B

C

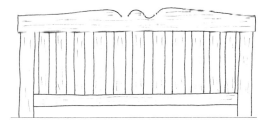

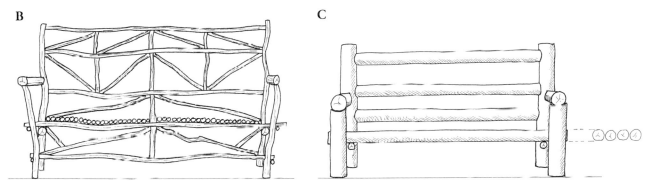

FIG 6.28
Some different patterns for the backs of garden benches

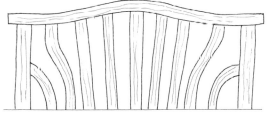

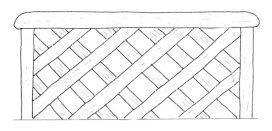

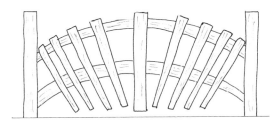

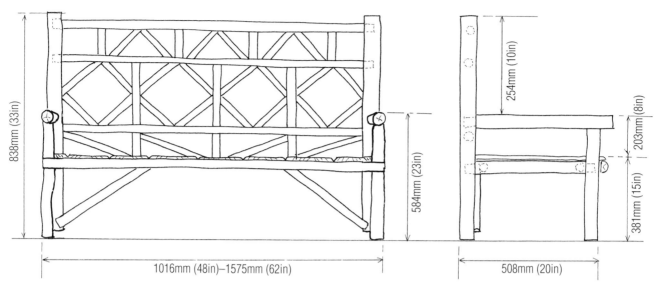

FIG 6.29
A 19th-century pole bench with a typically
complicated pattern for the back

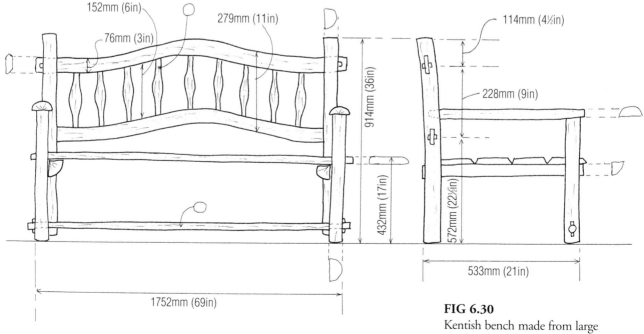

FIG 6.30
Kentish bench made from large
cleft poles of chestnut

Chapter 7 Post and Rung and Slab and Stick Furniture

Introduction

Making chairs has to be the supreme workshop craft of green woodworking. To make a chair from a tree is a special experience today, but at the peak of this trade it was an everyday occurrence for countless craftsmen. These pieces of furniture were not only made by the thousand, but also loved and used by all sections of the population. That there are very few examples of early vernacular furniture left today reflects the heavy use to which it was put.

There was very little sophisticated domestic seating before the 16th century. The earliest patterns were very heavy and solid in construction with a thick seat into which legs were mortised. Stools were far more common than chairs, and legs were rarely turned in the earliest examples. Use of the pole lathe made turned legs more widespread and added simple decoration to these otherwise functional items. By the 17th century turned decoration had become common, and to today's tastes many of the chairs were over decorated, with little wood left unturned.

As furniture became more widespread, so the number and range of styles available increased and the nature of chair-making changed from being a village craft performed by the local carpenter to an industry in which fewer but larger workshops or factories took the lead. We have very few paper records of the earliest chairs, but by Victorian times the major chair makers were producing catalogues illustrating over 140 different patterns. Many chairs were painted, sometimes to disguise the different woods used in the manufacture of an individual chair, but also to provide protection for chairs used out of doors. Despite this apparent organization, the making of chairs remained a piecemeal business. Legs and stretchers were made on pole lathes out in the woodland that provided the material from which they were turned. Making the seats and assembling the various components, however, was carried out by the chair maker in the workshop. The tradition of bodging chair legs in the Chiltern woods and similar areas has long since ceased, but the legacy of those skills remains, carried on in individual workshops throughout the world.

This development of chair patterns applied particularly to slab and stick furniture, but the history of post and rung furniture is less written about. It started around the same time as slab and stick, since an illustration in a 16th century book of trades shows such a chair, but few examples remain to us to see. No pole lathe is required to make a chair of this type, for the whole process, including the seats, can be carried out by hand tools. Post and rung chairs were developed most strongly in the North America, with the arrival of settlers from the Old World. It was not realistic to take furniture across the Atlantic, so making simple but effective furniture in those early years was a 'must' which post and rung filled admirably. Its most elegant and beautiful forms are found in Shaker furniture, and this style of chair rightly still finds favour today with chair makers around the world.

Post and Rung Stools and Chairs

The essence of post and rung furniture is exactly as described – four 'posts' or legs joined by a series of rungs (**fig 7.1** and **7.2**). There are usually two rungs joining each leg below those members that form the rim of the seat, although short stools only require one (**fig 7.3**). In a chair the back posts are continuous from the foot to the top of the back. This is the *sine qua non* of post and rung, never occurring on slab and stick furniture. Likewise, in an armchair the front posts continue above the seat line to support the arm (**fig 7.4**), while the bottoms of the posts may be connected to a curved bar to make a rocking chair (**fig 7.5**). Seats are applied to the frame after it has been made, and consist of woven bast, rush, or cloth. Chairs of this generic type may also be called 'Shaker', 'Brewster', 'Rush Bottom', and 'Ladder Back' – all terms that describe particular styles (**fig 7.6**).

Although turned posts and rails are sometimes seen, particularly on 'Brewster' chairs, it is more normal for all of the members to be made from clefts of wood fashioned to the required shape and finish using hand tools such as draw-knives and spoke-shaves. This imparts a unique visual and textural finish to the product that enhances and underlines the individual hand-made nature of every piece. Joints are mortice and tenon style, invariably round, and in the best furniture are 'blind' wedged (**fig 7.7**). This whole structure provides strength in a light, elegant chair.

Although the pattern described is largely fixed, there are areas where the craftsman can express his individuality.

Turning: the front posts, the upper part of the back posts and the front rungs can be turned (**fig 7.8**) using any of the patterns illustrated in **fig 7.31**. 'Brewster' chairs normally have short, turned members, joining the side rungs and back (**fig 7.9**).

Chair backs: these can be long or short (**fig 7.10**), which will in turn change the number of slats that are used. These 'slat-back' or ladder-back chairs have various patterns of slat which are quite characteristic of post and rail chairs, both in North America and England (**fig 7.11**). Another design common in post and rung chairs is the spindle back design (**fig 7.12**). It is normal for the spindles to be turned, but they can be plain sticks.

Seats: there are several choices of seating. Perhaps the most appropriate is the under-bark of trees such as elm, lime or hickory. With the outer bark removed the bast is pliable enough to weave into a seat. Different patterns of weaving are shown in **fig 7.13**. Other options are sea-grass (**fig 7.14**), rush or canvas. Finally it is possible to make the seat from thin slats of wood nailed to the frame, (**fig 7.15**).

Tips

- Use wood while it remains green.
- Dry the tenons, but keep mortises moist when assembling so that joints will tighten, rather than loosen, with time.
- Soften bast by soaking in water when required for weaving.
- Green wood shaved to a round shape will become slightly oval when seasoned; to achieve a true round shape shave again after seasoning.
- Shape the members forming the rim of the seat to an oval profile to support the seating material better.
- Ash, oak and hickory are the best materials, but must be straight grained and knot free.
- Chamfer the ends of all posts and rungs
- Finish with Danish oil or beeswax.

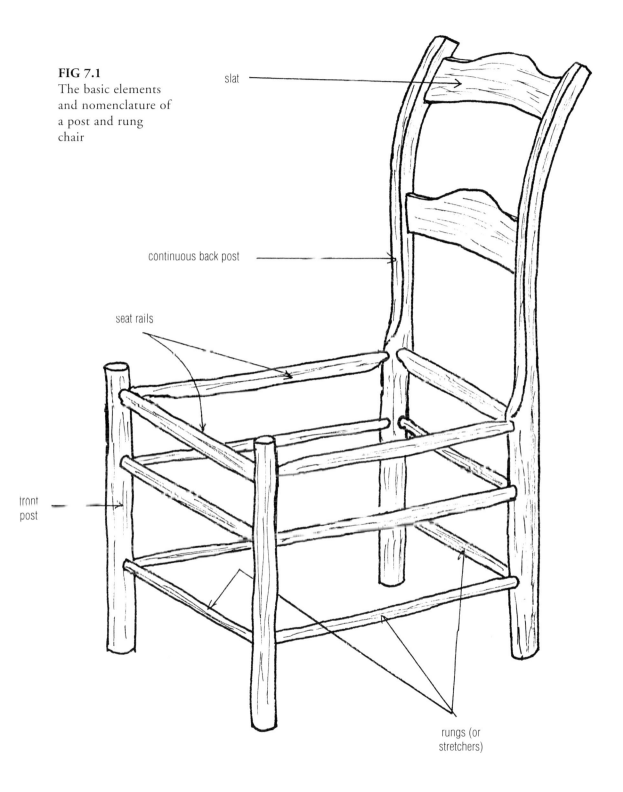

FIG 7.1
The basic elements
and nomenclature of
a post and rung
chair

slat

continuous back post

seat rails

front
post

rungs (or
stretchers)

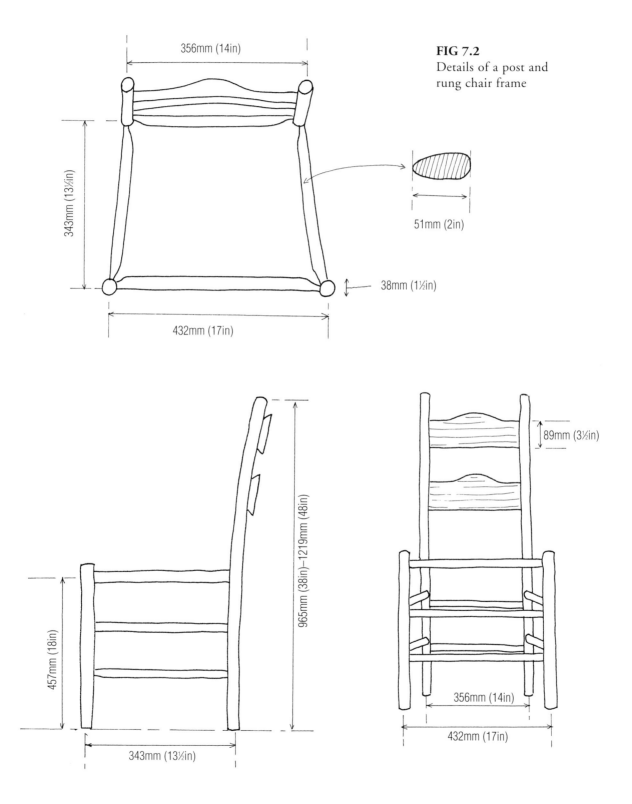

FIG 7.2
Details of a post and
rung chair frame

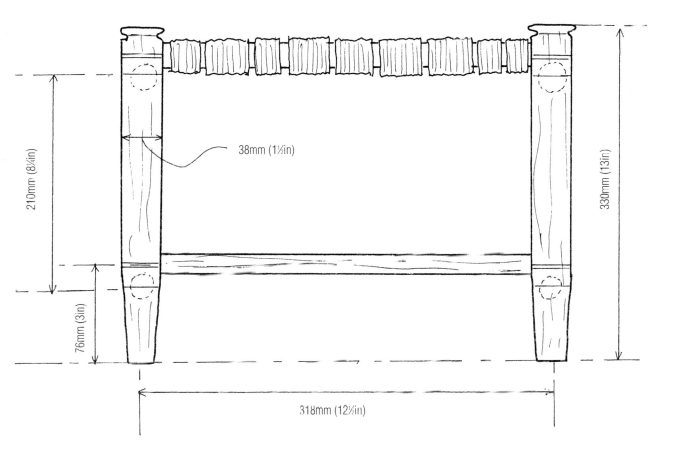

210mm (8¼in)

330mm (13in)

76mm (3in)

38mm (1½in)

318mm (12½in)

FIG 7.3
A low post and rung
stool requiring only
one set of stretchers

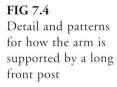

FIG 7.4
Detail and patterns
for how the arm is
supported by a long
front post

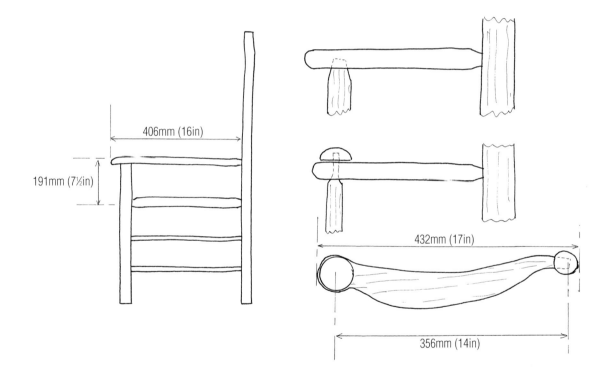

406mm (16in)

191mm (7½in)

432mm (17in)

356mm (14in)

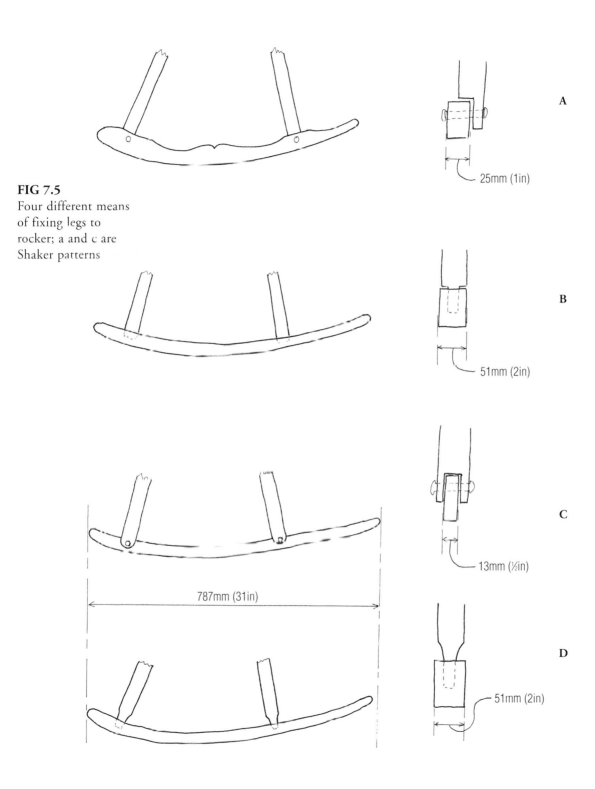

FIG 7.5
Four different means
of fixing legs to
rocker; a and c are
Shaker patterns

A

25mm (1in)

B

51mm (2in)

C

13mm (½in)

D

51mm (2in)

787mm (31in)

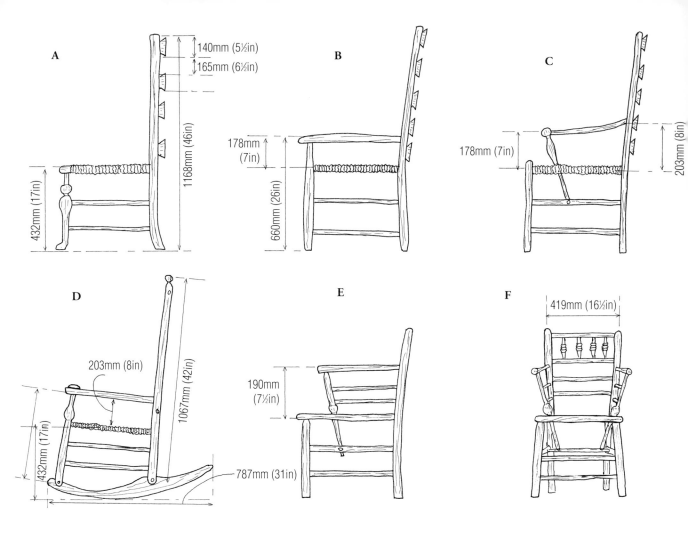

A

140mm (5½in)
165mm (6½in)
1168mm (46in)
432mm (17in)

B

178mm (7in)
660mm (26in)

C

178mm (7in)
203mm (8in)

D

203mm (8in)
1067mm (42in)
432mm (17in)
787mm (31in)

E

190mm (7½in)

F

419mm (16½in)

FIG 7.6
Some traditional patterns: a) 18th century; b) Pattern by E W Gimson, 1904; c) a 'Clisset' pattern; d) a shaker pattern rocking chair from the United States; e) and f) two views of a Sussex chair of *c.* 1875

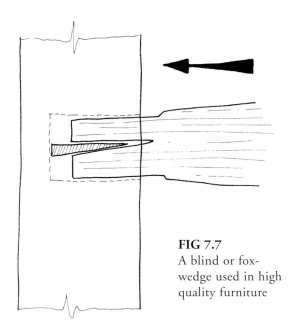

FIG 7.7
A blind or fox-wedge used in high quality furniture

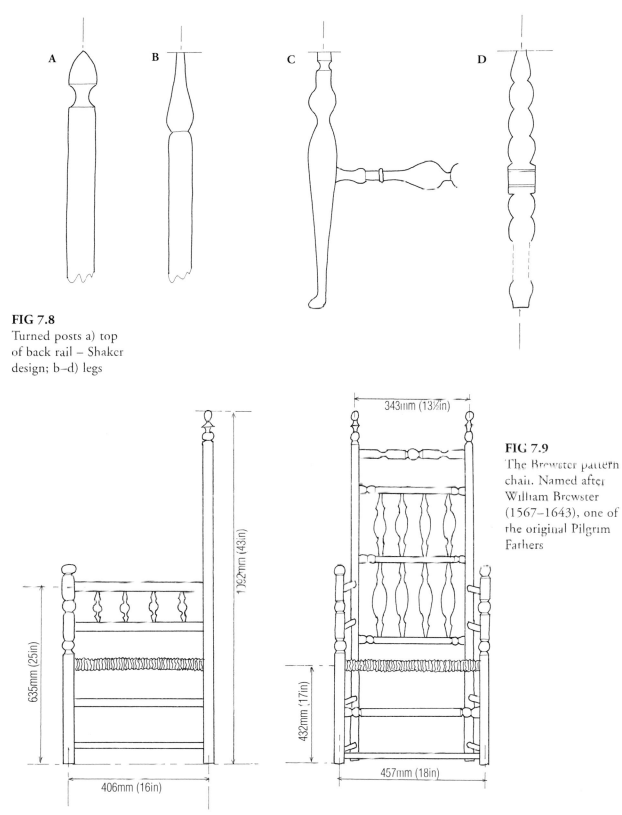

FIG 7.8
Turned posts a) top
of back rail – Shaker
design; b–d) legs

FIG 7.9
The Brewster pattern
chair. Named after
William Brewster
(1567–1643), one of
the original Pilgrim
Fathers

FIG 7.10
Typical chair heights: a) low stool;
b) normal stool; c) low-backed or
smoker's arm chair; d) normal
chair; e) high-backed arm chair

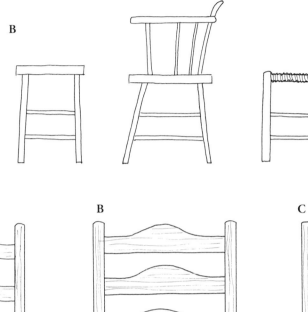

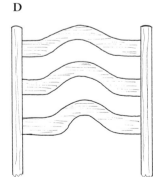

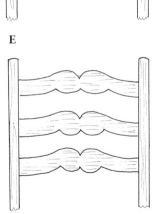

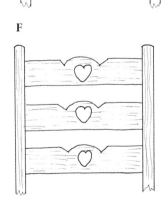

FIG 7.11
Patterns of ladder-back chairs with different
patterns of slats: a) an 18th century pattern;
b) Gimson's pattern – 19th century; c and d)
two Lancashire patterns of the 18th century;
e) Cupid bow; f) heart pattern (after Vosey)

FIG 7.12
Patterns of spindle-back chairs: a) unnamed; b)
Cumberland; c) Yorkshire; d) Lancashire; e) Sussex;
f) children's pattern from the United States

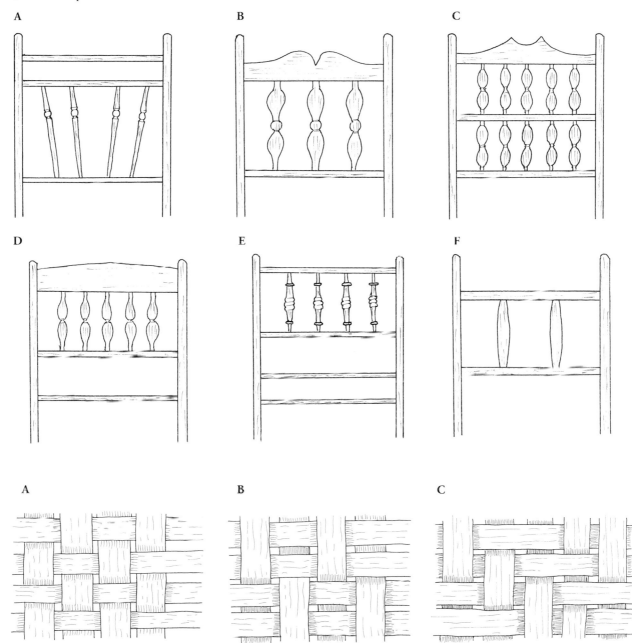

FIG 7.13
Patterns for weaving elm bast
seating: a) one over, one under;
b) two over, two under; c)
herringbone

FIG 7.14
Example of rush or sea-grass
seating

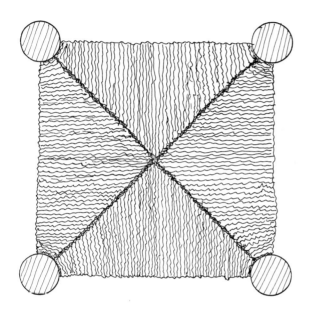

FIG 7.15
Seat composed of wooden slats
nailed or screwed to the seat
frame

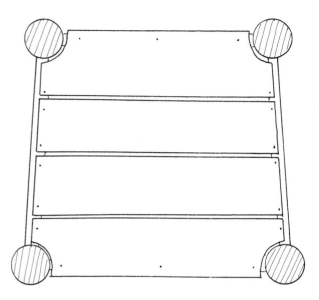

Basic Slab and Stick furniture

Slab and stick appears much as its description – a
thick slab forming the seat with stick legs mortised
into the underside. The additional sticks required to
form the back for a chair are separately mortised into
the slab from the top. The legs never extend above
the level of the seat to form the back or arms as they
do in post and rung chairs. Square-topped stools
with four legs are among the oldest examples of seats
that are either still in existence or can still be found
illustrated in old manuscripts.

Stools: I have seen the most basic type of stool (**fig
7.16**) made by coppice workers in Kent using only a
side axe, drill and twybil, as craftsmen must have
done for generations. Another simple pattern is the
milking stool, invariably based on a round slab and
three legs wedged into it (**fig 7.17**). Wedges are
oriented to prevent the slab splitting (**fig 7.18**).
Short stools with four legs usually have four

stretchers in either a box form or crossing between
the legs diagonally (**fig 7.19**). Where the stool seat is
the same height as a normal chair seat, or higher, the
number of stretchers may need to be increased. The
legs and stretchers can be either very plain and
shaped by draw-shave, or can be turned to any
of the patterns used for Windsor chairs.

Chairs: The slab that is at the heart of this furniture
tends to be thick and with a minimum of shaping on
the top surface. The actual shape of the slab can vary
from square to round or half round (**fig 7.20**). The
first slab and stick chairs were made by mortising a
back into the top of the slab. In early patterns the
mortices pass right through the slab and have wedges
driven in from the opposite side. Backs come in
various patterns, the simplest based on two or three
poles either on their own (**fig 7.21**), or with slats
added by way of a back rest. These chunky basic
patterns lend themselves to garden use rather than in
the drawing room. Pole backs can be either regular

in shape or consist of a series of natural curves that increase the visual interest and make the chair more comfortable (**fig 7.23**). One small advantage of this type of construction over post and rung is that the angle between the back and the seat, so essential to the chair's comfort, can be easily adjusted by angling the mortice holes rather than having to steam and bend the members.

It was from this basic slab and stick furniture that the elegant Windsor chairs developed. **Fig 7.22** illustrates examples of some very early 'Windsor' chairs that clearly show their slab and stick ancestry.

Tips

- Elm is the best material for the slab due to its resistance to splitting.
- The slab is best shaped to a concave top surface.
- Chairs will be more comfortable if the back is slightly angled to the slab.
- Stools and chairs are more stable if the legs are slightly splayed (*c.* 10 degrees).
- Chamfer all edges including the bottom of the legs.
- Furniture can be painted for outdoor use, otherwise finish with Danish oil or beeswax.

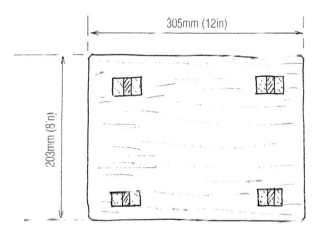

FIG 7.16
A very simple stool made
in the coppice

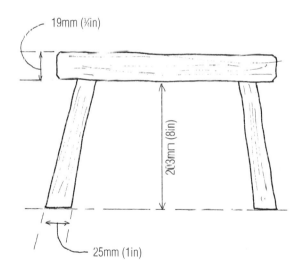

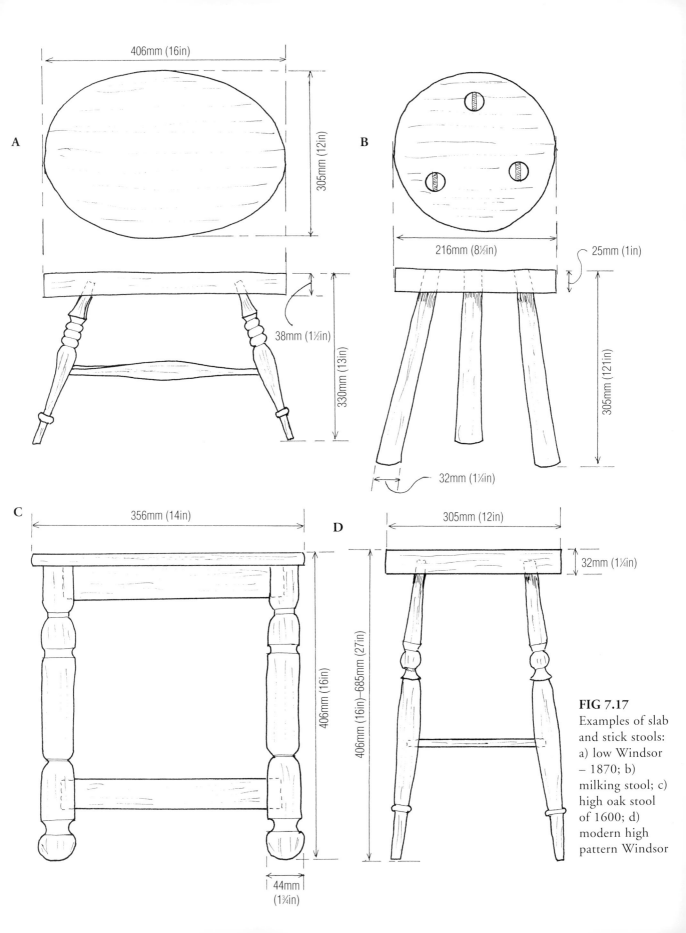

A

406mm (16in)

305mm (12in)

38mm (1½in)

330mm (13in)

B

216mm (8½in)

25mm (1in)

305mm (12in)

32mm (1¼in)

C

356mm (14in)

406mm (16in)

44mm (1¾in)

D

305mm (12in)

32mm (1¼in)

406mm (16in)—685mm (27in)

FIG 7.17
Examples of slab and stick stools: a) low Windsor – 1870; b) milking stool; c) high oak stool of 1600; d) modern high pattern Windsor

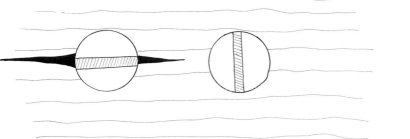

FIG 7.18
How wedges are oriented to the grain in order to avoid the slab splitting

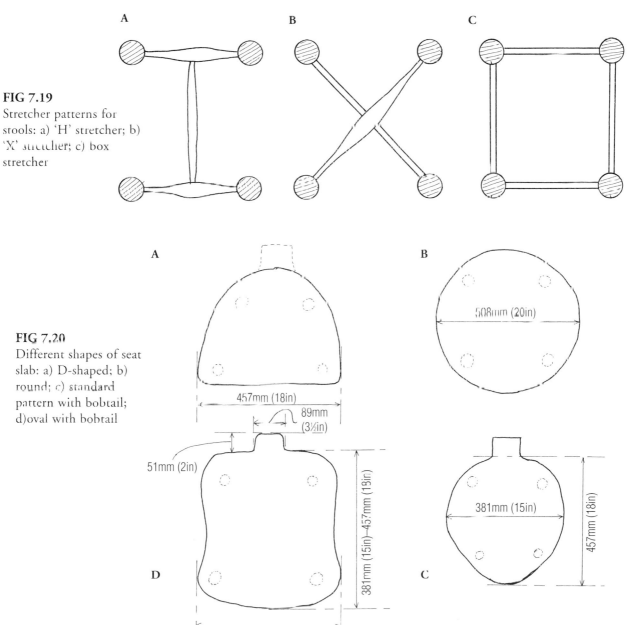

FIG 7.19
Stretcher patterns for stools: a) 'H' stretcher; b) 'X' stretcher; c) box stretcher

FIG 7.20
Different shapes of seat slab: a) D-shaped; b) round; c) standard pattern with bobtail; d)oval with bobtail

FIG 7.21
Examples of the most basic slab
and stick chairs

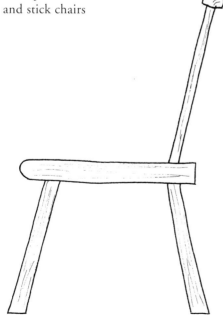

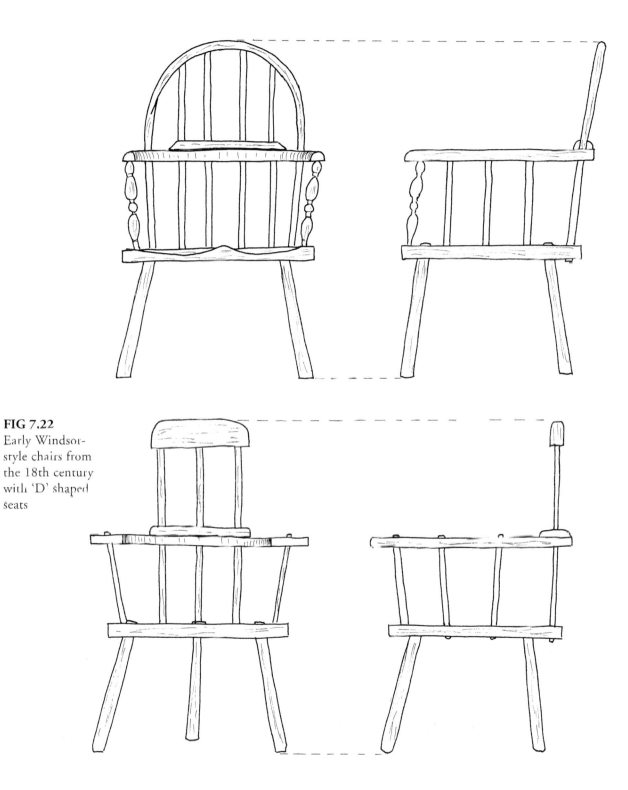

FIG 7.22
Early Windsor-
style chairs from
the 18th century
with 'D' shaped
seats

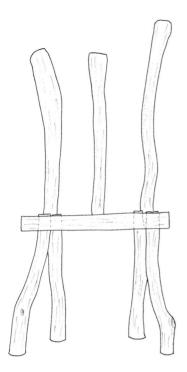

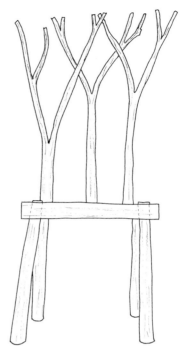

FIG 7.23
Use of natural sticks to make individually unique chair backs

Windsor-type Chairs

The real source of the name 'Windsor' for these chairs remains open to debate, but the most favoured explanation is that a majority of chairs made in the Chilterns were sold through the markets at Windsor. These chairs represent the ultimate form of slab and stick furniture, the finest being worthy of Chippendale and Sheraton. The key elements to Windsor chairs are shown in **figs 7.24** and **7.25**. The basis is a slab seat into which legs, back and arms (if fitted) are all mortised. The seat is shaped, and on a good chair varies considerably in thickness. The legs, all of which are turned, are fitted at a slightly splayed angle to the slab and are braced by stretchers. Backs come in a wide variety of patterns, and are usually angled to provide a comfortable sitting position. Arms are frequently fitted, forming an integral part of the back with one or more supports mortised into the seat. A distinctive part of the back of many

Windsor seats is the splat. This thin, flat member, which commonly forms the central component of the seat back, is usually intricately cut and incorporates a recognizable shape by which it is named (vase, wheel etc.). Together these features offer customers a wide choice. To simplify this complexity a range of patterns for the different parts of the chair is described.

Seats: Although the majority of seats conform to the variously curved outline with which we are familiar, seats can be perfectly round, half round, or fitted with a 'bob-tail' to support additional back braces. Almost without exception the top surface of the seat is shaped to a concave profile towards the back, forming the 'seat' (**fig 7.26**) while a central low ridge is left at the front to form the 'saddle'.

Backs (fig 7.27): Comb backs, made from a series of vertical sticks stretching between the seat to a top rail known as the comb or crest rail represent

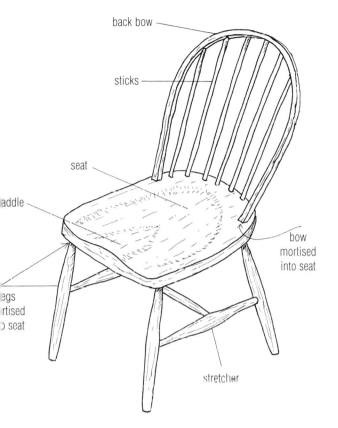

back bow

sticks

seat

addle

bow
mortised
into seat

egs
rtised
seat

stretcher

FIG 7.24
Basic patterns of a
Windsor chair

Some patterns are far less common. From the United States comes the loop-back chair and the unusual balloon back. Many patterns are regional in origin, and one of the most famous is the Mendlesham, from Suffolk, which combines the use of sticks, splat and balls (**fig 7.29**)

Crest Rails (**fig 7.30**): these are the rails into which sticks are mortised in the comb-back pattern. A selection is illustrated. The least common are rails with shaping at their bottom edge, and those with a strong curve are known as shawl crests.

Splats (**fig 7.31**): we have already described how splats fit into the back of chairs. Many of the patterns used have names that reflect the design incorporated in the splat. 'Wheel', 'vase', 'Prince of Wales', 'gothic' and 'heart' are all commonly used. There are of course many more, designed by individual craftsmen, and the subject probably warrants a book on its own!

Legs (**fig 7.32**): the turned pattern on the legs of a chair is another way that craftsmen are able to express their individuality. Legs vary from the simplest cylinders to complex turnery, and a range of patterns is illustrated. The basic Chiltern 'three bead' leg (**fig 7.32j**) has, without doubt, been produced more than any other kind of chair leg. Although it is most common for the front legs only to be patterned, the back legs are sometimes adorned with a simple pattern.

Stretchers (**fig 7.33**): there are several patterns of stretchers designed to provide the required rigidity to the legs. The first is a boxed stretcher system that is similar to that described for post and rung chairs. The commonest and simplest is the 'H' stretcher using swelled parts to give more material into which to mortise. Cow horn or crinoline stretchers are also much used. Turned decoration similar to that used in legs is common on the stretchers of better chairs (**fig 7.34**).

the earliest pattern. The sticks, numbering from four to eight, are mortised into both the crest and the seat. In some patterns a number of the central sticks are replaced by a flat splat. When the sticks are bunched at the seat and splay outwards to meet the crest rail, the back is called a fan, and is often braced by two sticks to a bob-tail. In some comb backs, the outer two sticks are replaced by flattened lathes, known as ribbon splats. Where all the sticks are replaced by narrow lathes the chair is called a lathe back. Lathe backs often have a sinuous rather than a straight back. A development of this style is the scroll back, where a deep top rail is mortised into the two curved side members.

Comb backs were replaced as the most common pattern by the bow or stick-back pattern. In this type the sticks are mortised into a curved bow that loops over from one side of the seat to the other (**fig 7.28**). As with the comb back, some of the central sticks are often replaced by a splat, and the wheel-back splat has resulted in the most popular chair pattern ever. Some backs are made with three splats and no sticks.

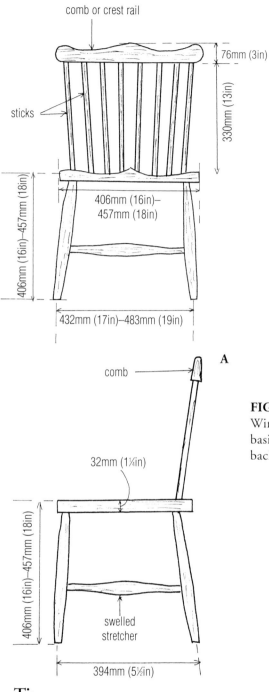

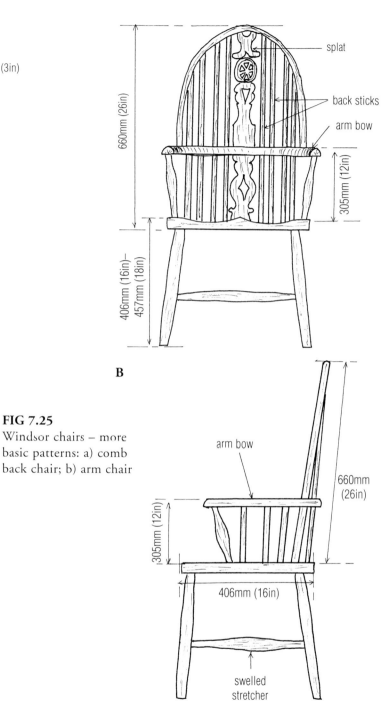

FIG 7.25
Windsor chairs – more
basic patterns: a) comb
back chair; b) arm chair

Tips:

- Deep shaping on the seat makes for a more comfortable chair.
- Elm is best for the seat or slab due to its resistance to splitting.
- Rockers can be added to the chairs but call for shorter legs.

- Keep patterns of any splats or leg turning patterns you devise or use, so you can easily repeat them.
- Good chairs have all their edges slightly chamfered, including all the cut edges of the splats.

406mm (16in)

406mm (16in)

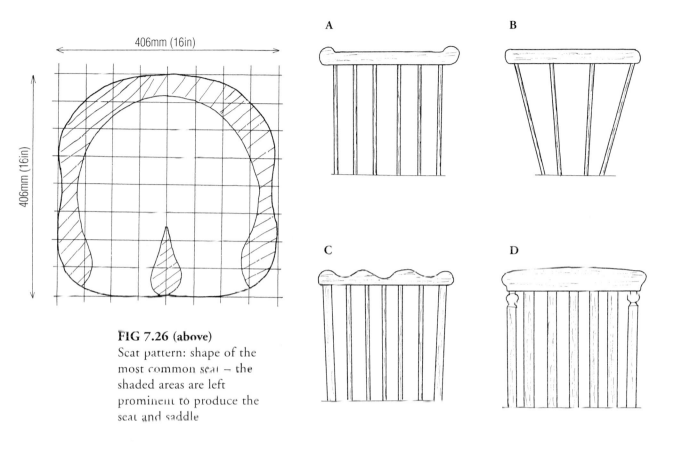

FIG 7.26 (above)
Seat pattern: shape of the
most common seat – the
shaded areas are left
prominent to produce the
seat and saddle

A B

C D

E F

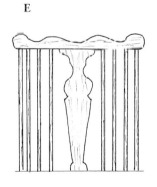

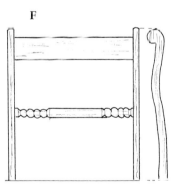

FIG 7.27 (right)
Patterns of comb-back
chairs: a) basic stick back
with eared comb; b) fan
back; c) ribbon slat and
stick; d) lathe back; e) splat
and stick; f) scroll back

A

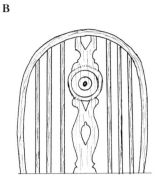

B

C

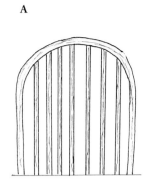
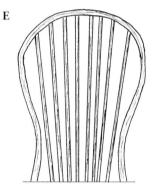
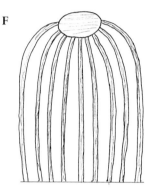

D

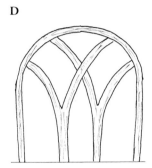

E

F

FIG 7.28 (above)
Patterns of bow-back chairs:
a) stick back; b) splat and
stick; c) splat and stick;
d) interlaced; e) loop back;
f) balloon back

FIG 7.29
Back of a Mendlesham
chair incorporating rails,
sticks, splat and balls

A

B

C

D

E

F

G

H

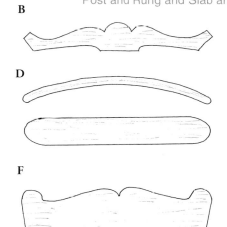

FIG 7.30
Patterns of crest
rails; patterns
with a deep curve
such as (d) are
called 'shawled'

A

B

C

D

E

F

G

H

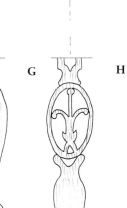

FIG 7.31
Some patterns of
splats: a) urn; b)
baluster; c) heart;
d) disc; e) wheel;
f) vase; g) Prince
of Wales; h)
Gothic

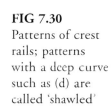

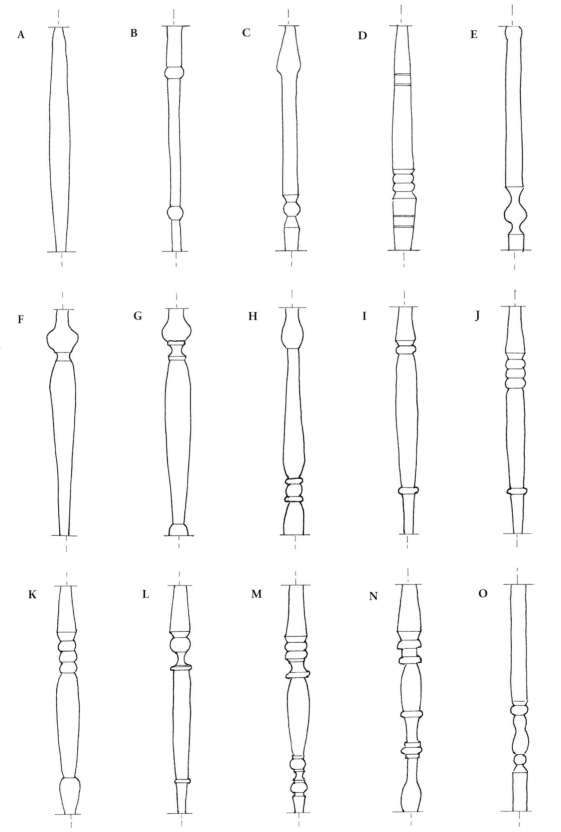

FIG 7.32
Patterns of
turned chair
legs: a) a simple
plain turned
'strut'; j) the
Chiltern three-
bead pattern –
probably the
commonest
pattern used

A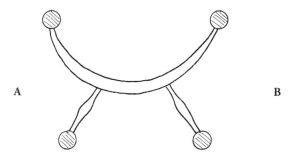

B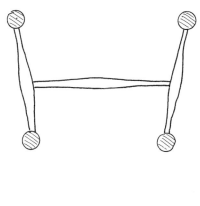

C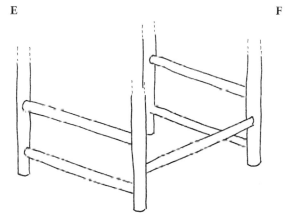

D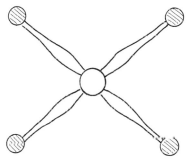

E

F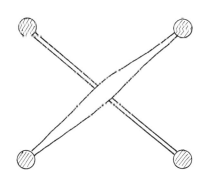

FIG 7.33
Patterns of stretcher arrangements: a) cow-horn or crinoline type; b) 'H' stretcher with swelled struts; c) double 'H' stretcher with sausage turning; d) 'X' stretcher with central ball; e) box stretcher; f) 'X' stretcher with one swelled strut

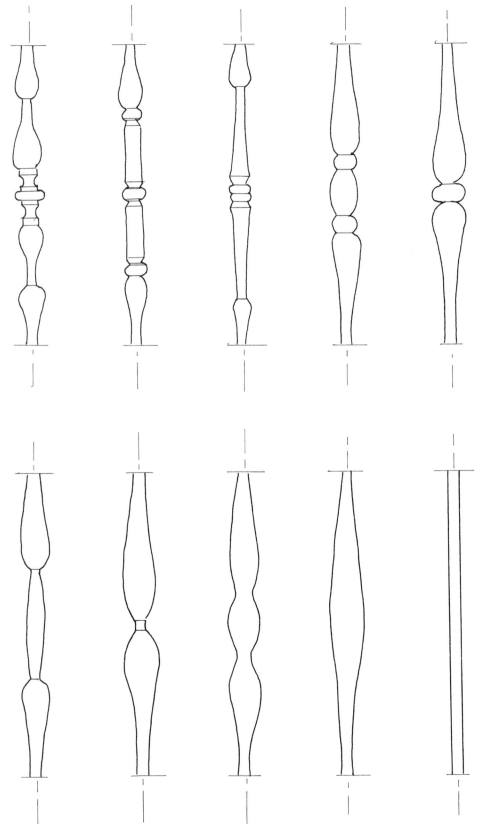

FIG 7.34
Patterns of
stretcher members.
Those with fancy
turning are most
commonly used at
the front of the
chair only

Chapter 8 Baskets

Introduction

Many hundreds of patterns for baskets have evolved over the centuries. They reflect, not only the range of jobs for which baskets have been used, but also their combination of light weight, strength and functionality. Like many green wood products, they reveal a strong local character often governed by the availability of raw materials that are specific to the area in which they are produced.

This account does not include willow baskets. That is a trade in its own right, and the patterns that have evolved warrant a whole book to themselves. Rather, this chapter describes baskets that fit the green woodworking trades, being made from round or cleft coppice wood. Some patterns, such as trugs, are well known, but others, made in various regions of France, may be new to other workers.

The uses we find for baskets span both home and workplace. Almost any task where small amounts of product need to be carried by one individual can be met by using a basket. Before agriculture became mechanized baskets were used to hold seed for broadcasting by hand. Stock and horses were fed from robust round baskets, while at the end of the year baskets were essential for harvesting fruit and vegetables. When dry goods were sold by the bushel (eight gallons) 'bushel baskets' were essential measures. Likewise baskets were used to move coal, transport fish, and to harvest shellfish. One quite unique item was the pottery crate. These remarkable structures could hold up to one ton of china and they transported product safely to most corners of the globe. While many of these uses have disappeared, the role of baskets in gardens and horticulture still supports a good trade for basket makers.

There are no artefacts remaining from the earliest days of basket making. No doubt the patterns relied heavily on round green wood (we know that woven hurdles were made in Neolithic times). Once the skill of riving wood into pliable clefts had been developed (a skill probably pre-dating steel tools such as the froe), woven baskets such as swills could be made. It is likely these skills evolved in parallel across much of Europe and North America.

Most of the baskets described rely on a stout frame to which thinner members are nailed or fixed by weaving. The frame determines the shape of the basket and its form is achieved nowadays by steaming and setting the individual members to shape. Once the craft reached this stage of development, the making of many baskets passed from individual craftsmen working in the coppice to workshops where large numbers of sets and jigs could be held. This process remains the same today, when not only are many of these baskets still made in small rural workshops, but also in the same villages where they have been produced for centuries.

Rigid cleft wood baskets

These baskets are all made from thin clefts of wood that can be bent to shape and nailed to a pre-shaped frame.

Trugs

Although we do not know precisely when the first trugs were made, there are records using this word dating from the 16th century. A Thomas Smith started making trugs in the 18th century at Hurstmonceaux, Sussex, and by the 19th century the company's trade was well developed. At this time they produced a catalogue describing some 14 different patterns of trug basket with 28 size options. Trugs are still made in this village today.

Trugs (**fig 8.1**) vary from square to oblong, the shape being defined by a cleft frame or rim that can be in one or two pieces (**fig 8.2**). Nailed to the frame are a series of thin planks or panels. After shaving these are pliable enough to bend but not to weave; depending on the size of basket either seven or nine are used (**fig 8.3**). They are nailed to the frame in a graceful curve and overlap one another so that the finished basket resembles a clinker-built boat. This probably accounts for the name 'trug', which in Norse means 'a shallow boat'. Strengthening panels are sometimes added at either end (**fig 8.4**). The panels are further secured by means of braces (**fig 8.5**), two in garden trugs, but five in a larger stable basket. Most garden baskets have a one-piece handle that circles the basket and is nailed to each panel. Larger baskets such as the bushel or stable basket use the rim at either end to form the handle (**fig 8.6**). Garden baskets are also usually fitted with two feet that

Table 8.1 Details of some different types of trug

Type	Length mm (in)	Width mm (in)	Number of panels	Features
Common/garden	241mm–711mm (9½in–28in)	127mm–381mm (5in–15in)	7	2 braces; feet optional; round or cleft handle
Decorative – square	203mm–254mm (8in–10in)	203mm–254mm (8in–10in)	7	White wood; no braces; feet; handle
Decorative – knitting	381mm–432mm (15in–17in)	152mm (6in)	7	White wood; two handles; feet
Horse feeding	457mm–610mm (18in–24in)	N/A	9	Round; no handle; three braces
Bushel basket	457mm–610mm (18in–24in)	356mm–381mm (14in–15in)	9	2 hand holds; 5 braces; no feet
Coal basket	445mm–584mm (17½in–23in)	241mm–305mm (9½in–12in)	9	Handle plus hand hold; feet; body tapered at one end
Trinket basket	178mm (7in)	102mm (4in)	5	White wood; feet; handle

keep the thin panels off wet ground and extend their life (**fig 8.7**). Although patterns of use in gardens and agriculture account for the majority of trugs, there are a number of fancy or special baskets (**fig 8.8**). These vary in function from holding coal to smaller 'white' (all bark removed) baskets for knitting and trinkets. Perhaps the most unusual is the Sussex flower and fruit gathering basket, in which a walking stick is inserted through the base of the trug holding it at a comfortable height that avoids the picker bending their back (**fig 8.9**). Details for some of these baskets are given in table 8.1.

Trug-making is still a very active craft, and modern green woodworkers are developing new designs that will add to customer choice. An example by Chris Thompson is illustrated in **fig 8.10**.

Tips:

- Use willow for planks and hazel or chestnut for handles and braces.
- Shape panels so they fill the space available.
- Overlap handle and rim using a secure scarfe joint (**fig 8.12**).
- Steam frames and handles so they bend to the shape required without fracturing.
- Use copper or galvanized nails that will not rust and are long enough to clench over.

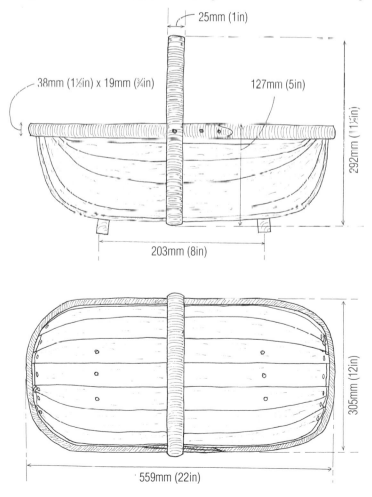

FIG 8.1
A basic garden trug with feet and no bracing

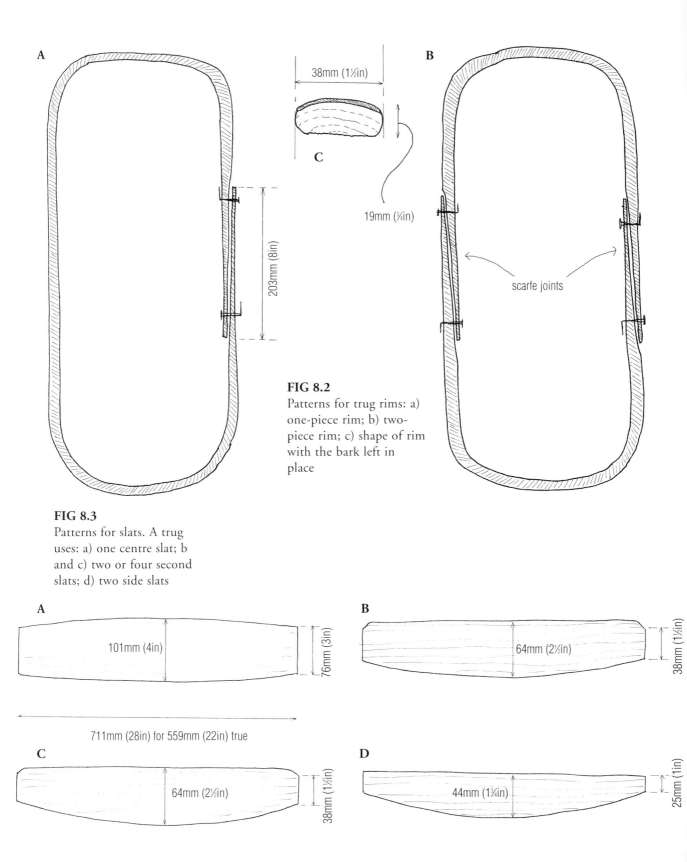

A

38mm (1½in)

C

B

203mm (8in)

19mm (¾in)

scarfe joints

FIG 8.2
Patterns for trug rims: a)
one-piece rim; b) two-
piece rim; c) shape of rim
with the bark left in
place

FIG 8.3
Patterns for slats. A trug
uses: a) one centre slat; b
and c) two or four second
slats; d) two side slats

A

101mm (4in)

76mm (3in)

711mm (28in) for 559mm (22in) true

B

64mm (2½in)

38mm (1½in)

C

64mm (2½in)

38mm (1½in)

D

44mm (1¾in)

25mm (1in)

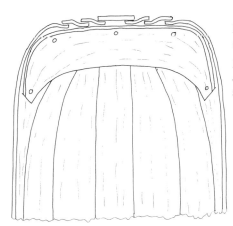

FIG 8.4
Optional strengthening
panel at the end of a trug.
Also note the way the slats
are overlapped.

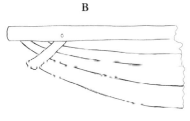

A

B

645mm (30in) x 381mm (15in) wide

152mm (6in)

FIG 8.5
Patterns for braces: a) two
braces on a garden trug; b)
five braces on a bushel trug

FIG 8.6
Rim handle for a trug: a) slats
cut out and ends nailed to the
end brace; b) side view

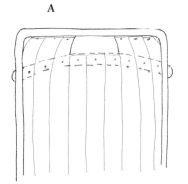

A

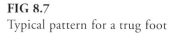

B

FIG 8.7
Typical pattern for a trug foot

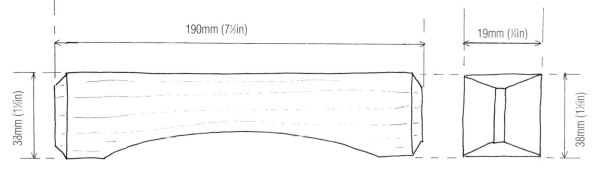

190mm (7½in)

19mm (¾in)

38mm (1½in)

38mm (1½in)

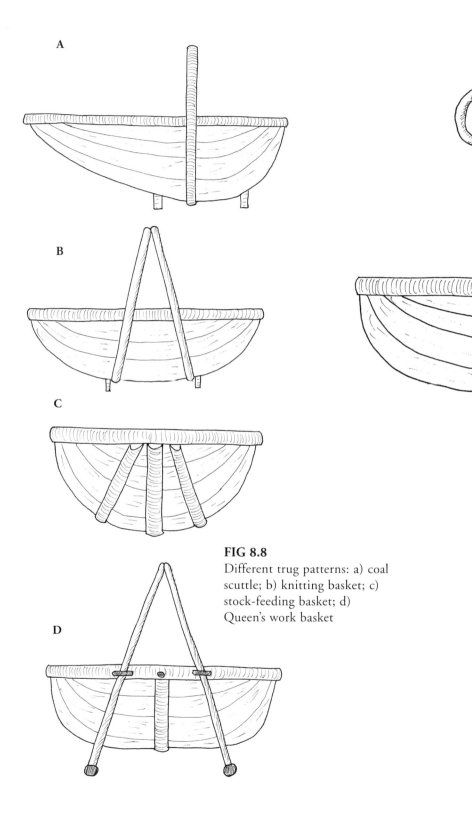

A

B

C

FIG 8.8
Different trug patterns: a) coal
scuttle; b) knitting basket; c)
stock-feeding basket; d)
Queen's work basket

D

FIG 8.9
The Sussex fruit
and flower gatherer

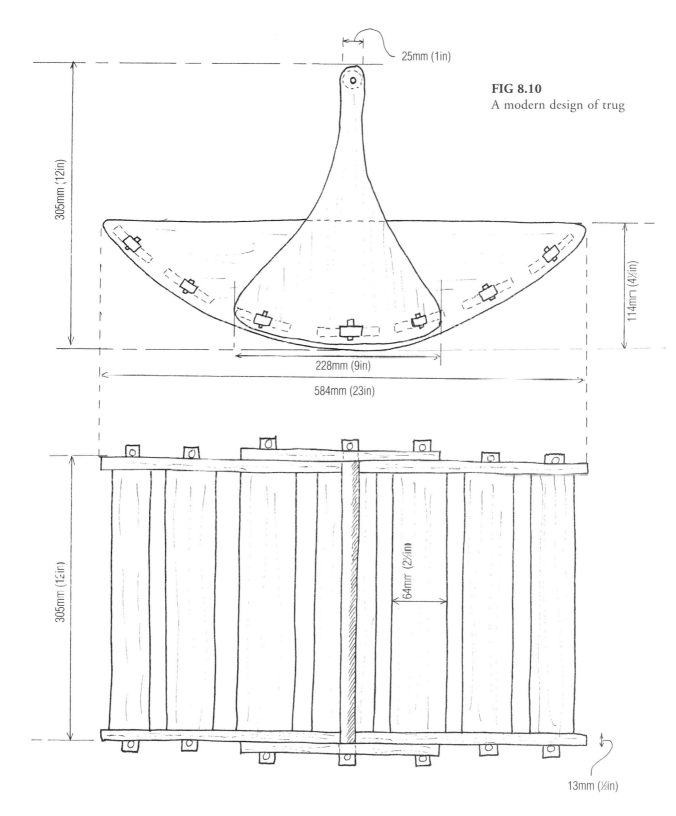

FIG 8.10
A modern design of trug

25mm (1in)

305mm (12in)

114mm (4½in)

228mm (9in)

584mm (23in)

305mm (12in)

64mm (2½in)

13mm (½in)

Devon Splint basket

These baskets are a particularly rugged pattern much used at markets in their home county. Splint baskets are made with a solid base and sides and with a hooped handle in round wood (**fig 8.11**). The panels that make up the sides are called splints, hence the name of the basket. Splints are fine clefts of straight-grained wood, rather like shingles. They are made in different widths to suit their position around the basket, but are cut with parallel sides so that while they all meet at the base of the basket, there is a gap between the splints at the top (**fig 8.12**). The splints are regularly placed around the basket, with 22 used in a large basket, and 18 in a smaller pattern. Each one is nailed to both the base and the top rim,

which define the shape and size of the finished basket. The sides are strengthened by another hoop that passes around the outside of the splints at about their mid point (**fig 8.13**).

Tips:

- Use straight grained knot free wood to obtain even straight clefts for the splints.
- Pre-drill holes at ends of splints so they do not split when the nails are driven home.
- Splints and base can be made from ash, oak or chestnut; rims and handles are best made from hazel with the bark on.
- Handles and rims are best steamed and set to the shape required.

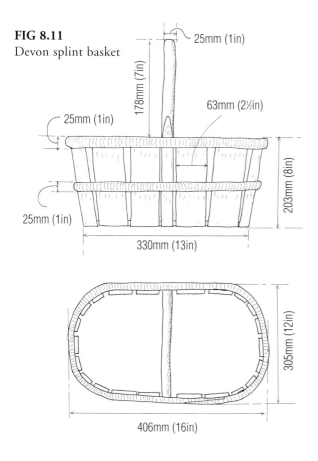

FIG 8.11
Devon splint basket

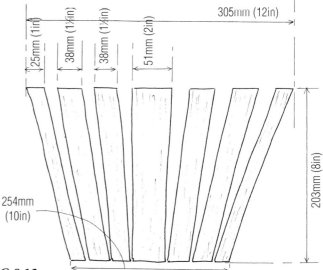

FIG 8.12
Pattern of splints to give a splay at the end of the basket

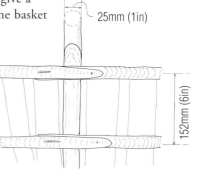

FIG 8.13
Pattern of rim, side loop and handle on a splint basket

Haute-Vienne basket (France)

This basket, which is light and strong, is used in its home region for collecting fruit, vegetables and mushrooms (**fig 8.14**). It is made entirely from stout clefts of ash wood (**fig 8.15**) that are steamed and set to the required shape. The shape and size of the basket is determined by the four horizontal hoops that pass round its periphery. These are cut so that their ends have a long overlap that can be nailed together to form a closed loop and they are held in place by the handle, which loops the entire basket. The longitudinal members form both the base and the ends of the basket. All of the components are nailed to each other, in order to form a light, rigid structure.

Tips:

- Ash is the best wood for these baskets, giving even straight clefts that are easily steamed to shape.
- Remove the bark to avoid bark beetle.
- Trim all spears from the clefts so they are safe and smooth to the touch.
- Use copper or galvanized nails.
- Use a device to hold the steamed clefts to the required shape until 'set'.

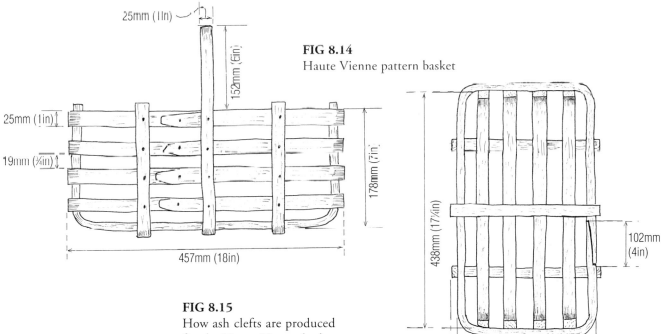

25mm (1in)

152mm (6in)

25mm (1in)

19mm (¾in)

178mm (7in)

457mm (18in)

FIG 8.14
Haute Vienne pattern basket

438mm (17¼in)

305mm (12in)

102mm (4in)

10mm (⅜in)

FIG 8.15
How ash clefts are produced for the Haute Vienne basket

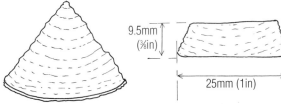

9.5mm (⅜in)

25mm (1in)

Woven cleft wood baskets

These baskets are made from cleft wood that is flexible enough to be woven. They require a frame to provide shape and rigidity to the finished item.

Swills or spelks

These remarkable baskets have been made for centuries across much of Europe and put to a wide range of uses where their rugged simplicity serves them well. In England there are 15th century records (Barratt) of 'spelks' (swills) made in Cumbria, where the coppice oak required for the body of these baskets grows plentifully and in the right quality. Swills are still made in this region but now in very small volumes. Similar baskets are made both in France and in the Appalachian region of the United States, where white oak provides the perfect raw material.

A basic swill (**fig 8.16**) is based on an oval rim or 'bool' to which the ribs (spelks) are attached by a combination of binding, weaving and inserting them through slits in the bool (**fig 8.17**). The ribs form the warp of the weave and are fitted first, looping over the width of the oval. The 'taws' are then woven through the ribs to form the final body of the swill. Gaps are left at either end so the rim can be used as the handle (**fig 8.18**). Swills are made while the wood is moist and pliable, and as they dry the clefts tighten, become harder and set to shape, producing a tough, resilient basket.

Some patterns of swill basket are associated with particular uses and are given different names. Baskets from Furness were reputedly made with a closer weave than those made in Wyre or North Devon, to the extent that powders could be held in them. Side swills are designed to be carried on the hip and have a round rod built into the rim to act as a handle on the opposite side to the hip (**fig 8.18**). Seed baskets were made with a kidney shaped indentation so it fitted comfortably against the hip, and seed skeps were fitted with straps to go over the user's shoulder (**fig 8.19**). Morecambe Bay Cockle baskets are round, fitted with a loop handle and are quite deep (**fig 8.20**). Scoops, used for shovelling coal or similar materials, are shallow at one end and have a handle at the other in order to work as their name suggests (**fig 8.21**). Potato skips use much narrower clefts, which may be hazel ash or willow, but have a construction similar to a swill. Wiskets, on the other hand, which are made in Wales, have their oak or hazel ribs running along the length of the basket, handles at the sides and hazel for weavers (**fig 8.22**).

Tips

- Allow a good overlap where the ends of the rim are joined. They can be notched, nailed or bound together (**fig 8.23**).
- Wood is best seasoned before use – it will shrink less in the final product.
- Weavers must be boiled before riving and kept moist while the basket is being made to prevent them fracturing.
- Different widths of weavers will help to fill the weave properly.
- Hazel, ash or birch are normally used for the rim. Oak and ash make the toughest weavers, but must be straight-grained, knot-free stems about 30 years old.
- It is best to trim weavers of any spears that may be protruding.

Table 8.2 Details of some different types of cleftwood basket

Type	Sizes mm (in)	Detail
Basic swill	Length 406mm–1016mm (16in–40in) Width 508mm (20in) Depth 203mm (8in)	Even oval shape; rim handle grips at ends as required; ribs transverse across the basket
Side swill	Length 609mm (24in) Width 457mm (18in) Depth 127mm (5in)	Shape a flattened oval with a rod handle at one side
Seed basket (side slop)	Length 559mm (22in) Width 356mm (14in) Depth 127mm (5in)	Kidney shaped basket with a 'rim handle' grip at one side
Seed lip	Length 609mm (24in) Width 457mm (18in) Depth 127mm (5in)	Flattened oval shape with a leather shoulder strap and a turned 'nib' handle at one side. Made from ash and willow in Southern England
Cockle basket	Diameter 914mm (36in) Depth 152mm (6in)	Deep round basket with a loop handle across the centre
Potato skip	Length 609mm (24in) Width 406mm (16in) Depth 127mm (6in)	Oblong basket with well rounded corners; rim handles at both ends; ribs transverse across the basket; may be in ash or willow
Wisket	Length 660mm (26in) Width 432mm (17in) Depth 127mm (6in)	Ribs longitudinal; rim handles at both sides; may be in willow or hazel

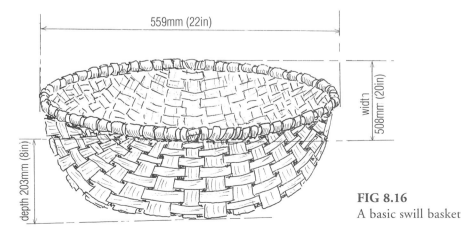

559mm (22in)

width
508mm (20in)

depth 203mm (8in)

FIG 8.16
A basic swill basket

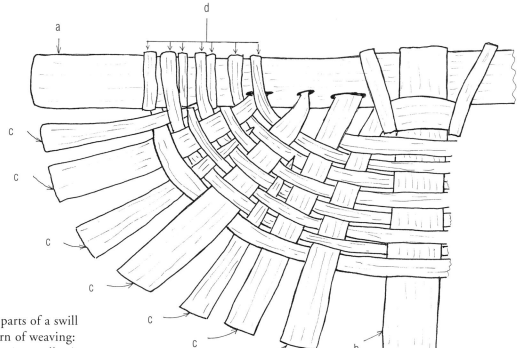

FIG 8.17
Detail of the parts of a swill
and the pattern of weaving:
a) bool; b) lapping spelk; c)
spelks; d) taws

FIG 8.18
Patterns of swill handles:
a) bool spelk cut away
and taws turned over to
make a gap; b) a round
rod built into the rim as a
handle

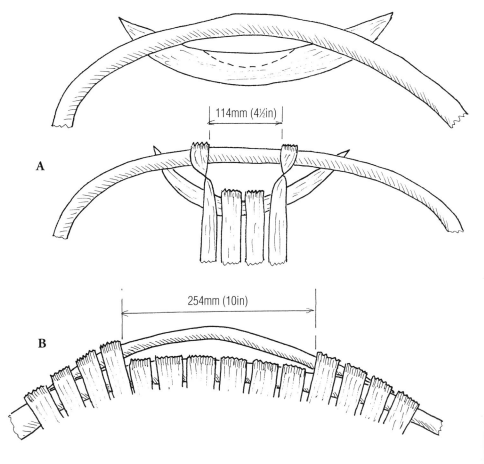

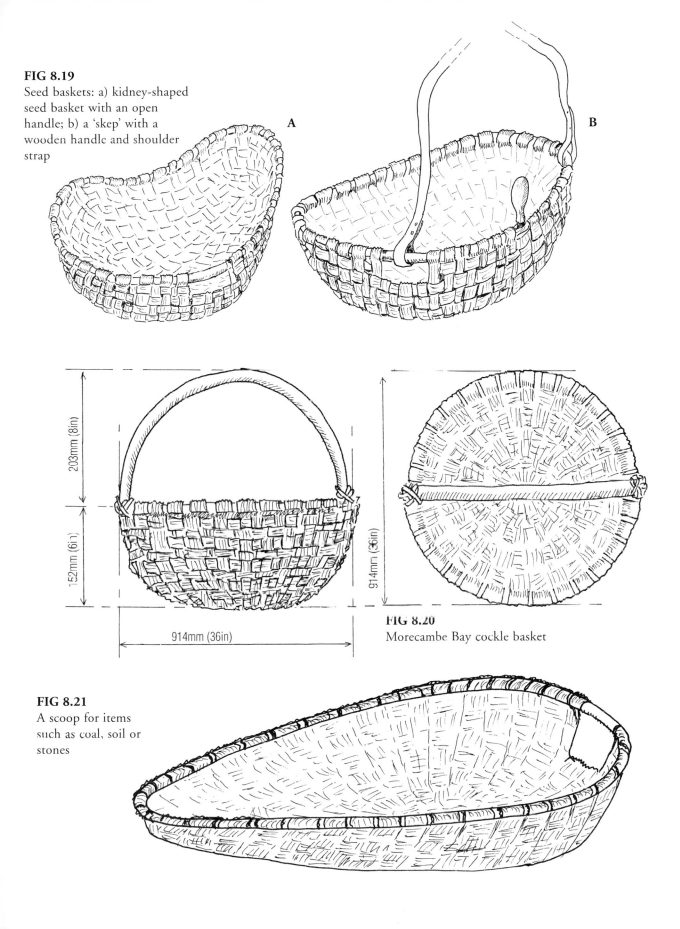

FIG 8.19
Seed baskets: a) kidney-shaped seed basket with an open handle; b) a 'skep' with a wooden handle and shoulder strap

A

B

203mm (8in)

152mm (6in)

914mm (36in)

914mm (36in)

FIG 8.20
Morecambe Bay cockle basket

FIG 8.21
A scoop for items such as coal, soil or stones

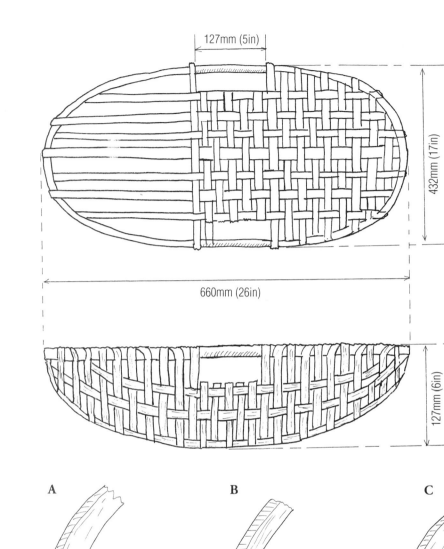

127mm (5in)

432mm (17in)

660mm (26in)

127mm (6in)

FIG 8.22
A wisket. Note that the finished basket has a tighter weave than illustrated

A

B

C

FIG 8.23
Patterns of scarf joints: a) nailed; b) tied; c) notched (usually tied as well)

Melon Basket, United States/ Landes, France

There is a long tradition of cleft oak baskets in both France and the United States. The baskets described here are typical basic patterns, the principles of which are applicable to other types.

The melon basket is based on a round rim and handle that are fixed at a right angle to one another in the same way as a trug (**fig 8.24**). The Landes basket uses the same principle, but the ribs are wider and tapered at their ends (**fig 8.25**). This gives a more robust basket. The scarf of the rim is tied together and/or notched (**fig 8.23**) and the rim and handle are fixed together by a binding of peeled oak or ash. Ribs are inserted into this binding, which then enables flat clefts to be woven through them in order to produce the body of the basket. Weavers are joined as shown in **fig 8.26**.

Tips

- Oak is the best wood for these baskets, although ash can be used.
- Use straight-grained, knot-free wood.
- Uses as many ribs as needed to provide a tight weave.
- Use moist but seasoned wood – it will be easier to weave and will not shrink too much on drying.

Ardeche basket (France)

These lovely rectangular baskets (**fig 8.27**) are made from thin, wide clefts peeled from ash or willow logs. These are interwoven to form an oblong basket with more or less right-angle corners at the base and ends. There is a rim of cleft hazel with the bark still on, to which the clefts are tied by means of a thin strip of elm bast laced through holes in the ends of the clefts (**fig 8.28**). The basket is finished with a looped hazel handle, cleft and trimmed in the same way as that for a trug.

Tips

- Material and its preparation are the same as for swills.
- Elm bast for the tying can be stored dry until used. It must then be soaked to make it pliable.
- Ensure that holes cut in the ends of the clefts for binding them are carefully cut so that they do not split.

Vendée basket (France)

This is a French pattern of a swill in which the oval basket is divided into two halves, separated by a round hazel pole that forms the handle (**fig 8.29**). Details are similar to those given for swills.

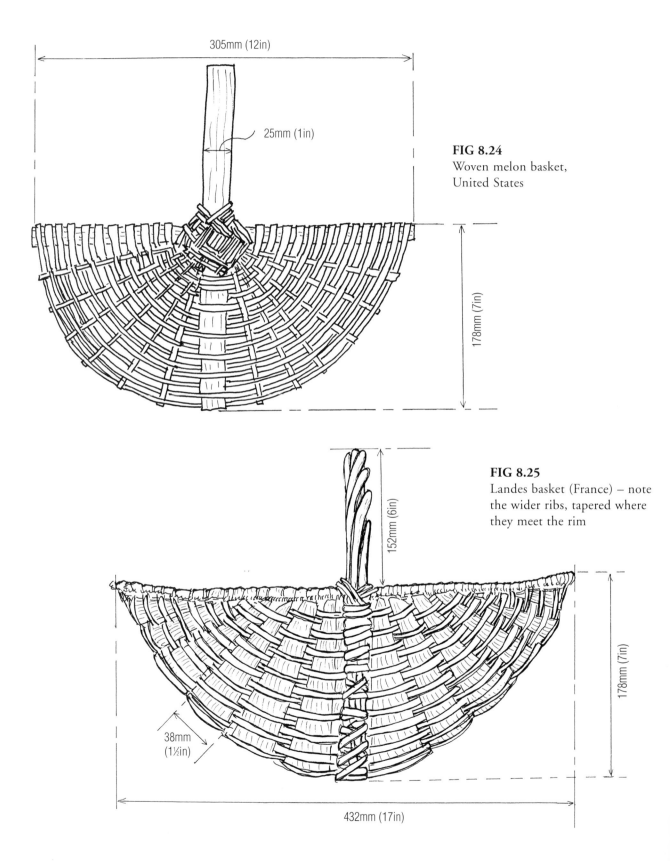

305mm (12in)

25mm (1in)

178mm (7in)

FIG 8.24
Woven melon basket,
United States

152mm (6in)

178mm (7in)

38mm
(1½in)

432mm (17in)

FIG 8.25
Landes basket (France) – note
the wider ribs, tapered where
they meet the rim

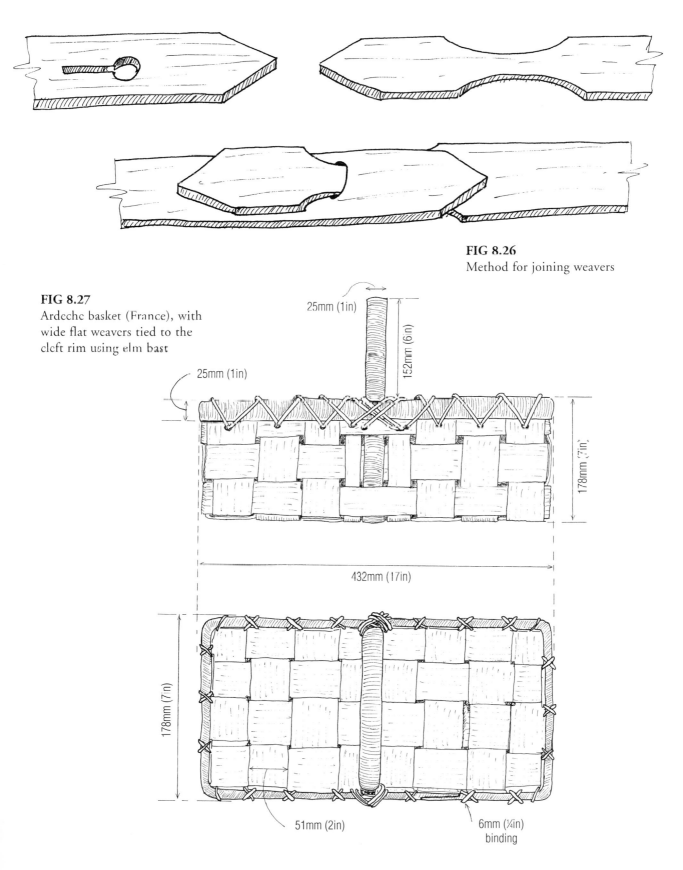

FIG 8.26
Method for joining weavers

FIG 8.27
Ardeche basket (France), with
wide flat weavers tied to the
cleft rim using elm bast

25mm (1in)

152mm (6in)

25mm (1in)

178mm (7in)

432mm (17in)

178mm (7in)

51mm (2in)

6mm (¼in)
binding

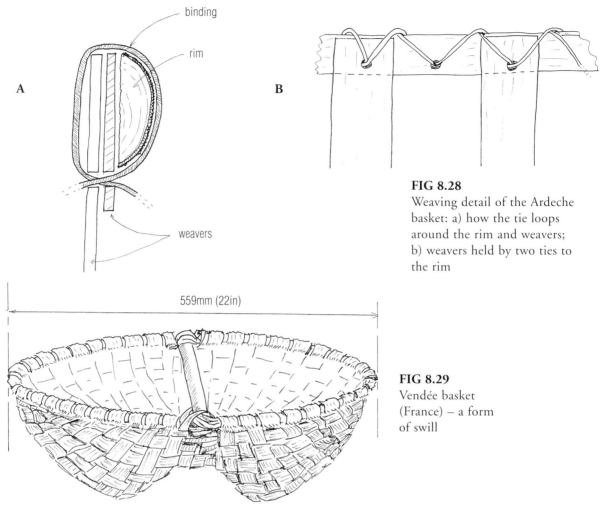

A

binding

rim

weavers

B

FIG 8.28
Weaving detail of the Ardeche basket: a) how the tie loops around the rim and weavers; b) weavers held by two ties to the rim

559mm (22in)

FIG 8.29
Vendée basket (France) – a form of swill

Round Wood Baskets

These baskets mainly make use of round or half-round wood in their manufacture, rather than cleft material.

Crates

Crates are no longer made in England, supplanted by disposable cardboard boxes. In their day, with the help of copious amounts of straw, they were the baskets in which chinaware was transported from the potteries. Older patterns of crate had a solid top frame and curved base (**fig 8.30**). More modern versions use a pattern based on a combination of cleft heads and round rods (**fig 8.31**). These round rods form the base and the sides of the crate, passing through holes in the cleft members. The hazel rods are also wound to form a withe that can be tied.

Tips

- Use hazel, chestnut or birch for the heads, but hazel for all of the smaller rods because they can be wound to form a withe.
- Remove bark from the heads – there is then no chance of bark beetles attacking them.
- Heat the hazel rods so they can be bent to shape without splitting.
- Jam wedges into the mortice holes to form tight joints (**fig 8.32**).

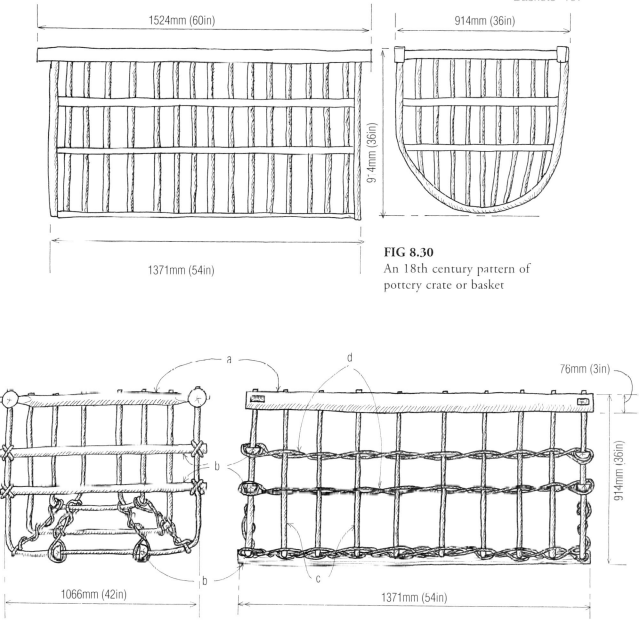

FIG 8.30
An 18th century pattern of pottery crate or basket

FIG 8.31
A current pottery crate showing: a) round heads; b) cleft end rods and keel rods; c) round bows; d) and round 'twilley' rods that can be woven and knotted

FIG 8.32
Wedging the bows into the heads of the crate

Deux Sèvres basket (France)

This French basket is trug-like in shape, but uses half-round rods, sometimes flattened at the ends, instead of flat planks (**fig 8.33**). This produces gaps between the rods through which rubbish and soil can fall, making it the ideal basket for collecting vegetables, its traditional use.

The basket is based on a roughly oblong rim and a loop handle that fixes to it at right angles. Two looped braces, one at either end, fit to the rim and supply additional support to the round rods that curve along from one end of the basket to the other. No feet are used.

Tips

- Steam and set rods to shape for rim and handle.
- Use copper or galvanized nails long enough to clench over.
- Drill the rods where they are nailed near their ends in order to prevent them splitting.
- Handle can be round or cleft, in both cases with the bark left on.
- Hazel is the best wood for these baskets.

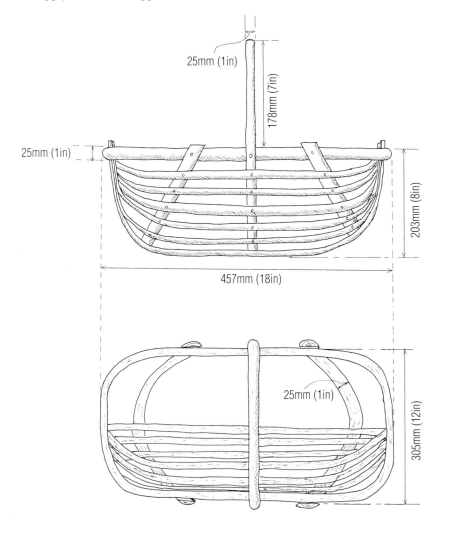

FIG 8.33
Deux Sèvres basket (France) made from hazel rods

Chapter 9 Toys, Games, the Outdoors and a Final Few

Introduction

This chapter contains a miscellany of products that are not related, but are historic, useful and beautiful.

Wooden toys and games reflect an age before television, plastic and computers. Games then were very basic, often based on manual skills. Games such as skittles were played socially, often in the village pub where a skittle alley was a common attraction. We cannot know with accuracy when many of these games started, but we do know, for example, that the Romans did play a number of similar games using wooden pieces. Many of these games reflect the adage that simplest is best – still providing great enjoyment today. Patterns for a few of the simplest toys and games are given here. These items are cheap and easily replaceable as they always have been – essential for the rough life they lead.

The 'outdoor' items are well known and still in demand. Wooden tent pegs, for example, are still made in quantity because they work so well. Walking sticks remain as popular and as useful as ever and their history for both personal defence and support must go back to the very dawn of our activities. We will never know who made the first boot jack and saved millions of muddy hands by this simple device, so effective if the dimensions are right. Wooden clothes pegs are almost a thing of the past, again reflecting the increased use of plastic and wire versions and doing many a traveller out of his craft. Their classic peg with its tin band is shown for posterity. Wooden sheep feeders are less common. Two classic patterns from the south of England are described, both rugged and effective in use.

This chapter finishes with items that did not fit easily elsewhere, but which I have included because they underline the range of beauty and versatility that can be achieved by green wood products. For example, 'grass vases', when turned from figured wood and filled with dried grass flower heads, reveal the beauty of wood simply and effectively. Mushrooms, large and small, demonstrate how simple artefacts can catch people's imagination – we cannot make enough of them! Hazel nutcrackers made from ash wood shows how good design produces a tool both effective and good to use. And finally the wooden balance from the *Mary Rose* describes better than words how elegance and function can be combined in an everyday item.

Toys

Five basic, timeless wooden toys, common across many continents, are described. There must be a book full of others to be described!

Whistles: Whistles are great fun. They can be made from bark-on sticks or turned from small clefts (**fig 9.1**), the latter allowing more freedom in the appearance of the product. A hole is drilled along about two-thirds of the body length. This can be drilled all the way through, but then the end must be filled with a plug (**fig 9.2**). Some patterns have a transverse hole in the end to allow a string to be looped through (**fig 9.1**). A 'V' mouth is cut out near to the mouthpiece end, and the hole between this and the mouthpiece is partially blocked by a 'fipple' (**fig 9.2**), which accelerates the air to create the 'whistle'. The precursor to the children's whistle was the countryman's 'bird call'. Changes in the size of the whistle's body will alter the pitch of the note.

Baby's Rattle: This is the classic test piece for trainee pole-lathe turners, who are always assured it looks more difficult than it is. The rattle comprises two to four loops that are loose but captive on a stem with a handle at one end (**fig 9.3**), and a knop at the other to retain the rings. It is simple, effective and safe.

Rattle/bird scarer: Also known as a crow starver in the United States the oldest rattle relies on two boards loosely bound to a third that has a handle (**fig 9.4**). More modern versions have a thin wooden reed that 'clacks' against wooden teeth as the body of the rattle is rotated (**fig 9.5**). In my youth they were also a necessary accoutrement for football supporters. The star wheel bearing the wooden teeth is fixed to the handle and the flexible reed is held securely at the far end of the body from the teeth. The free end of the reed just overlaps the teeth and makes a loud clack as it springs from one tooth to the next (**fig 9.5**). Two gears and reeds can be used (**fig 9.6**).

Tops: In Victorian times tops were a common site in the streets of our cities. Good tops have a wide diameter, a shallow angle from the point (**fig 9.7**), and, for outdoor use, a metal tip so that hard ground will not blunt it (**fig 9.8**). The shape should distribute the weight of the top to give the best gyroscopic effect, which results not only in the top spinning for longer, but also staying upright longer. Sizes vary enormously from very small

patterns for use on the table top, to those larger tops used outdoors. Traditional tops were used with a whip which enabled a very high speed of rotation to be achieved. This requires a suitable 'neck' to accommodate the cord (**fig 9.8** and **9.9**). Humming tops have holes in the body that create the humming noise when the top rotates (**fig 9.9**).

Ball and Cup or 'billboquets': In this classic toy a ball is attached by a fine cord to a wooden cup, rather like a golf tee, on a handle (**fig 9.10**). The purpose of the toy is to swing the ball up into the air and catch it in the cup. A groove beneath the cup retains the string, and in the pattern illustrated the base is flat to allow the toy to stand upright when not in use. Additional patterns of this game vary from using a flat round plate with seven cups, each scoring a different value, to one with a spike and cap in place of the cup and ball (**fig 9.11**).

Spade: This is the classic one piece sea-side spade similar to those used by all of us at one time or another (**fig 9.12**). The earliest patterns of these spades were not cranked, but were straight along their whole length.

Tips

- Hard, dense wood is best for tops – elm, hornbeam and box particularly. Ash is good for ball and cup.
- Almost any wood can be used for other toys
- Clean as many fibres as possible from the central hole in the whistle – seasoned wood is best.
- Wood for these items is best seasoned for at least six months before use, resulting in less shrinkage and cleaner cuts.
- Fipples for whistles must be well seasoned, so they don't shrink and fall out.

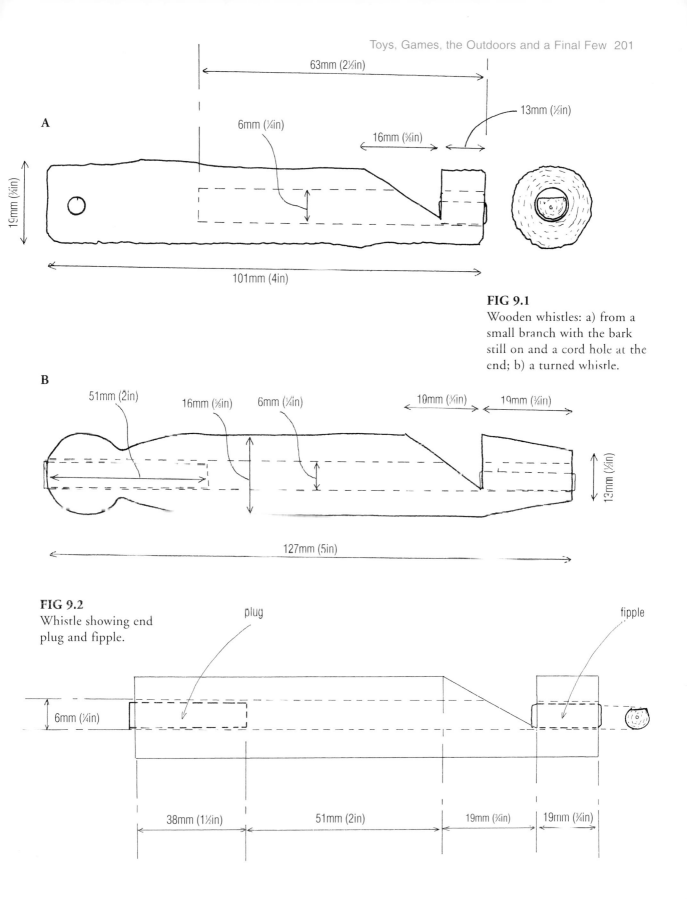

A

63mm (2½in)

13mm (½in)

6mm (¼in)

16mm (⅝in)

19mm (¾in)

101mm (4in)

FIG 9.1
Wooden whistles: a) from a small branch with the bark still on and a cord hole at the end; b) a turned whistle.

B

51mm (2in)

16mm (⅝in)

6mm (¼in)

10mm (⅜in)

19mm (¾in)

13mm (½in)

127mm (5in)

FIG 9.2
Whistle showing end plug and fipple.

plug

fipple

6mm (¼in)

38mm (1½in)

51mm (2in)

19mm (¾in)

19mm (¾in)

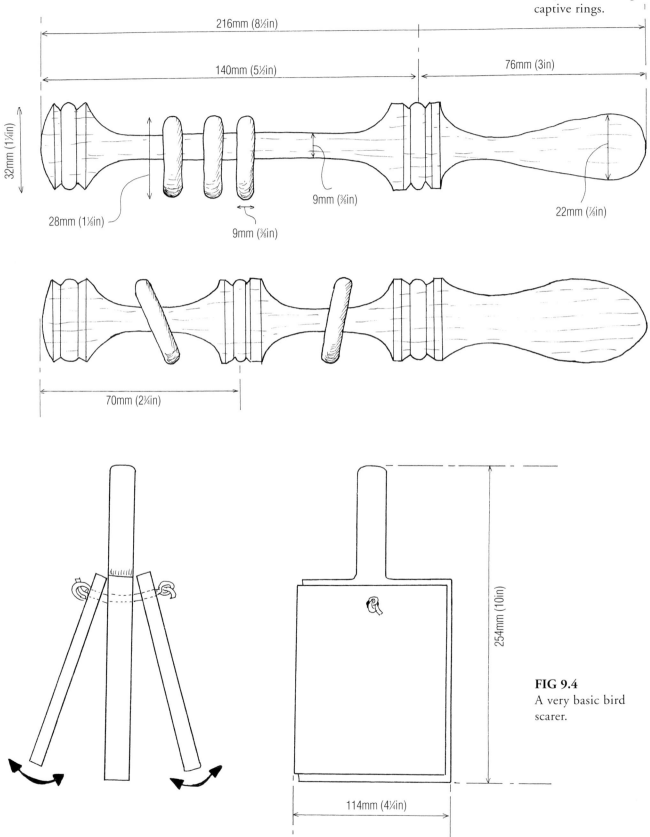

FIG 9.3
Baby's rattles using captive rings.

216mm (8½in)

140mm (5½in)

76mm (3in)

32mm (1¼in)

28mm (1⅛in)

9mm (⅜in)

9mm (⅜in)

22mm (⅞in)

70mm (2¾in)

254mm (10in)

114mm (4½in)

FIG 9.4
A very basic bird scarer.

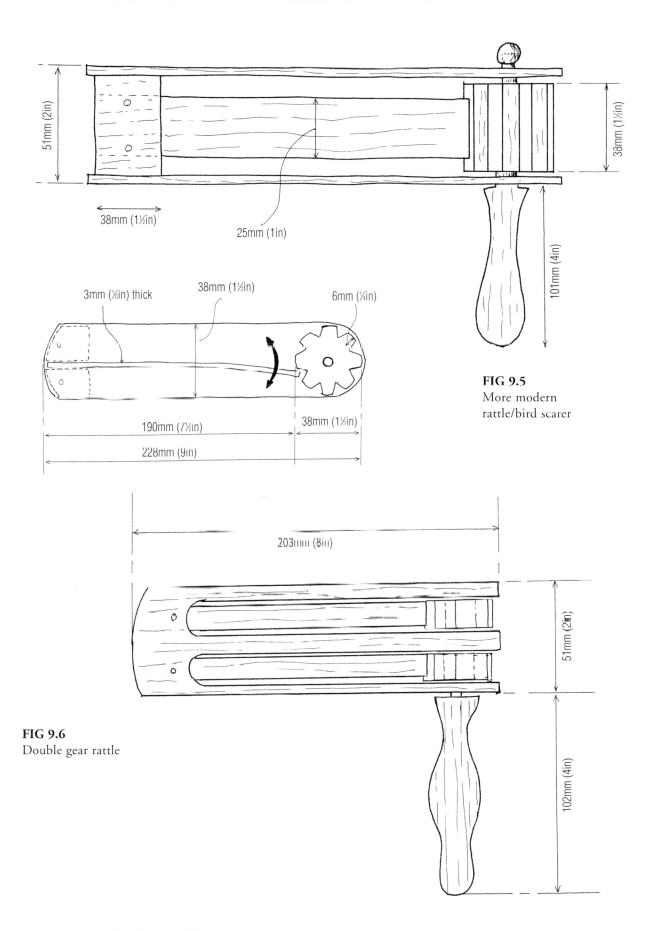

51mm (2in)

38mm (1½in)

25mm (1in)

38mm (1½in)

101mm (4in)

FIG 9.5
More modern
rattle/bird scarer

3mm (⅛in) thick

38mm (1½in)

6mm (¼in)

190mm (7½in)

38mm (1½in)

228mm (9in)

203mm (8in)

51mm (2in)

102mm (4in)

FIG 9.6
Double gear rattle

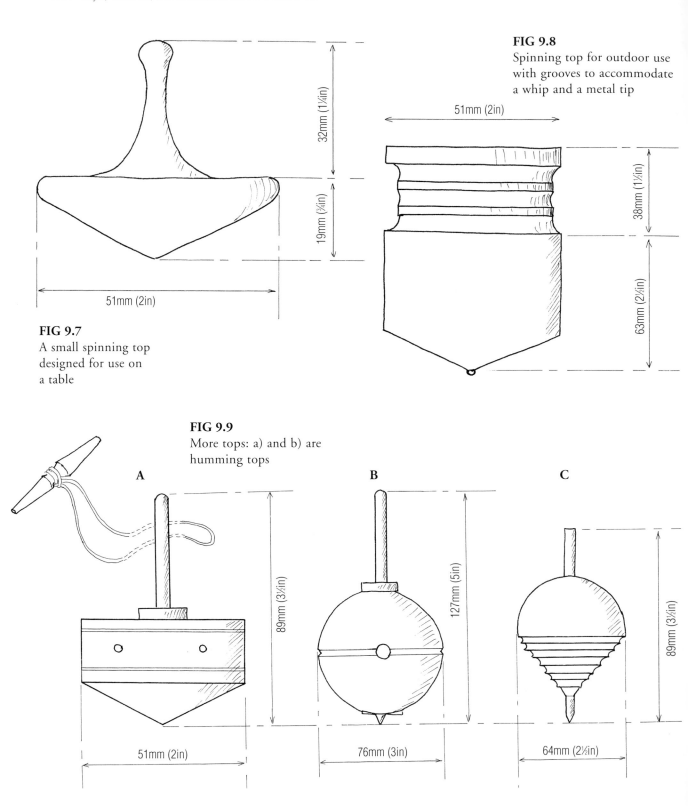

FIG 9.8
Spinning top for outdoor use
with grooves to accommodate
a whip and a metal tip

32mm (1¼in)

19mm (¾in)

51mm (2in)

FIG 9.7
A small spinning top
designed for use on
a table

51mm (2in)

38mm (1½in)

63mm (2½in)

FIG 9.9
More tops: a) and b) are
humming tops

A

B

C

89mm (3½in)

127mm (5in)

89mm (3½in)

51mm (2in)

76mm (3in)

64mm (2½in)

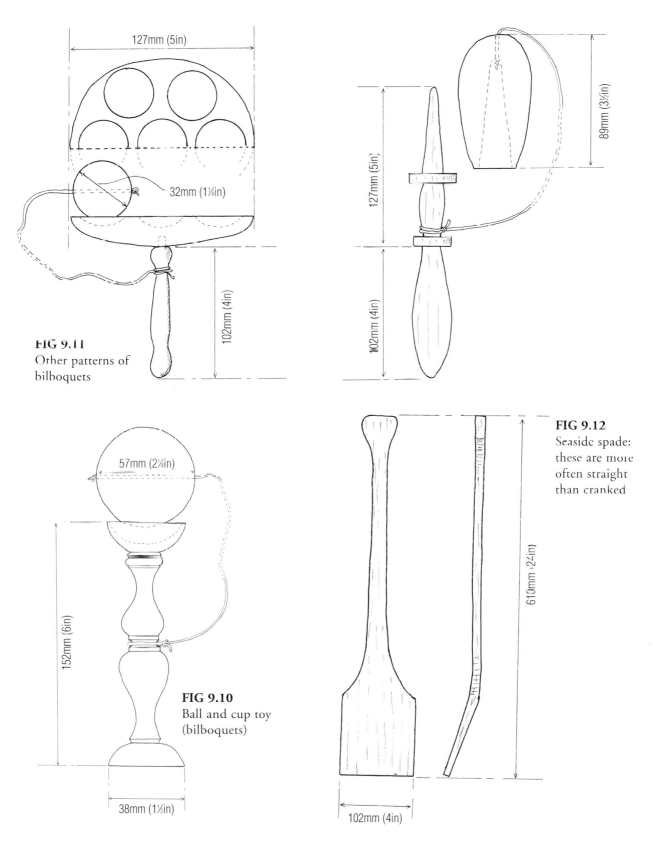

127mm (5in)

32mm (1¼in)

102mm (4in)

FIG 9.11
Other patterns of
bilboquets

89mm (3½in)

127mm (5in)

102mm (4in)

57mm (2¼in)

152mm (6in)

FIG 9.10
Ball and cup toy
(bilboquets)

38mm (1½in)

FIG 9.12
Seaside spade:
these are more
often straight
than cranked

610mm (24in)

102mm (4in)

Games

Here are some basic games using wooden products.

Skittles or nine pins: there can be few people who have not played this game, including its modern transatlantic counterpart, ten-pin bowling. Traditionally skittles were played in a wooden alley surrounded by a low wall. This ensured some safety as well as considerable noise. Both ball and skittles (**fig 9.13**) are made from a heavy wood, resistant to splitting. Skittle patterns vary from extremely simple to bottle-shaped with decorative turned rings (**fig 9.13b**), while the base is narrowed to a size that will allow it to fall over with some ease. Size and weight vary with individual taste. A 'cheese' was often used in place of a ball (**fig 9.14**).

Tip cat: I imagine that bat and stick is the older of the batting games – it being easier to get a stick than a ball – particularly before the advent of the pole lathe. In bat and stick there is a turned or shaved round, short bat, similar to a modern rounders bat, and a short stick tapered to each end from the centre (**fig 9.15**). The player lays the stick on a hard surface, then hits one end of it with the bat, flipping the stick into the air; as it descends he hits the stick again to see how far it will go. Furthest wins! Patterns are very basic, but the bat can be decorated with beads.

Trap ball: This is a more sophisticated form of tip cat. The ball is held on a 'shoe' – a base that contains a rocking arm, one end of which holds the ball. When the free end of the rocking arm is hit down with the bat, the ball is projected into the air and is then hit as far as possible with the flat bat (**fig 9.16**).

Bat and ball: A ball and bat is all that is required for games like rounders. The ball can be turned to any size as required, but about the size of a tennis

ball is the most common. It is normal to have a knop or bead at the end of the bat handle, often shaped to retain a string binding which is put around the handle to improve the grip (**fig 9.17**).

Cricket: we cannot miss our national bat and ball sport! Stumps are simply a long cylinder, the bottom end pointed and with a rim that ensures the stump penetrates the ground by a fixed distance (**fig 9.18**). At the top is a depression to retain the bails. The bails sit on top of the stumps, and that part not resting on the stump is usually decorated with beads. A couple of Victorian patterns are shown in addition to a modern bail (**fig 9.19**). Note the different lengths of the plain portion at either end of the bail – remember that both bails rest on the centre stump and so are shorter at that end.

Two-person ball and cup: In this game the ball is entirely free, and each player has a turned, hollow cone (**fig 9.20**). The ball is thrown from one player to another and must be caught in the cone.

Quoits: this was a popular family game in which wooden rings are thrown to land over a spike in (or on) the ground (**fig 9.21**). This game started by using horseshoes and a metal pin.

Tips:

- Ash or Hickory are the best woods for sports items due to their ability to resist sudden shocks.
- Balls and skittles are best made in dense woods resistant to splitting – hornbeam, box and elm are favourites.
- Wood is best when at least part seasoned before use, to avoid excessive splitting.
- A polyurethane finish can be applied once the item is seasoned.

FIG 9.13
Three patterns of skittle: a)
traditional; b) decorated; c)
bottle shaped; d) ball

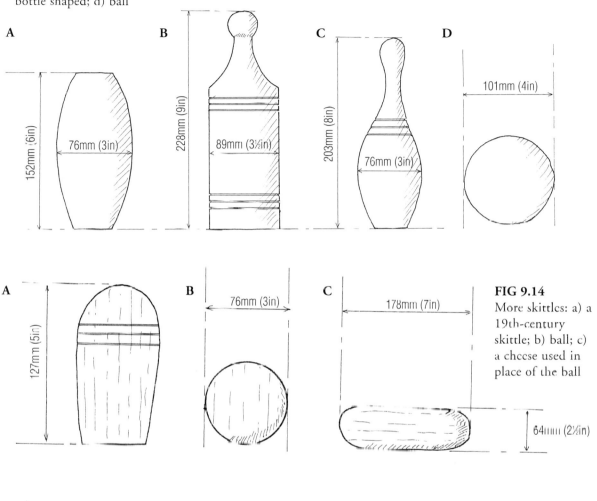

FIG 9.14
More skittles: a) a
19th-century
skittle; b) ball; c)
a cheese used in
place of the ball

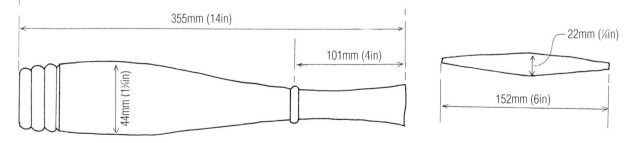

FIG 9.15
Tip cat

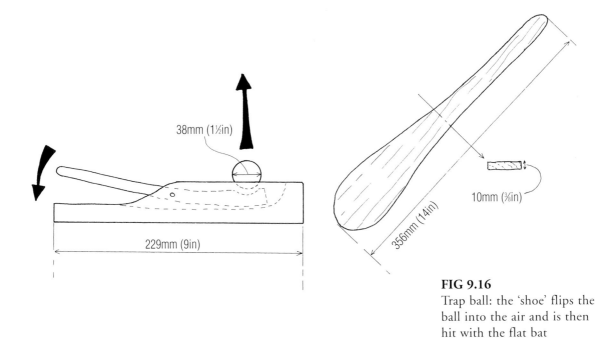

38mm (1½in)

229mm (9in)

356mm (14in)

10mm (⅜in)

FIG 9.16
Trap ball: the 'shoe' flips the
ball into the air and is then
hit with the flat bat

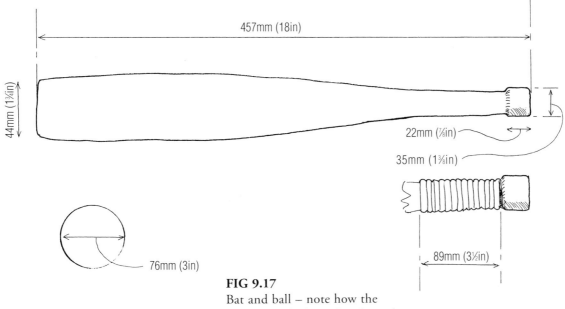

457mm (18in)

44mm (1¾in)

22mm (⅞in)

35mm (1⅜in)

76mm (3in)

89mm (3½in)

FIG 9.17
Bat and ball – note how the
handle can be bound with cord
to improve grip.

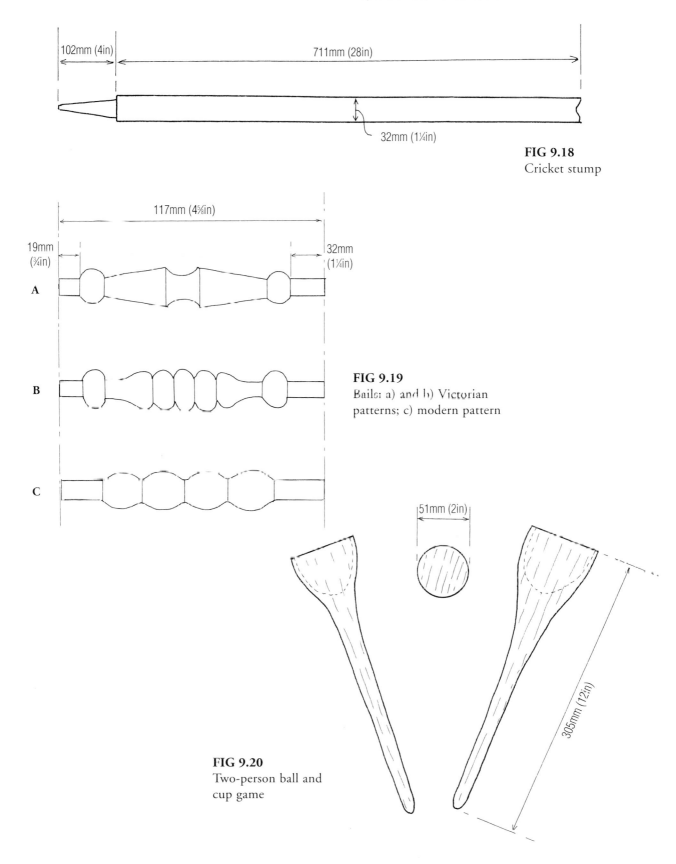

102mm (4in)

711mm (28in)

32mm (1¼in)

FIG 9.18
Cricket stump

117mm (4⅝in)

19mm
(¾in)

32mm
(1¼in)

A

B

FIG 9.19
Bails: a) and b) Victorian
patterns; c) modern pattern

C

51mm (2in)

305mm (12in)

FIG 9.20
Two-person ball and
cup game

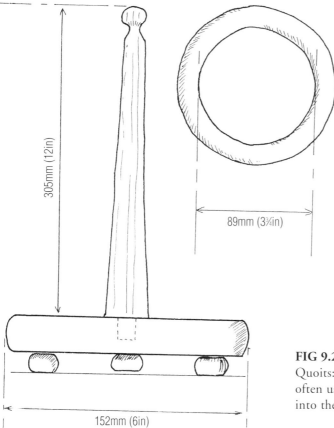

305mm (12in)

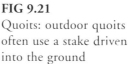

89mm (3¼in)

152mm (6in)

FIG 9.21
Quoits: outdoor quoits
often use a stake driven
into the ground

Out of Doors

These products have no more affinity with each
other than their use outdoors.

Tent pegs: to put a perspective on how common
these products were, it is estimated that some fifty
million pegs were used during World War II.
Although pegs are made in all parts of the country,
the Chiltern woods have been a major source, for
the beech that grows there so well makes fine pegs.
There is still a strong market today among
recreational campers and for marquees. And with
good reason, for cleft wooden pegs, with their
ribbed surface and subtle shape, grip the ground
better than their metal or plastic counterparts. Pegs
come in a wide range of sizes (see table 9.1), but
all are made to the same pattern (**fig 9.22**). They
are made from clefts riven from poles at least
152mm (6in) in diameter (see **fig 9.23**). Key

points in the pattern are: A small square tip that
will not turn; chamfering around the notch so as
not to fray the ropes; chamfering at the head end
to avoid splitting when hit.

Clothes pegs: Green woodworker's traditionally
made several patterns of clothes pegs. First a
turned one-piece peg with a sawn and shaved
mouth (**fig 9.24**). This has a bead at the head end
and the jaws of the mouth are rounded so they do
not snag. Second is the two-piece cleft and shaved
peg held together by a tin strip (**fig 9.25**). The
halves are shaved to produce an open mouth and
smooth jaws. The tin strip goes close to the head
and is pinned to one of the clefts. This pattern is
often associated with travellers, being sold from
door to door, but all wooden pegs are now largely
supplanted by plastic and wire spring pegs. Lastly,
peg makers produced a heavy blanket peg, the
body of which was usually turned (**fig 9.26**).

Table 9.1 Dimensions of tent pegs (see also fig 9.22)

Length (a) mm (in)	Width (b) mm (in)	Head (c) mm (in)	Tip (d) mm (in)	Head End (e) mm (in)	Thickness mm (in)
457mm (18in)	44mm (1¾in)	114mm (4½in)	6mm (¼in)	32mm (1¼in)	22mm (⅞in)
305mm (12in)	41mm (1⅝in)	89mm (3½in)	6mm (¼in)	25mm (1in)	19mm (¾in)
228mm (9in)	38mm (1½in)	63mm (2½in)	6mm (¼in)	25mm (1in)	16mm (⅝in)
152mm (6in)	35mm (1⅜in)	44mm (1¾in)	4mm (³⁄₁₆in)	22mm (⅞in)	16mm (⅝in)

Sheep feeders: These are simple cages, into which hay or other fodder can be placed for feeding sheep. They are so designed that the animals can only get their heads inside the feeder, thus preventing them trampling and spoiling the food. There are two main patterns. The first, of all cleft wood, is a long narrow cage with hoops mortised into a heavy bottom frame which sits on the ground. This pattern maximizes the number of animals that can feed at any one time (**fig 9.27**). The second pattern is a round cage of woven hazel rods, the uprights of which can be driven into the ground. This type requires a mould to hold the uprights in place while the cage is woven (**fig 9.28**). Both are remarkably rugged and will last five or six years out of doors.

Navvy's spade cleaner: anyone digging heavy soil will appreciate this simple device (**fig 9.29**). It is a hardwood wedge with a simple handle and is used to scrape the mud off the blade of a spade or similar tool. It was devised and used by the Victorian navvies who gave us our railways and who reckoned 'it was worth another man to them'.

Boot jack: and when you have finished digging you will need a 'jack' to remove your muddy boots. A boot jack is a flat board, raised at one end, which has a U-shaped piece removed from it so it can grip the heel of a boot (**fig 9.30**). The other foot rests on the board to hold the jack steady while the boot is removed. There is some variation in the design of the member that lifts the board to

the required angle, and all of the edges are chamfered to avoid splitting and spears. The only significantly different pattern I have seen is one from Derbyshire in which the board has a boot-sized hole in it rather than a 'U' (**fig 9.31**). This stops the boot flopping over as it is removed. Boot jacks were sometimes hinged in their centre (either way) to allow them to be folded for storage.

Walking Sticks: sticks are very personal to the user and invaluable companions at work and play. They have a well-used terminology for their various parts (**fig 9.32**). There are three main generic patterns of stick, but a multitude of detailed decorative differences that are not covered here.

One-piece sticks range from straight, smooth ash or hazel plants, to sticks with shaped knobs from coppice stools, to various curved handles for walking, nutting or shepherding (**fig 9.33**).

Thumb sticks can have a natural fork, a scalloped or shaped fork, or a fork made from a piece of deer antler (**fig 9.34**).

Two-piece sticks in which a shaped head in bone or wood is fitted to a good straight or honeysuckle twisted shank (**fig 9.35**). Different patterns for fixing head to shank are shown in **fig 9.32**.

The length of the shank in all sticks varies with both use and the users personal preference, but fall between hip and shoulder height.

Priest: this short heavy club is used by fishermen to despatch their landed fish by means of a sharp blow to the head (giving it the last rites – hence the name). It is often weighted in the head and the cavity sealed with a plug (**fig 9.36**).

Tips

- Make tent pegs with freshly felled wood. Avoid knotty wood.
- Beech, ash or chestnut are best for tent pegs.
- Never use oak or chestnut for clothes pegs – they will stain the clothes.
- Remove all spears from sheep feeders to avoid injury to animals.
- Hazel, ash, blackthorn and chestnut make the best walking sticks, and are best seasoned under cover for six months before final trimming.
- Use dry heat or steam to soften sticks before bending or straightening, and always keep green poles tied in bundles to keep them straight while seasoning.
- A polyurethane finish is best for sticks.

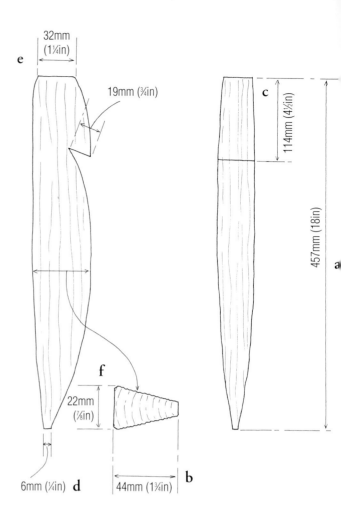

FIG 9.22
Cleft tent pegs – normal pattern

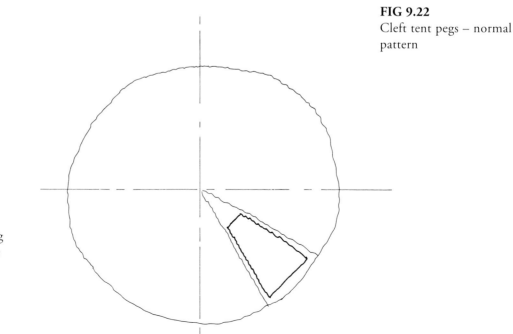

FIG 9.23
How a cleft tent peg is taken from a pole

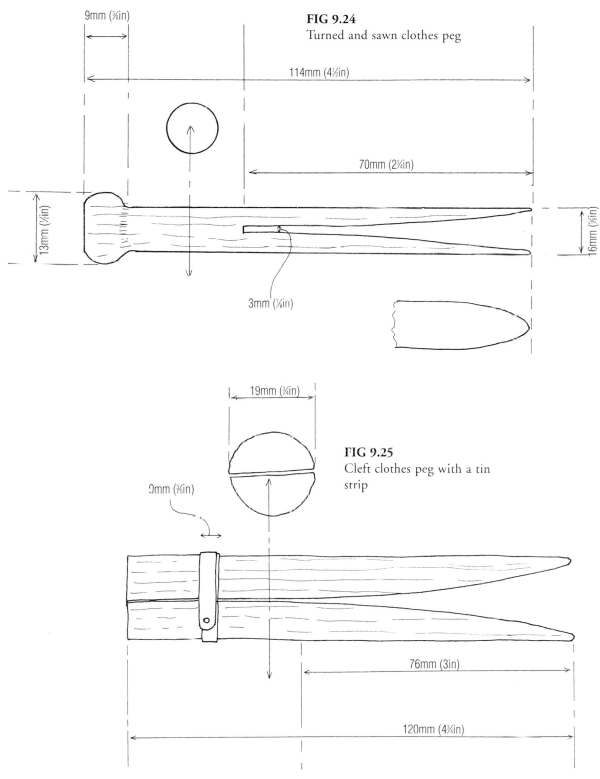

9mm (⅜in)

FIG 9.24
Turned and sawn clothes peg

114mm (4½in)

70mm (2¾in)

13mm (½in)

16mm (⅝in)

3mm (¼in)

19mm (¾in)

FIG 9.25
Cleft clothes peg with a tin
strip

9mm (⅜in)

76mm (3in)

120mm (4¾in)

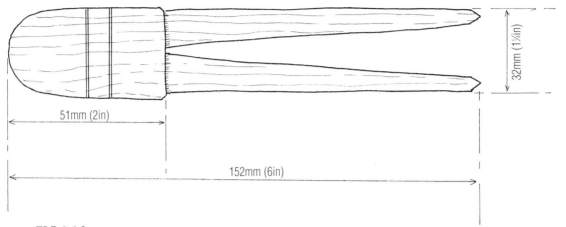

FIG 9.26
Blanket peg

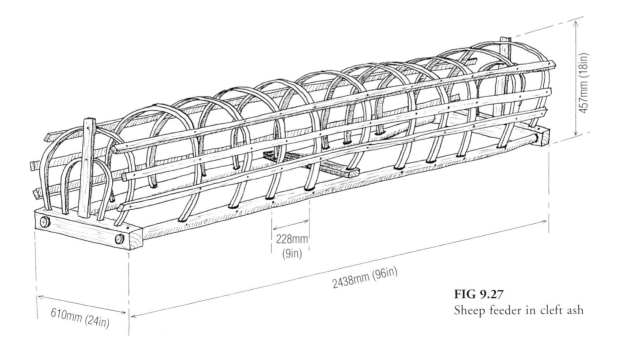

FIG 9.27
Sheep feeder in cleft ash

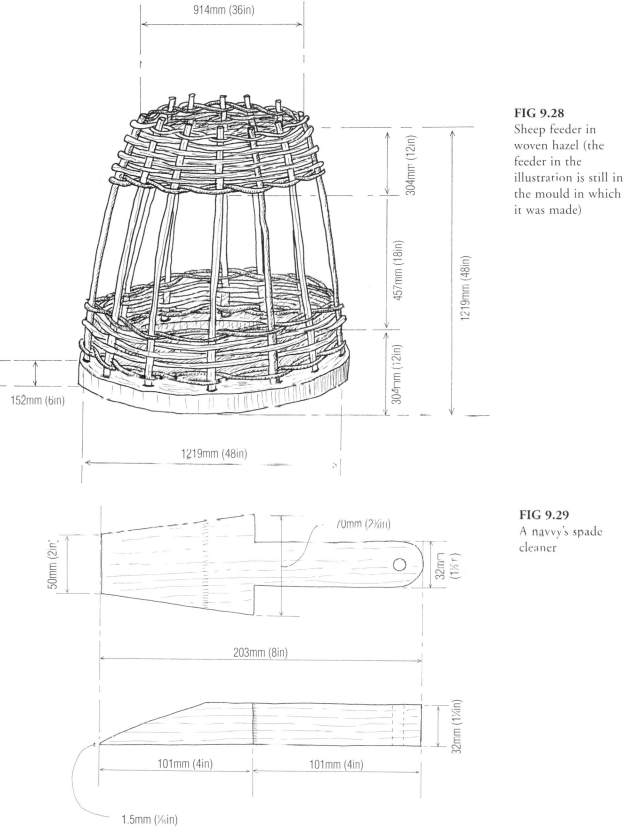

914mm (36in)

304mm (12in)

457mm (18in)

1219mm (48in)

152mm (6in)

304mm (12in)

1219mm (48in)

FIG 9.28
Sheep feeder in woven hazel (the feeder in the illustration is still in the mould in which it was made)

FIG 9.29
A navvy's spade cleaner

70mm (2¾in)

50mm (2in)

32mm (1¼ r)

203mm (8in)

32mm (1¼in)

101mm (4in)

101mm (4in)

1.5mm (¹⁄₁₆in)

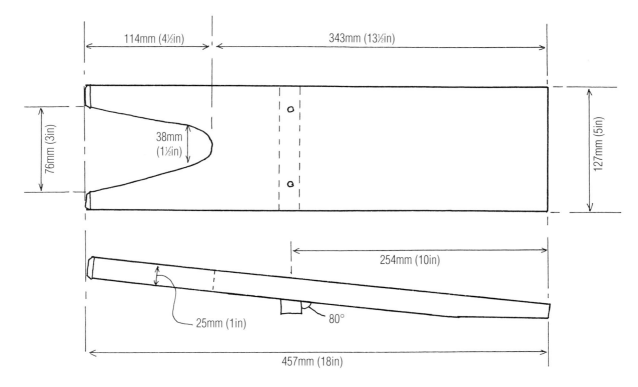

114mm (4½in)

343mm (13½in)

38mm (1½in)

76mm (3in)

127mm (5in)

254mm (10in)

25mm (1in)

80°

457mm (18in)

FIG 9.30
A basic boot jack

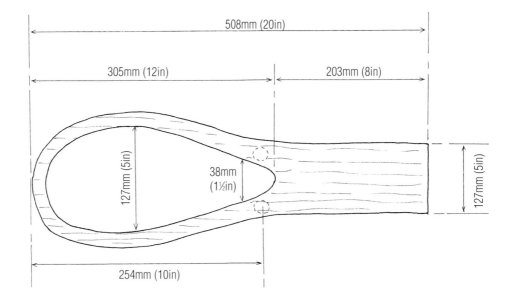

508mm (20in)

305mm (12in)

203mm (8in)

127mm (5in)

38mm (1½in)

127mm (5in)

254mm (10in)

FIG 9.31
A boot jack from
Derbyshire

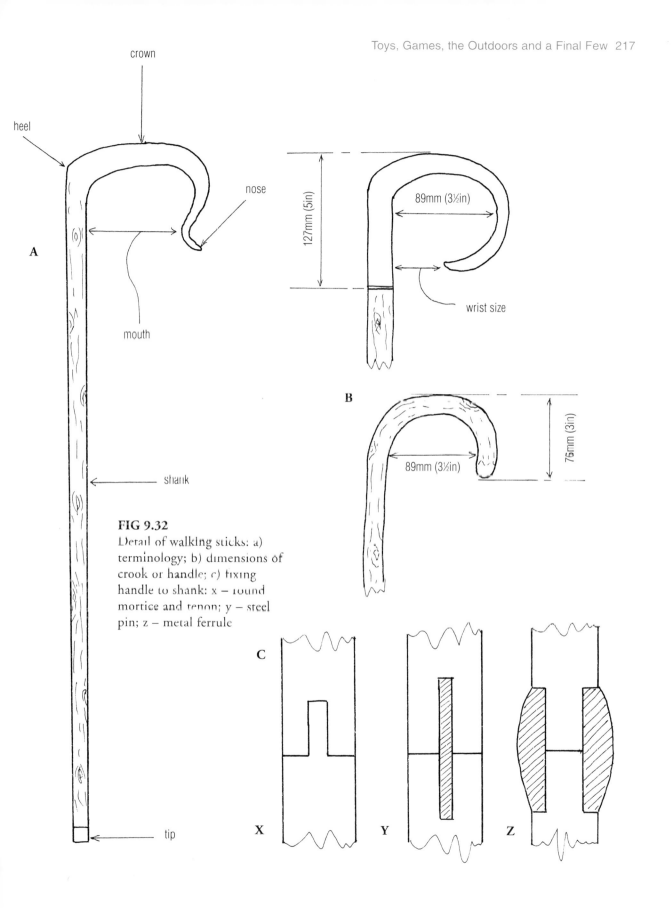

crown

heel

nose

A

mouth

127mm (5in)

89mm (3½in)

wrist size

shank

B

76mm (3in)

89mm (3½in)

FIG 9.32
Detail of walking sticks: a)
terminology; b) dimensions of
crook or handle; c) fixing
handle to shank: x – round
mortice and tenon; y – steel
pin; z – metal ferrule

C

tip

X

Y

Z

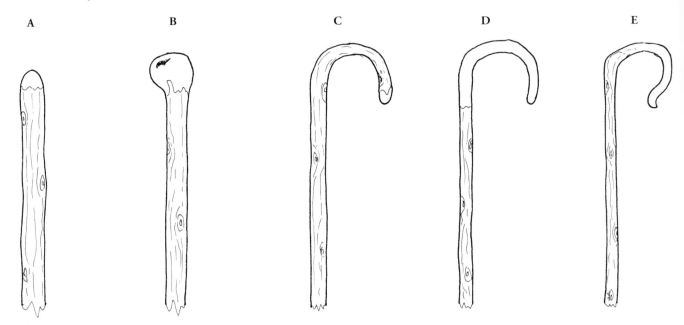

FIG 9.33
Varieties of one piece stick: a) straight ash
plant; b) knop stick from a coppice stool; c)
normal bent-handled walking stick; d)
Suffolk 'nutting' stick with bark removed
from handle; e) classic crook stick

FIG 9.34
Thumb sticks: a) horn crotch fitted to
straight shank; b) natural fork or 'V';
c) shaped 'V' to fit the thumb better

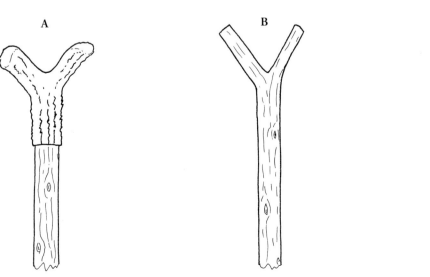

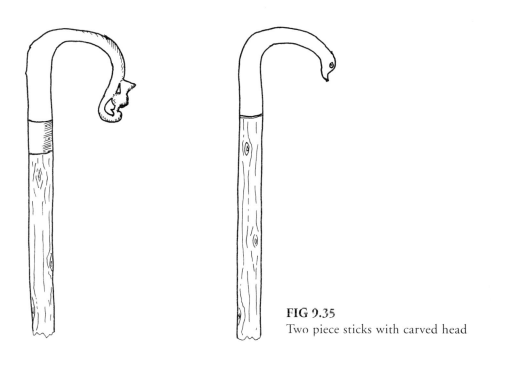

FIG 9.35
Two piece sticks with carved head

FIG 9.36
A Priest – note the cavity at the end to hold
a lead weight

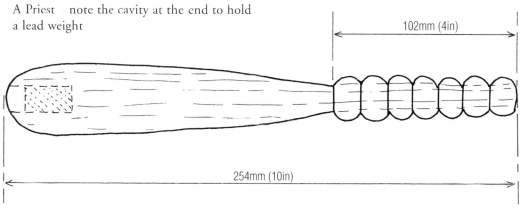

102mm (4in)

254mm (10in)

A Final Few

To end this pattern book I have selected a few pieces that do not fit elsewhere, but which nevertheless seem to epitomize the range, function and fun of green woodworking.

Grass Vases: these turned items are shaped like a vase, but have a deep narrow-diameter hole from the top (**fig 9.37**). They are designed to hold stems of dried grass, which complement so well the colour and texture of the wood used.

Wood Sculptures: most people will be familiar with small turnery shaped to resemble common fungi. They are frequently turned from round wood, leaving some bark in place to increase the decorative effect (**fig 9.38**). Large toadstools used as garden decoration and/or seats are really loved by children – we cannot make enough! (**fig 9.39**). Rough sculpture or carving can come in many patterns, but those that appeal most are human forms. Those illustrated are derived from the ancient cultures of Easter Island and Africa (**fig 9.40**). These can be small enough to fit on a shelf, or large enough to stand on the floor.

Hazel Nutcrackers: there are three ways to open hazel nuts: hitting them with a hammer, using leverage, and using screw pressure. Most nutcrackers use leverage and the pattern of an elegant and effective pair in regular use is shown in **fig 9.41**. They are notched so as not to crush the kernal when fully closed. A range of older patterns of nutcrackers is shown in **fig 9.42**. An example of a screw nutcracker is shown in **fig 9.43**. In these elegant devices the nut is placed in the cavity and pressure applied to it by turning the screw until the shell cracks. Much better than a hammer! A larger cavity is needed for walnuts.

Balances: called balances rather than scales, since neither of the patterns illustrated has a scale (**fig 9.44**). The hand-held pattern is 16th century from the *Mary Rose*, with a simple rocking bar from which hang two shallow pans, and pivoted in an inverted U-piece handle. The more usual pattern of balance is designed to stand on a table and its U-piece is the other way up, although both balances function in the same way. As green wood artefacts combining function with elegance, they are hard to beat.

Napkin rings: It is much less common today for linen napkins to be used. Rings are rarely wider than 50mm (2in), and may be decorated on the outside with beading (**fig 9.45**).

Darning mushrooms: sadly socks and gloves are rarely repaired today – they are rather thrown away. When they were repaired, however, a darning mushroom was used. Patterns for use with socks and gloves are illustrated (**fig 9.46**), together with an unusual egg-shaped pattern for socks.

Tips

- When using whole round wood for turning it should be thoroughly seasoned first to avoid radial splits (very slow seasoning after turning is the second best).
- Balances and turned mushrooms are best in close-grained wood such as beech.
- Mushrooms can be varnished or polished for indoor use.
- Nutcrackers are best treated with oil from time to time in order to prevent them becoming too brittle.
- When carving, the use of clefts rather than whole round wood will reduce some of the drying splits – but in the larger pieces this can add to the attraction.
- Use a metal pin as the pivot in the balance – it will reduce friction and increase the sensitivity of the instrument.

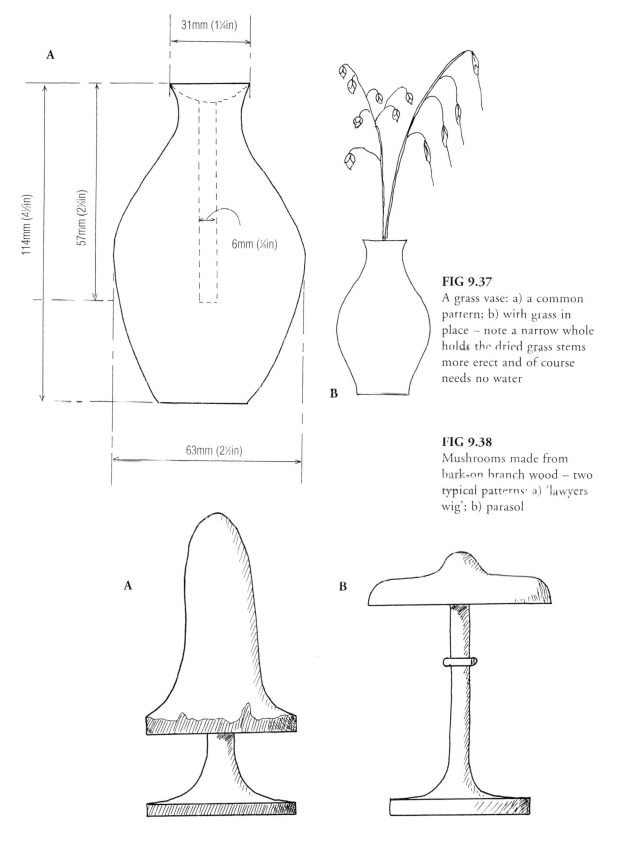

A

31mm (1¼in)

114mm (4½in)

57mm (2¼in)

6mm (¼in)

63mm (2½in)

FIG 9.37
A grass vase: a) a common pattern; b) with grass in place – note a narrow whole holds the dried grass stems more erect and of course needs no water

B

FIG 9.38
Mushrooms made from bark-on branch wood – two typical patterns: a) 'lawyers wig'; b) parasol

A

B

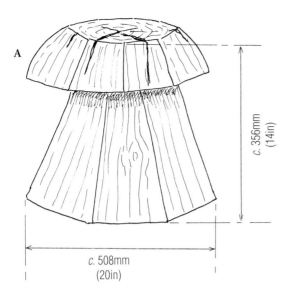

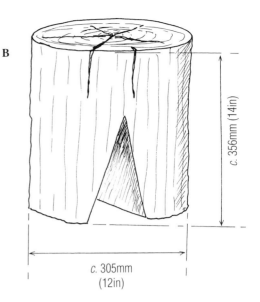

FIG 9.39
Garden ornaments: a) mushroom; b) stool. These large items are shaped using a chain saw

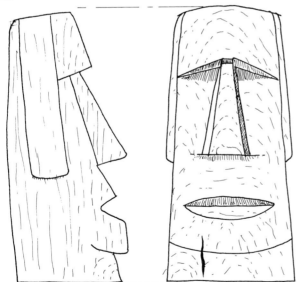

FIG 9.40
Green wood sculptures: a) copy of an Easter Island head shaped from a cleft; b) face carved onto a large round log – hence the drying splits – for indoor or outdoor decoration

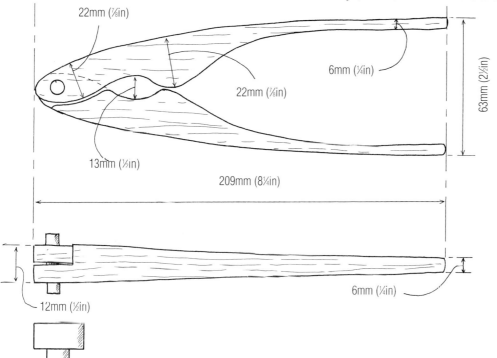

22mm (⅞in)

22mm (⅞in)

6mm (¼in)

63mm (2½in)

13mm (½in)

209mm (8¼in)

12mm (½in)

6mm (¼in)

FIG 9.41
Hazel nutcrackers –
pair in ash wood –
note the wooden pin
that acts as the hinge

FIG 9.42
Range of nutcrackers: pair
(d) are made from one piece
of wood, steam-bent at the
hinge

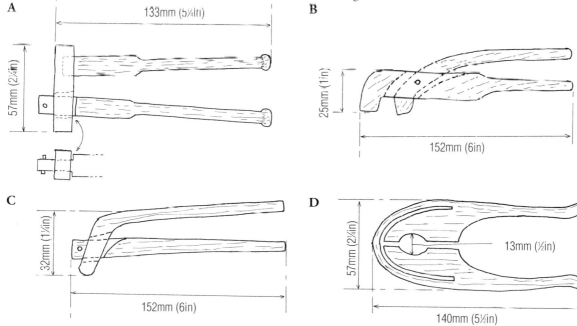

A

133mm (5¼in)

57mm (2¼in)

B

25mm (1in)

152mm (6in)

C

32mm (1¼in)

152mm (6in)

D

57mm (2¼in)

13mm (½in)

140mm (5½in)

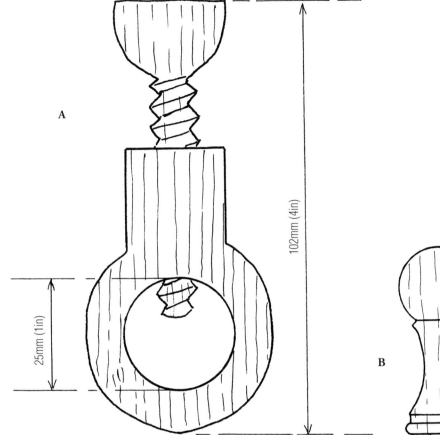

A

102mm (4in)

25mm (1in)

B

140mm (5½in)

25mm (1in)

FIG 9.43
Screw nutcrackers: a)
for the pocket; b) for
the table

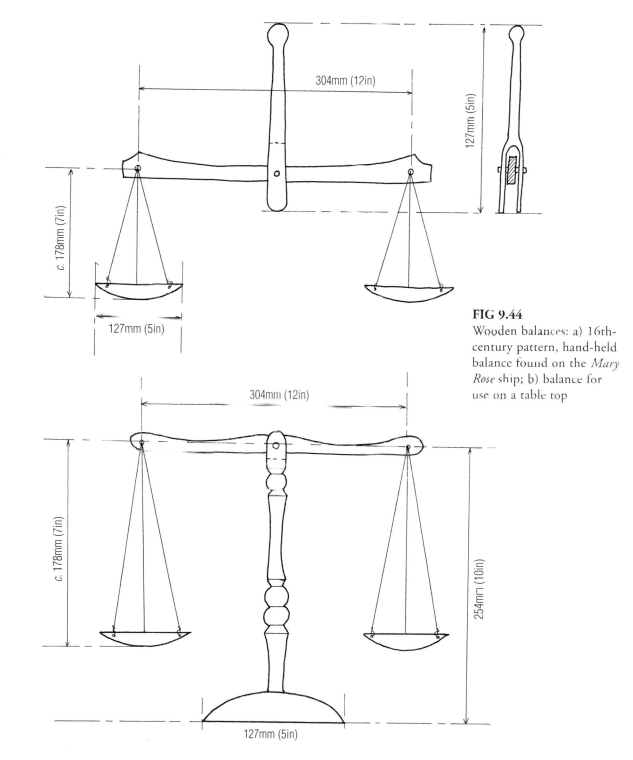

A

304mm (12in)

127mm (5in)

c. 178mm (7in)

127mm (5in)

FIG 9.44
Wooden balances: a) 16th-century pattern, hand-held balance found on the *Mary Rose* ship; b) balance for use on a table top

B

304mm (12in)

c. 178mm (7in)

254mm (10in)

127mm (5in)

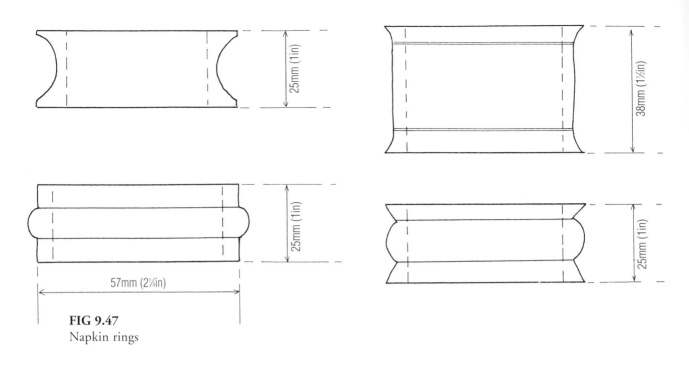

FIG 9.47
Napkin rings

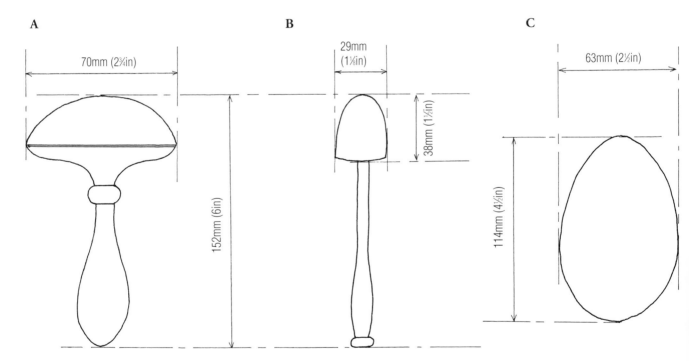

A

70mm (2¾in)

152mm (6in)

B

29mm (1⅛in)

38mm (1½in)

C

63mm (2½in)

114mm (4½in)

FIG 9.46
Darning mushrooms: a)
mushroom for socks; b)
mushroom for glove fingers;
c) a darning egg

Appendix: Cutting Plans

This appendix illustrates how detailed working and cutting plans should be produced before any work is started. These plans are the first step in converting the sketched pattern into a real object or piece of furniture. From these plans you can determine the raw material required and any special tools and devices needed before work starts.

Furniture includes some of the more complex artefacts green woodworkers make, so I have chosen two examples from this group to demonstrate what

you will need to do. The first is a garden bench; the second a slab and stick chair. There are two elements to each of these plans:

1. A drawing of the piece from at least two elevations that shows where all the parts fit and their dimensions, plus sketches of any key detail.

2. A tabulated cutting list that includes all the parts required, the number of them, their sizes, and finally any relevant comments.

Appendix Table 1: Cutting list for two seat round-wood garden bench

Item	Number	Size in mm (in)	Notes
Front legs	2	584mm (23in) x 76mm (3in) diameter	Use 76mm (3in) poles
Rear legs	2	838mm (33in) x 76mm (3in) diameter	Use 76mm (3in) poles with curve if possible
Back rails	2	1219mm (48in) x 51mm (2in) diameter	Chamfer ends to fit 32mm (1¼in) mortice holes
Back sticks	6	254mm (10in) x 38mm (1½in) diameter	Chamfer ends to fit 25mm (1in) mortice holes
Seat supports	2	533mm (21in) x 38mm (1½in)	Quarter clefts from 102mm (4in) poles
Seat slats	6	4 slats at 1219mm (48in) x 89mm (3½in) x 25mm (1in)	Clefts from large poles made into 'planks'
Arms	2	559mm (22in) x 38mm (1½in)	Half clefts of 76mm (3in) poles
Back braces	2	As required	Use half clefts from round poles, then size and shape to fit as required
Side braces	4	As required	Use half clefts from round poles, then size and shape to fit as required
Front Rail	1	1219mm (48in) x 51mm (2in) diameter	Chamfer ends to fit 32mm (1¼in) mortice holes

FIG A1
Detailed drawing for a round wood
garden bench to go with the cutting plan,
with detail of how the seating slats fit to
their support.

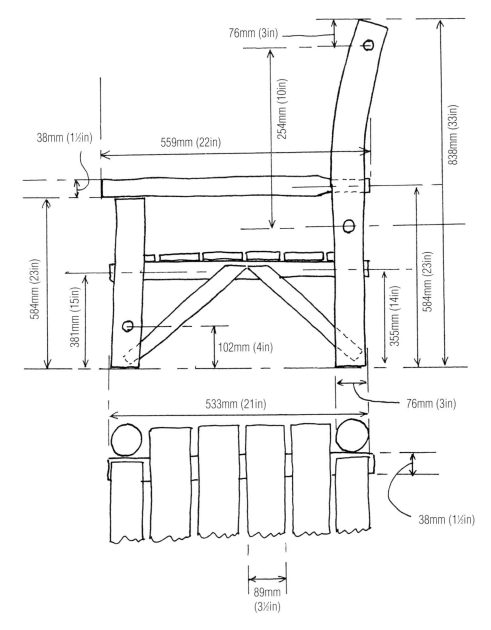

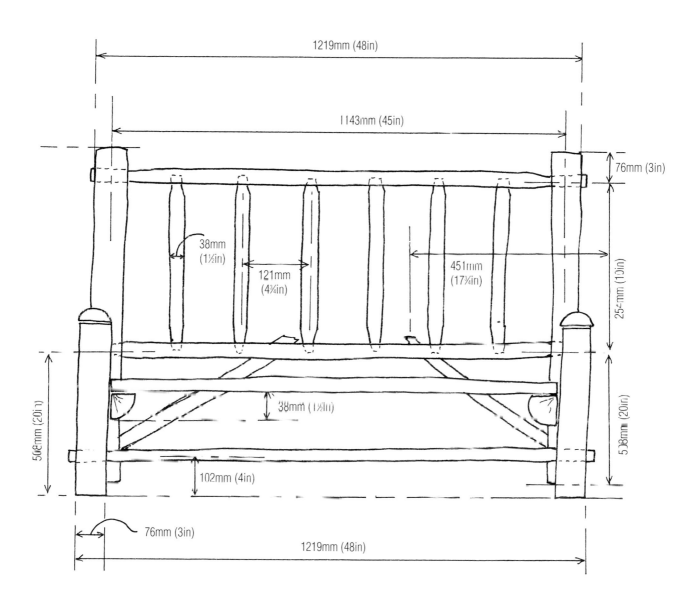

FIG A2 (below)
Details of the garden bench: a) Shape of the
back sticks; b) approximate shape required for
end braces so that they fit to both the legs and
the seat support; c) staggering of the mortice
holes for the back rails – used to angle the
back when curved back legs are not available.

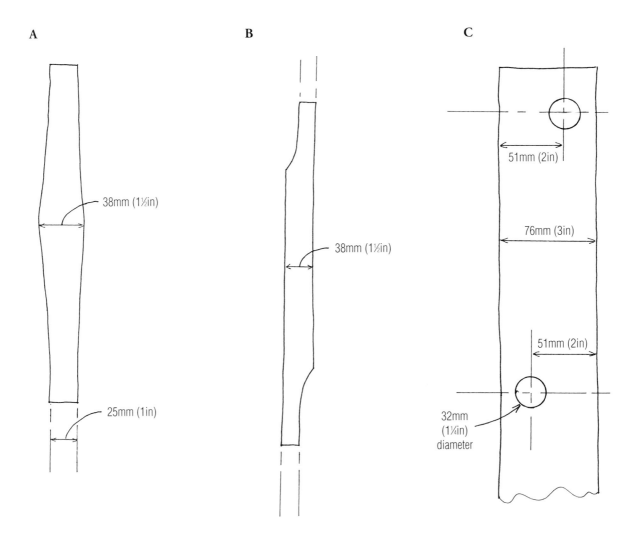

A

38mm (1½in)

25mm (1in)

B

38mm (1½in)

C

51mm (2in)

76mm (3in)

51mm (2in)

32mm
(1¼in)
diameter

Appendix Table 2: Cutting plan for slab and stick chair

Item	Number	Size in mm * (Imperial in brackets)	Notes
Seat	1	343mm (13½in) x 349mm (13¾in)	Note curved shape in plan
Centre back sticks	2	327mm (12⅞in) x 16mm (⅝in)	Taper ends to fit 11mm (⁷⁄₁₆in) mortice holes
Outer back sticks	2	324mm (12¾in) x 16mm (⅝in)	Taper ends to fit 11mm (⁷⁄₁₆in) mortice holes
Turned back sticks	2	324 mm (12¾in) x 38mm (1½in)	Taper seat end to 25mm (1in) and comb end to fit 16mm (⅝in) mortices
Comb	1	413mm (16¼in) x 09mm (3½in) x 19mm (¾in) thick	See drawing for shaping of this item
Front legs	2	441mm (17⅜in) x 38mm (1½in)	Taper end to fit 25mm (1in) mortices
Back legs	2	432mm (17in) x 38mm (1½in)	Taper end to fit 25mm (1in) mortices
Side stretchers	2	314mm (12⅜in) x 29mm (1⅛in)	Swelled at centre – ends to fit 16mm (⅝in) mortice hole
Centre stretcher	1	295mm (11⅝in) x 25mm (1in)	Swelled at centre – ends to fit 16mm (⅝in) mortice hole

FIG A3 (opposite)
Detailed drawings of a slab
and stick chair to go with
the cutting plan.

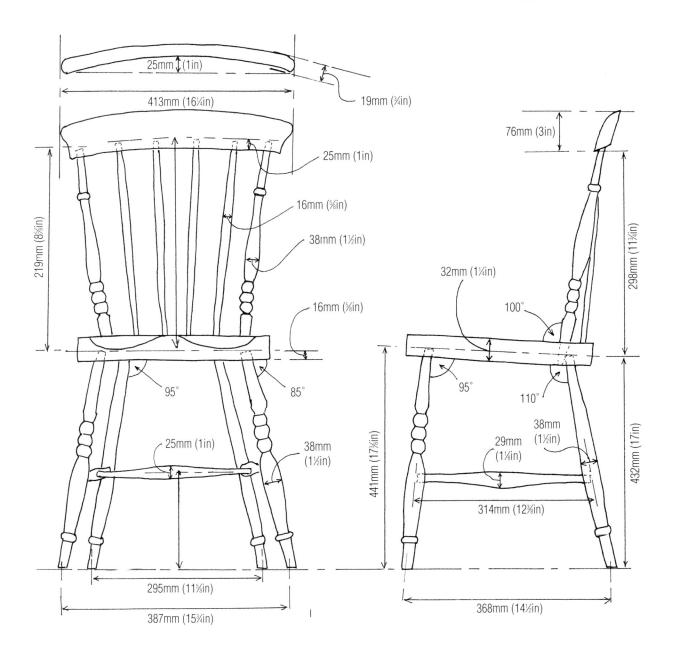

25mm (1in)

413mm (16¼in)

19mm (¾in)

25mm (1in)

16mm (⅝in)

38rnm (1½in)

16mm (⅝in)

219mm (8⅝in)

95°

85°

25mm (1in)

38mm (1½in)

441mm (17⅜in)

295mm (11⅝in)

387mm (15¾in)

76mm (3in)

32mm (1¼in)

100°

298mm (11¾in)

95°

110°

38mm (1½in)

29mm (1⅛in)

432mm (17in)

314mm (12⅜in)

368mm (14½in)

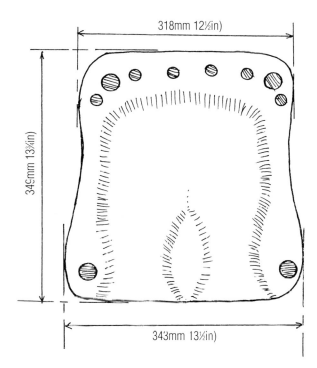

318mm 12½in)

340mm 13¾in)

343mm 13½in)

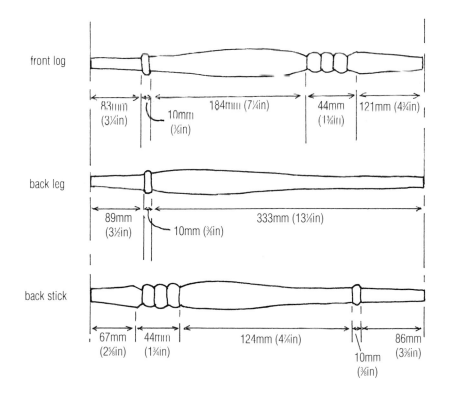

front log

83mm
(3¼in)

10mm
(⅜in)

184mm (7¼in)

44mm
(1¾in)

121mm (4¾in)

back leg

89mm
(3½in)

10mm (⅜in)

333mm (13⅛in)

back stick

67mm
(2⅝in)

44mm
(1¾in)

124mm (4⅞in)

10mm
(⅜in)

86mm
(3⅜in)

A

B

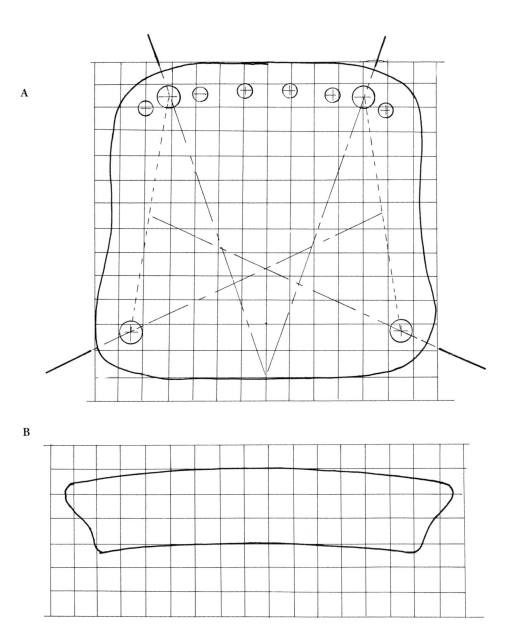

FIG A4
Detail of slab and stick chair: a) seat on 25mm
(1in) squared paper showing how the holes are
positioned and the angle of the legs determined
(after Abbott). Hatching shows the seat is shaped by
removal of wood. Note that leg and centre stick
holes do not pass right through the seat.

FIG A5
Typical angles used for slab
and stick seating.

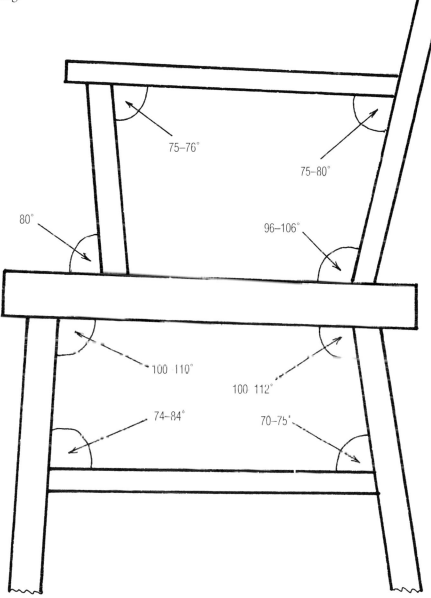

75–76°

75–80°

80°

96–106°

100–110°

100–112°

74–84°

70–75°

Bibliography

No woodworker exists in a vacuum. We are all influenced to a greater or lesser extent by what we see around us and by the advice of others. I have listed in this appendix the books that have had the greatest effect on my work, and have also received the greatest acclaim by woodworkers in general. Some of them are here because of their fund of patterns; others because of their advice on 'how to'. And knowing 'how' gives the woodworker the opportunity to develop new patterns.

Abbott, M, *Green Woodwork: Working with Wood the Natural Way*, Guild of Master Craftsman Publications, 1989

Alexander, J D Jnr, *Make a Chair from a Tree: An Introduction to Working Green Wood*, Astragal Press, 1994

Barratt, M, *Oak Swill Basket Making in the Lake District*, M Barratt, 1983

Crispin, T, *English Windsor Chairs*, Allan Sutton, 1992

Edlin, H L, *Woodland Crafts in Britain*, Batsford, 1949

Geraint Jenkins, J, *Traditional Country Craftsmen*, Routledge and Keegan Paul, 1978

Hart, E, *Walking Sticks*, Crowood, 1986

Hasluck, P N, *The Handyman's Book*, Cassell, 1903

Langsner, D, *Country Woodcraft*, Rodale Press, 1978

Langsner, D, *The Chairmaker's Workshop*, Lark Books, 1997

Levi, J, *Treen for the Table*, Antique Collectors Club, 1998

Mack, D, *The Rustic Furniture Companion*, Lark Books, 1996

Pinto, E H, *Treen and Other Wooden Bygones*, G Bell and Sons, 1969

Rogers, E, *Making Traditional English Wooden Eating Spoons*, Woodland Craft Supplies, 1997

Salaman, R A, *Dictionary of Woodworking Tools c. 1700–1970*, Unwin Hyman, 1989

Sparks, I, *The English Country Chair*, Spur Books, 1973

Tabor, R, *Traditional Woodland Crafts*, Batsford, 1994

Tabor, R, *The Encyclopedia of Green Woodworking*, Eco-logic Books, 2000

Warnes, J, *Living Willow Sculpture*, Search Press, 2001

Wood, R, *A History of the Wooden Plate*, Robin Wood, 2002

Wood, R, *A Short History of Drinking Bowls and Mazers*, Robin Wood, 2002

Index